Life in ACTION

**Abundant Life.
Radical Action.**

365 DAYS OF DEVOTION

by LIFE ACTION

Life in Action

First Printing – 2016

Printed in the United States of America.

Copyright ©2016 Life Action Ministries and Tim Grissom.
Published by Life Action Ministries
P.O. Box 31, Buchanan, MI 49170
269-697-8600
www.LifeAction.org

Design and layout by Life Action Media
Buchanan, Michigan

ISBN 978-1-934718-61-2

INTRODUCTION

It has been said that revival is "falling in love with Jesus all over again" and that it involves renewed life from the Holy Spirit. Is that what your soul needs this year?

Life in Action was designed to encourage and challenge you to seek God personally—to live out the biblical principles that lead to life transformation. The content is predicated on the simple command put forth in James 1:22 to "be doers of the word, and not hearers only." That's why each daily reading begins with Scripture, offers practical life application teaching, and then presents a key question to ponder or an action step to take.

At Life Action Ministries, we believe that genuine revival begins when people respond to God's Word in the following six critical areas:

Humility. The Scriptures explain that "God opposes the proud, but gives grace to the humble" (James 4:6). In humility, therefore, we seek His grace by admitting our own great need, throwing off our self-sufficiency, and bowing prayerfully before our Lord.

Honesty. Confession of sin avails us of the forgiveness and cleansing of God (1 John 1:9). Experiencing personal revival always involves honestly dealing with our sins—both those committed against God and those committed against other people.

Repentance. Seeking God's face is not merely an exercise in rituals or words; it is really a change of direction. Repentance involves turning from our sins so we can obey God instead of self. As Paul wrote to the Ephesians, we must "put off" the old self and "put on" the new identity Christ died to provide for us (Ephesians 4:17–24).

Forgiveness. Experiencing God's forgiveness is one of the greatest blessings of the Christian life, and God requires that we pass that same blessing on to others who have offended, hurt, or taken from us (Ephesians 4:32). As we come close to God for spiritual renewal, we must release the bitterness we hold and clear our sin accounts with others, extending forgiveness to those who have wronged us and seeking it from those we have wronged.

Obedience. From a position of humble repentance, we are now ready to say yes to Jesus in every category of our lives. He is worthy of our obedience in everything from daily habits to major decisions. Even our thoughts and motivations are important to Him (Luke 6:46).

Seeking His Kingdom First. Obedience to God leads us to a complete reprioritization of life. The ultimate aim of spiritual renewal is that each of us would walk with God, that we would demonstrate His love in a dark world, and that we would be a part of fulfilling the Great Commission task in our generation (Matthew 6:33; Mark 16:15).

This devotional guide has been designed to assist you in responding biblically to the Lord, so that His power and presence will fill your life, family, and future.

May God richly bless you as you seek Him!

The Life Action Team

ACKNOWLEDGMENTS

We wish to express our gratitude to Tim Grissom, who authored these daily readings based on Life Action's teachings and principles. Tim currently serves as Senior Editor for FamilyLife Publishing, and previously served on Life Action's staff for fourteen years. He is also co-author of our small group devotional curriculum focused on personal revival, entitled *Seeking Him*.

---

*"Return to me, and I will return to you,
says the LORD of hosts" (Malachi 3:7).*

Are you responsive to God? In a world of noise, anxieties, and untamed thoughts, God's voice may seem faint. Our own spiritual indifference is generally the culprit. We've trained ourselves to ignore His promptings.

Perhaps you've allowed yourself to drift. You do have every intention of returning fully to God someday, but you want to go just a little farther in your chosen direction, under your own power. God can wait.

Frankly, such thinking is as foolish as it is sinful. Why would we ignore the One who loves us and longs for us to enjoy Him?

Prior to the Welsh Revival (1904–05), Evan Roberts became greatly concerned over the spiritual indifference of the church. He began preaching a four-point sermon that invited the lost to salvation and the backslidden to personal revival. The points were:

1. Confess all known sin, receiving forgiveness through Jesus Christ.
2. Remove anything in your life that you are in doubt or feel unsure about.
3. Be ready to obey the Holy Spirit instantly.
4. Publicly confess the Lord Jesus Christ.

Over 150,000 were converted, and countless lives were transformed. Nothing is gained by ignoring God. To delay responding to Him is to postpone the very joy, peace, and rest that our souls yearn for.

YOUR LIFE IN ACTION

Do you need to respond to God in light of any of
Evan Roberts' four points? What do you need to do?

"You looked for much, and behold, it came to little.
And when you brought it home, I blew it away.
Why? declares the LORD of hosts.
Because of my house that lies in ruins,
while each of you busies himself with his own house" (Haggai 1:9).

Delayed obedience is disobedience. Spiritual procrastination—the idea of saying, *Yes, God . . . but tomorrow, not today*—unmasks a stubborn heart rather than a surrendered one.

In the early days of a new year, many of us are thinking about ways we want to change. We love the idea of new beginnings. Yet in the making of resolutions and commitments, of launching ourselves into new or renewed disciplines, we should ask, *Are my priorities God's priorities?*

Haggai describes God taking issue with His procrastinating people. This was a season of national restoration; the people were returning to their homeland after years in exile. God had lifted their burden.

But rather than responding in grateful obedience, they rushed back into the life they wanted, rebuilding, planting, harvesting, working. But God's house stayed in ruins. Worship was put on hold. The temple ruins eventually blended into the landscape, turning neither heads nor hearts . . . all because of spiritual procrastination.

Take caution as you think of ways you want to change or improve in this New Year. Remember that holy intent without godly action is really nothing more than self-indulgence. Put nothing—*nothing*—above seeking God with all your heart. Say to Him, *Yes, God . . . today*.

YOUR LIFE IN ACTION

Are your priorities God's priorities? In what ways have you
been intending to obey God, but have not yet done so?

GOD'S FOLLOW-THROUGH

I am sure of this, that he who began a good work in you
will bring it to completion
at the day of Jesus Christ (Philippians 1:6).

God is not a quitter. He finishes everything He starts. Think of the implications this truth holds for you personally.

Philippians 1:6 points to the greatest promise of God's follow-through, that His saving you began a work that He will complete. It is a sanctifying work with no pauses or stops.

We should be both humbled and encouraged that God has taken our spiritual maturation upon Himself rather than leaving it to our best efforts. We did nothing to gain God's affection; salvation is a gift, not a prize. God initiated, we responded. And as it was with salvation, so it is with sanctification. It is God's work continued.

You may have grown cold toward Christ in comparison to where you once were, but you have not stopped His work in you. God is more committed to your spiritual formation than you will ever be, even on your most spiritually vibrant day.

Oh, the blessed rest that comes through knowing that God's work will continue in us and will be completed! God does not pick us up, wind us up, and drop us off. His presence is constant, and His activating grace is unending.

YOUR LIFE IN ACTION
Who or what are you truly relying on today for your growth
as a Christian? If it is not Christ Himself, then acknowledge your
need of Him, and thank Him for His faithfulness.

_It is God who works in you, both to will and to work
for his good pleasure (Philippians 2:13)._

What you need is not another of your own pep talks, conjuring up the spiritual motivation to do, say, and think the right things today. Here's a reminder that will prove much more inspirational: "It is God who works in you."

Here the Scripture speaks of _work_ as the evidential progress of our salvation, not things we must do to become or remain a Christian. "To work for his good pleasure" refers to works the body of Christ does to spiritually mature and to advance the gospel. Every Christ follower has work to do. What is yours?

We want to do works that please God ("to work"), and we want to _want to_ do works that please Him ("to will"), yet we often take it upon ourselves to try to muster holy intent, to coax ourselves into godly behavior. But we don't have to do that. God provides the compulsion along with the capacity. Ours is not a need for self-motivation, but for quieting our heart and embracing what God has already put there.

Philippians 2:12 instructs us to "work out your own salvation with fear and trembling." Clearly, willing and working for God's good pleasure are not matters to take lightly. They are God's means of displaying His glory to the world, like a light in a dark house or a city on a hill (Matthew 5:14-16). Give yourself over to God that He might show Himself through your circumstances, whether a cause to engage, a task to complete, a person to love, or a challenge to endure.

YOUR LIFE IN ACTION

What is the work God is giving you to do that will
display His glory to the world?

Not that I have already obtained this or am already perfect, but I press on to make it my own, because Christ Jesus has made me his own. Brothers, I do not consider that I have made it my own. But one thing I do: forgetting what lies behind and straining forward to what lies ahead, I press on toward the goal for the prize of the upward call of God in Christ Jesus (Philippians 3:12–14).

The truth of Philippians 1:6, that God is the one who brings us along in spiritual maturity, should give our souls rest. It means we do not have to earn God's trust. We don't have to wake up in the morning and worry about whether He will pay any attention to us today.

However, a soul at rest is not a soul in neutral. For while it is "God who works in you," He does so in a way that drives you to "work for his good pleasure" (Philippians 2:13). Those who know Christ are motivated by Him to intentional living and purposeful activity.

Paul described his life with phrases like "press on" and "straining forward." Do these sound nonchalant to you? Or do they sound like a person who, though "accepted in the beloved" (Ephesians 1:6), still gives himself daily to the noble work of God's kingdom? Our work is a heavenly calling rooted in love for our Savior and compassion for those still at enmity with Christ.

So work hard today in the kingdom. Pray, serve, share, give, love, forgive, take your thoughts captive, sacrifice, put the interests of others ahead of your own . . . all from the position of a soul at rest. With your everlasting peace already certain, let your heart be motivated by the love God has poured into you. Carry the gospel forward. Press on!

YOUR LIFE IN ACTION

Be intentional about your faith today. Look for opportunities
to acknowledge God and serve others.

> *. . . that I may know him and the power of his resurrection,*
> *and may share his sufferings,*
> *becoming like him in his death (Philippians 3:10).*

Saul (Paul) was an overachiever. He was a man of ancestral pedigree and unmatched religious zeal. He never stopped trying to be a better man, always ready to protect his people from threats. As a defender of his culture and beliefs, he was greatly respected, even feared.

Then he met Jesus, and (at the risk of sounding cliché) *everything* changed, from the way Paul would live the rest of his life to the way he would face death. So stirred and redirected were Paul's passions that everything about his life became centered on Christ.

Paul no longer tried to deal with his sin through ceremonial duty (fix this by doing that) but through faith in the uninterrupted grace of Christ's death and resurrection. He also no longer dreaded the ending of his existence and the fear that perhaps he had not done enough. Instead he would face death as the last momentary suffering that must be endured just before the dawning of eternal day.

To *know* Christ and the power of His resurrection, to *share* in His sufferings, to *become like* Him in His death—this Christ-centered approach to life shaped all of Paul's thinking and doing . . . as it can and should shape yours. This is what it means to live according to the gospel—appropriating the resurrection power of Christ to your struggle with sin, to your need to forgive, to your understanding of what is important to do today, to your present suffering in whatever form it may take, and to the death you will one day encounter.

YOUR LIFE IN ACTION

What changes do you need to make in order to truly
center your life on Christ?

Rejoice in the Lord always; again I will say, rejoice.
Let your reasonableness be known to everyone.
The Lord is at hand (Philippians 4:4–5).

The verses surrounding those above mention a wide range of circumstances, including the affection of a devoted disciple maker, two quarreling women, a call to prayer and thanksgiving, and a grid for right thinking. In the midst of these, Paul lays out two matters of perspective that could stabilize the heart of every Christian:

Be always rejoicing in the Lord. John Fletcher was a Methodist theologian and contemporary of John Wesley. He was a man of prayer who often greeted friends with the question, "Do I meet you praying?" To Fletcher, prayer was the default activity of the Christian heart; so he expected—or certainly hoped—that the friends he greeted were praying at that very moment. We should hope the same about rejoicing. One Christian might greet another by saying, "Do I meet you rejoicing?" and hope that always the answer would be yes.

Rejoicing should not be a reaction based on our moods and circumstances, but rather the normal posture of our redeemed hearts, because we who were dead in our sins have been made alive together with Christ (Ephesians 2:1, 5)! Sadly, we often forfeit rejoicing by forgetting that Christ did more than heal us, He brought us back to life.

Be always expecting Christ's return. The fulfillment of a promise is as certain as the one who made it. This is the reason we know, and the only reason we need, that Christ will return . . . *perhaps today*. Keep your heart in a posture of expectation. Christ *is* coming! Press on!

YOUR LIFE IN ACTION

Reset your heart to a posture of joy by remembering your salvation and thanking God for it. How would you approach today differently if you really believed this could be the day of Christ's return?

*Our citizenship is in heaven, and from it we await a Savior,
the Lord Jesus Christ (Philippians 3:20).*

The relatively short letter of Philippians makes at least five references to the return of Christ and to eternity: "the day of Jesus Christ" (1:6); "the day of Christ" (1:10; 2:16); "our citizenship is in heaven" (3:20); "the Lord is at hand" (4:5).

The anticipation of Christ's return and of our dwelling eternally with Him is a motivation found again and again in Scripture. Jesus often emphasized it in His teaching, as seen in one of His last earthly encounters with His disciples: "If I go and prepare a place for you, I will come again and will take you to myself, that where I am you may be also" (John 14:3).

No doubt these men were sad at the thought of being separated from the Messiah, and intimidated at the mission He had given them (Mark 16:15). Jesus reassured them that He would return and take them to be with Him forever. This is a promise for every believer.

If we're honest, we'll have to admit that we generally give more thought and preparation to vacations, outings, and dinner parties than we do to Christ's return and eternity. We treat them in almost mythical terms, like compelling ideas wrapped in wishful thinking.

But let us be reminded by Jesus' very words: "I will come again and will take you to myself." This is more certain than whatever you have on your calendar for today. Your plans may change. His will not.

YOUR LIFE IN ACTION

In what ways do you find the coming return of Christ and
spending eternity with Him to be motivating?

> *When [God] summoned a famine on the land*
> *and broke all supply of bread, he had sent a man ahead of them,*
> *Joseph, who was sold as a slave (Psalm 105:16–17).*

Suffering, in the life of a Christian, always has a context that is beyond that person's life and lifespan. God is always doing more than we can see at any given moment.

This does not mean that God is a cosmic manipulator, knocking our lives against others in uncaring ways. It means that He is building His kingdom, and you are playing a part that is beyond the hardships of today. God may give you a glimpse of what your role is, and He may not. Sometimes the lessons to be learned, the changes to be made, and the blessings to be received are not fully known until the next generation, or even the next.

Joseph is a good example. He suffered many setbacks, insults, false accusations, and broken hopes. Brothers and friends turned against him. The favored son became an inmate. Yet this was all part of God's plan; Joseph was the man God had sent ahead.

We may hope for God to explain Himself, to tell us why we are in a storm; God is not put off by our asking. But we must understand that sometimes our suffering indicates that we have been sent ahead. It may not be to save a starving nation, as in the case of Joseph, but it may be to turn the tide of your family from spiritual darkness to light, or to display the grace of God within your circle of friends and neighbors, or to set about an unbelievable chain of events that will bring the gospel to a people group you don't even know exists.

YOUR LIFE IN ACTION

What people in your life or family history has God sent ahead to accomplish His purposes?

There arose a new king over Egypt,
who did not know Joseph (Exodus 1:8).

Count Nikolaus von Zinzendorf, who helped found the Moravian Church, used to tell their missionaries in training to "preach the gospel, die, and be forgotten." In doing so he emphasized a principle Christians in every century should live by: Do not live for fame. It has no value.

Can you imagine the once legendary Joseph, whose run from prisoner to prince, from pit dweller to national treasure, becoming a John Doe in the chronicles of Egypt? Yet that's exactly what did happen. Joseph the Vice Pharaoh became Joseph the Unknown.

Notoriety didn't matter to Joseph, though. Nor should it matter to any who serve in God's kingdom. We are all and only devoted to the fame of our Savior.

When John the Baptist said, "'I am not the Christ, but I have been sent before him.' . . . He must increase, but I must decrease" (John 3:28, 30), he unlocked the *how to* in the command to humble yourself (1 Peter 5:6). True humility comes not from self-deprecation but from Christ-exaltation, from making much of Him!

There is a parallel principle that we should also remember: God will not forget you. As one upon whom God has set His love, you are always in His sight and under His care. This is better—always better—than fame.

YOUR LIFE IN ACTION

Which is better, fame or God's unbroken attentiveness?
Why is it better?

*[Nehemiah said to the people], "Do not be afraid of them.
Remember the Lord, who is great and awesome, and fight for your brothers,
your sons, your daughters, your wives, and your homes" (Nehemiah 4:14).*

What will you allow to motivate you today? This is a bigger question than, "What motivates you?" You have a choice in the matter; you elect your own influencers. You will be driven to do certain things for certain reasons, and you choose the reasons.

In the book of Nehemiah, a group of people were busy doing God's will, rebuilding the wall and gates around Jerusalem. They were organized, unified, and dedicated, but they were also under a verbal attack that threatened to get physical. Their God-hating enemies intended to do whatever was necessary to stop the God-pleasing progress.

Nehemiah could see that the enemies' words were having an effect. As the threat level increased, the people were getting fearful and distracted, and the work was slowing down. Nehemiah then spoke words of motivation that restored their courage. He told them to remember God and to fight on behalf of those who could not.

Sometimes God calls us to do a work that is discouraging. When confident that we are doing His will, we should remind ourselves that God's glory matters most. Our perseverance demonstrates that God is worthy of unflagging allegiance and trust.

So, when resistance comes, *remember Him*. Furthermore, remain faithful for the sake of others, protecting them and providing for them according to God's will. *Remember them*.

YOUR LIFE IN ACTION

How do you typically respond to resistance, even when you know you are doing God's will? Is your motivation generally centered on the glory of God and the good of others, or on your own desires?

If you, O Lord, should mark iniquities, O Lord, who could stand?
But with you there is forgiveness, that you may be feared (Psalm 130:3–4).

All forgiveness is not equal. The consequences of one offense may not be anywhere near as severe as the consequences of another. Furthermore, one wronged person may be of very little threat to exact punishment, while another may put the offender's life in jeopardy.

Get caught taking a dollar from the coffee shop tip jar, and at worst you'll be asked never to come back. Get caught robbing a bank, and you're facing prison time. If the manager of the coffee shop forgives you, you put the dollar back and suffer some embarrassment, rightly so. But if the bank forgives you, you get your freedom back.

We fear most the one whose power for taking revenge is greatest, and we hold in highest regard the one who, though able to punish severely, forgives completely.

Every illustration falls short when describing God and His ways, but the point here should be clear. Frankly, the capacity of God's vengeance is restrained only by His counter-capacity to forgive. Therefore, we can rest in God's forgiveness. We can even enjoy it and delight in it. But the one thing we should never do is take it lightly.

The fear of God can be a difficult thing to understand, and many would rather not think of God in such terms. Yet the Bible tells us that "the fear of the Lord is the beginning of wisdom" (Proverbs 9:10). We must learn to fear the One whose power for exacting revenge and forgiving sinners is and always will be unmatched.

YOUR LIFE IN ACTION

Describe what it means to fear the Lord.

There is one whose rash words are like sword thrusts,
but the tongue of the wise brings healing (Proverbs 12:18).

God gave us the ability to speak, to communicate with one another. We should be careful to use that ability *ex modo prescripto*, that is, in the manner prescribed. Proverbs 12:18 is one of many portions of Scripture that prescribes the proper way to communicate. Here we find a simple contrast of how one might use his or her words.

In the first case, there is the person who is rash and careless in speech. He is dangerous with his words and is likely to injure the one who hears them. Inwardly, the listener recoils and wants to get away from the one who speaks. The symbolism of a sword emphasizes the point all the more, depicting an ongoing assault of words that will wear the opposition down, and setting up a final and lethal jab.

In the second case is a person who is not only careful with word selection but whose purpose is to heal and help. His goal is not for the other party to lose so that he may win, but to help so that neither loses. This he does with caution, precision ("A word fitly spoken is like apples of gold in a setting of silver" Proverbs 25:11), and pure intent.

Communication is not just about words; it is about life and relationship, about serving others and lifting them up, and yes, at times correcting them. This is using the ability to speak in the manner God prescribed.

Speak carefully today.

YOUR LIFE IN ACTION

As you approach every conversation today, picture yourself putting your sword in its sheath. This may seem silly, but the symbolism will help.

They forgot God, their Savior, who had done great things in Egypt, wondrous works in the land of Ham, and awesome deeds by the Red Sea (Psalm 106:21–22).

Do you remember what your life was like before Christ controlled it? While it is good and healthy to avoid recalling specific acts of sin, it is helpful to remember the hopelessness of your life before Christ, and even better to think about the people, events, and circumstances He used to draw you to Himself. In other words, remember the great things God did to bring you out of your "Egypt."

In many biblical accounts, people's spiritual decline can be traced back to their forgetting the works of God. As a countermeasure, throughout both the Old and New Testaments, God's people are encouraged to remember. And they were not to keep these memories to themselves but to tell them to one another. In this way, their own faith was bolstered, others were encouraged, and God was publicly exalted.

Remembering the works of God in your life and in the lives of friends and family can set your heart on a path of thanksgiving, praise, and faith. Be intentional rather than passive about such remembering. Talk to yourself and to others about the goodness of God and how He brought you out of Egypt.

YOUR LIFE IN ACTION

Look for an opportunity today to tell a friend about a way that God has worked in your life.

---

*The people who survived the sword found grace in the wilderness.
. . . I have loved you with an everlasting love;
therefore I have continued my faithfulness to you (Jeremiah 31:2–3).*

God's love for His children is eternal, assuring them of an ultimate future filled with never-ending joy. In the meantime, however, they will encounter seasons of barrenness that may draw them down to near despair. Yet even in those times, they can endure because of their future and certain hope. They can find grace in the wilderness.

Ecclesiastes 3:11 says that God has "put eternity into man's heart." First Corinthians 15:19 gives a corresponding thought where Paul declares, "If in Christ we have hope in this life only, we are of all people most to be pitied." In both passages, as well as in Jeremiah 3, we are encouraged to approach life in the context of eternity. This means that in Christ, we long for the eternal and perfect future, and its coming reality makes some of life enjoyable and all of it endurable.

Does today hold hardship for you? Know that there is coming a day of eternal rest. Long for it. Does today hold celebration for you? Know that this will be only a foretaste of never-ending joy. Taste it. Does today present a difficult decision? Know that the God who inhabits eternity dwells in you. Rest in Him.

Be strong and take courage. Do not give in to thoughts of despair. The wilderness is but a season you must pass through on your way Home.

YOUR LIFE IN ACTION
What do you think of when you think of heaven and eternity?

"Am I not allowed to do what I choose with what belongs to me? Or do you begrudge my generosity?" (Matthew 20:15).

Never would we dare give God advice, but we often question and silently scold Him. Our jealousy is proof.

Matthew 20 records a parable that calls attention to God's great generosity. The storyline is this: A landowner is looking to hire some day laborers to work in his vineyard. He finds some, they agree to the wage he offers, and they go to work. A few hours later, in need of more laborers, the landowner hires a few more. This happens at least three more times. Finally, at the end of the work day the laborers line up to receive their pay. Those who worked the entire day are tired and dirty, but also happy because they expect to get paid more than the rest. But to their shock, they are paid the same as those who worked only one hour. It wasn't *fair*.

Then the landowner explained that what they were really quarreling over was not their wage (remember, he paid what they agreed to), but his generosity. Twelve-hour pay for one hour of work was a blessing, regardless of who received it.

Our reaction can be much the same as the jealous laborers'. When God blesses us, we rejoice. But if God blesses someone we consider undeserving, we may feel jealous, or even angry. Shouldn't our response be the same any time we see God's grace in action, whether toward ourselves, people we like, or even people we don't like?

After all, who *really* deserves God's goodness?

YOUR LIFE IN ACTION

Look for ways God shows His goodness and grace to others today, and say a prayer of thanksgiving each time you see it.

So [Hagar] called the name of the LORD who spoke to her,
"You are a God of seeing," for she said, "Truly here I have seen
him who looks after me" (Genesis 16:13).

God sees you, always. Be glad that He does. Hagar was running away to save her life and her baby. God saw what was going on, and He sent an angel to reassure her. The angel told Hagar to go back to the people and place she had fled; God would watch over her. Hagar rejoiced: "You are a God of seeing." She knew that never being out of God's sight meant never being out of His care.

Another woman found the same sense of hope and relief when she, too, realized that God saw her. At a well one day, Jesus drew the truth out of her, breaking through her inhibitions of shame and remorse, opening her soul to receive the living water of eternal forgiveness. So elated was she at being "found out" and forgiven, she urged everyone in her village—all of whom would have known of her shady past—"Come, see a man who told me all that I ever did" (John 4:29).

It is good to be seen and known by God. This matter of being found out, however momentarily painful it may be, is but a prelude to the outpouring of God's great mercy.

Hagar would tell you, as would the woman at the well and every person who has ever encountered the God of mercy. Do not try to run or hide from God. Run to the God of seeing, to the One who knows all that you ever did. Be found out. Receive His mercy.

YOUR LIFE IN ACTION

Are you glad today that God sees and knows everything about you?
Tell Him. Are you wishing you could hide something from God?
Confess your sin to God, and receive His forgiveness.

Blessed be the God and Father of our Lord Jesus Christ, the Father of mercies and God of all comfort, who comforts us in all our affliction, so that we may be able to comfort those who are in any affliction, with the comfort with which we ourselves are comforted by God (2 Corinthians 1:3–4).

All who live will suffer affliction. All who are alive in Christ will be comforted by God in their affliction. All who have been comforted by God should become comforters to others in their affliction.

We are often taught in Christian circles how to be responsible stewards of our money, time, and talent in order to serve and support the kingdom-building work of God. We see ourselves as the manager of these things rather than the owner, knowing that all we possess we have been given (1 Corinthians 4:7). Therefore, we are ready to pass some or all of it on to others as God directs.

And so it is with comfort. We should not keep it to ourselves.

Do you remember your darkest days, when your suffering was indescribable . . . when you thought the oppression might literally kill you? Do you also remember the comfort of God that made you able to endure? Are you even now amazed that you survived the soul trauma and emerged with peace rather than in pieces?

Don't keep that comfort to yourself. Someday, perhaps today, there will be a person in your sphere of influence whose sense of hopelessness is as deep as yours once was. God wants you to carry His comfort to them—a comfort only He can provide and only you can deliver.

YOUR LIFE IN ACTION

Reflect on the times and ways God has comforted you.
Thank Him, and then pray for those you know
who are presently in a time of suffering.

"He has helped his servant Israel, in remembrance of his mercy,
as he spoke to our fathers, to Abraham and to his offspring forever."
". . . to show the mercy promised to our fathers and to remember
his holy covenant" (Luke 1:54–55, 72).

God's promises are kept fresh by His mercy. Generations may pass between God's first proclamation of a promise and its fulfillment, but never will one of His promises be broken.

To break a promise, God would have to forget both the promise and His own mercy. This would be more than a mental lapse—it would mean God ceasing to be Himself. An unkept promise would indicate a diminishing of God's mercy, a declining of His divinity.

For this reason, when Mary learned that she was carrying the Christ child (Luke 1:54-55), and when Zechariah began to prophesy on the day John the Baptist was born (v. 72), both rejoiced in the great covenant-keeping God. Their joy went far beyond their own lives and times, all the way back to the ancient days of a promise made and the ever-present mercy of God in bringing it to fulfillment. God showed indescribable mercy on the day He fulfilled His promise, just as He had been showing mercy every day leading up to its fulfillment.

Those who wait for the promises of God to be fulfilled should live with a sense of spiritual anticipation and intention. The fact that Christ has not yet returned gives evidence to the very mercy that assures us this promise will be seen. "The Lord is not slow to fulfill his promise . . . but is patient toward you, not wishing that any should perish, but that all should reach repentance" (2 Peter 3:9).

YOUR LIFE IN ACTION
Are you in the habit of expecting Christ's return at
any moment? How would your life be affected if you were
to live with that sense of anticipation?

---

*When the angels went away from them into heaven, the shepherds
said to one another, "Let us go over to Bethlehem and see this thing
that has happened, which the Lord has made known to us" (Luke 2:15).*

What started out as just another night of sheep-watching duty
turned into a heavenly encounter, and then a divine one. The
familiar sights and sounds of the countryside were suddenly eclipsed
by the presence of a heavenly messenger.

Seeing that they were nearly overcome with fright, the angel spoke:
"Fear not, for behold, I bring you good news of great joy," followed by
the astonishing announcement that the Messiah had arrived. God
had come to earth, in a village nearby. Suddenly a countless host of
angels were proclaiming in full-throated joy: "Glory to God in the
highest!" How does one go back to work after that?

Isn't it reassuring that such grand news came first to such ordinary
people? These men would truly wonder over getting to spectate, let
alone participate in the activity of God. Even more, they could not
and would not remain still or silent. When they were finally able to
speak, they said to each other, *Let's go!* They knew God hadn't told
them about this wondrous occurrence to keep it to themselves.

Was it any less wonderful when Christ the Redeemer made Himself
known to you? Did you then, and do you still, respond as the shepherds? Do you seek and worship Him? Do you proclaim the good
news of His coming? Do you marvel that, having neither more nor
less advantage than the shepherds, you were given news of the Savior?

YOUR LIFE IN ACTION

Take time to marvel over the fact that you have been given the
opportunity to hear and respond to the gospel. Find a way to express
your admiration to the Savior, in prayer or in song.

Jesus, perceiving in himself that power had gone out from him, immediately turned about in the crowd and said, "Who touched my garments?" . . . But the woman, knowing what had happened to her, came in fear and trembling and fell down before him and told him the whole truth. And he said to her, "Daughter, your faith has made you well; go in peace, and be healed of your disease" (Mark 5:30, 33–34).

All that mattered to this woman was getting to Jesus. After years of suffering, she was desperate. This dear lady was down to her last hope. Suffering had brought her to singular faith in Christ alone. She believed, rightly so, that He was the only one who could help her.

God had so arranged matters that Jesus was in her vicinity that very day (divine appointments often look like coincidence to us), so she put all her energy into getting to Him. Something (Someone) told her that if she could just touch Jesus' garment, she would be healed.

This biblical story is not a promise of physical healing to everyone. Other sick people in the crowd that day perhaps went away as ill as when they arrived. The point is this: Regardless of the nature or cause of your suffering, even if self-inflicted due to your sinful choices, know that there is One and only One who cares about you supremely.

In your desperation, move *toward* your Savior, not away from Him. Seek to touch His garment. He truly is the Wonderful Counselor and Prince of Peace (Isaiah 9:6). The hardships we encounter shape us more than most other events and circumstances. Desperation will activate either our fear or our faith.

YOUR LIFE IN ACTION

Are you in a season of hardship and suffering right now?
Are you moving toward Christ?

"When you are invited, go and sit in the lowest place,
so that when your host comes he may say to you, 'Friend, move up higher.'
Then you will be honored in the presence of all who sit at table with you.
For everyone who exalts himself will be humbled,
and he who humbles himself will be exalted" (Luke 14:10–11).

Humble is both an adjective and a verb; it is something you *are* as well as something you *do*. If humble is what you want to be, then humbling yourself is what you must do.

Jesus used the occasion of a dinner party to emphasize the importance of being humble. Having accepted an invitation to eat in the home of a leader of the Pharisees, and noticing the haughty approach the other guests took in choosing their seats, Jesus spoke words of rebuke, correction, and instruction. He ended with the clear warning that humility does come to all eventually, but those who choose it for themselves escape the shame and pain of a crashing ego.

Many of us have to be humbled (verb) in order to be humble (adjective). Why? Because each time we try to humble ourselves, we are sparring with a fallen nature that is used to getting its way.

We often resist the opportunities God presents us for humbling ourselves, like those who saw themselves worthy of a seat of honor. Christ disapproved of their haughtiness, knowing that in their case it was the very thing that kept them from believing in Him. Pride always blinds us to the spiritual riches that are in Christ.

YOUR LIFE IN ACTION

What circumstances has God brought into your life recently
that He might be using to humble you?

*Blessed is the one whose transgression is forgiven, whose sin is covered.
Blessed is the man against whom the LORD counts no iniquity,
and in whose spirit there is no deceit (Psalm 32:1–2).*

What does it mean to be an *honest* person? A question like that is often answered through contrast. In the absence of dishonesty, an honest person does not tell lies, cheat, or falsely accuse others.

The holy Scriptures hold a higher view of human virtue than we are naturally inclined to consider. As our personal attributes undergo sanctification by the Holy Spirit, we begin to see the deeper and greater things that drive our behavior. We know that honesty does not really stem from our choosing not to do or not to say certain things, but rather from being a person "in whose spirit there is no deceit."

The state of our honesty is revealed mostly through our responses to the Holy Spirit. When He speaks, do we submit or ignore? Do we obey, delay, or even refuse Him? When we sin, we are sometimes inclined to hide it from God—as if that were possible—by giving Him the silent treatment. This reveals a spirit of deceit.

Is your soul languishing in deceit? Are you ignoring God, rationalizing that He doesn't know what you don't admit? The Psalmist puts you on notice that a dishonest soul is feeble and miserable, but forgiveness—along with blessing and vitality—await just on the other side of confession. "I acknowledged my sin to you, and I did not cover my iniquity; I said, 'I will confess my transgressions to the LORD,' and you forgave the iniquity of my sin" (v. 5).

YOUR LIFE IN ACTION
Have you been allowing any sin to linger in your life,
to the point that you no longer bring it before God in prayer?
Break the spirit of deceit today and confess it.

The grace of God has appeared, bringing salvation for all people, training us to renounce ungodliness and worldly passions, and to live self-controlled, upright, and godly lives in the present age, waiting for our blessed hope, the appearing of the glory of our great God and Savior Jesus Christ (Titus 2:11–13).

God is demanding. Every member of His household must be pure, holy, and perfect. If you are His, this is what He requires of you. Can you deliver?

Of course you can't. No one can. And God knows that. For this reason, He has met His own demands through Jesus Christ, His perfect, sinless, holy Son. This is grace, and like meeting the person who will become your most intimate friend, salvation is but your first encounter with grace. From that point on, grace will always be with you.

Titus 2:12 points out that grace functions to train us in godly living. We are not perfect, but we are being perfected. This is a process God will complete in each of us at the appearing of Christ when eternity dawns. Each day, from now until then, God will be at the divine work of shaping us by His grace. There will never be any down time. Grace is always active within us.

You will view today more highly if you'll remember that it is a training day, a day when God is working in you to make you more like His Son. Whatever else your plans and hopes are for today, nothing matters more than this heavenly activity.

YOUR LIFE IN ACTION

Describe what a "self-controlled" or "upright" or "godly"
life would be in terms of your specific circumstances.
In what ways is God training you right now?

The LORD is good to those who wait for him, to the soul who seeks him. It is good that one should wait quietly for the salvation of the LORD. . . . The Lord will not cast off forever, but, though he cause grief, he will have compassion according to the abundance of his steadfast love; for he does not afflict from his heart or grieve the children of men (Lamentations 3:25–26, 31–33).

We sometimes waste time and energy trying to find courage, when usually it is courage that finds us. The problem is, in its approach courage isn't terribly appealing. It looks a great deal like loneliness.

Have you ever felt as if you were the only person left on the planet? Or the first person to ever feel pain so deeply? The last one standing after a fierce battle, but about to fall yourself, and there's no one left to care if you do? Ironically, because loneliness may be the most universal of human emotions, the world is crowded with lonely people. Everyone feels lonely sometime.

Here's some perspective for the lonely child of God: You're never really alone in your loneliness. Whatever circumstance put you there—illness, grief, personal failure, shame, depression, even the wrongdoing of others—it was God who opened the door. He either allowed you or ushered you into the isolation chamber. This is His place for you for now. And there, alone with Him, you'll learn things you'd never experience in a crowd.

"The evidences of courage may be public, but the substance of it is always forged in loneliness" (Andrée Seu).

YOUR LIFE IN ACTION

Do you find yourself in a time of extended loneliness? Are you trying to receive from others what God Himself wants to give you? Begin journaling what God is teaching you about Himself.

Whether you eat or drink, or whatever you do, do all to the glory of God.
Give no offense to Jews or to Greeks or to the church of God, just as I try to
please everyone in everything I do, not seeking my own advantage,
but that of many, that they may be saved (1 Corinthians 10:31–33).

Do we stop our reading of 1 Corinthians 10 too soon? Many who are familiar with the "do all to the glory of God" phrase in verse 31 may be surprised at what follows: instructions for applying this exhortation to interpersonal relationships. "I try to please everyone with everything I do." Just as Scripture specifies that we cannot love God while not loving our brother (1 John 4:20), so neither can we glorify God without serving and helping others in a gospel-centered way.

Many have accepted an "It's not about me, it's about God" mentality, and that's a good outlook to have, as far as it goes. But we must go on to the successive biblical teaching that leads us to also embrace an "It's not about me, it's about you" love for our neighbors and friends. For then, when we must put a name and face on someone that we *have to* love, especially those who make it a challenge to do so, we come upon the true living out of biblical Christianity. Our obedience to the high calling of loving and serving others is the true telling of our love for God.

Such a calling is beyond us. It exceeds our ability every day and, if we're honest, exceeds our desires most days. But as with all things God requires of us, He has already made provision. Our example is Christ Himself, "who for the joy that was set before him endured the cross, despising the shame" (Hebrews 12:2). Therefore, seek always to show not *your* best display of love, but Christ's.

YOUR LIFE IN ACTION

What matters most to you—that people like you, or that they know Jesus loves them? What opportunities is God giving you to serve others in such a way that they might be open to hearing the gospel?

Jesus, knowing their thoughts, said, "Why do you think evil in your hearts? For which is easier, to say, 'Your sins are forgiven,' or to say, 'Rise and walk'? But that you may know that the Son of Man has authority on earth to forgive sins"—he then said to the paralytic—"Rise, pick up your bed and go home." And he rose and went home (Matthew 9:4–7).

When it comes to the matter of sin, there are three truths we must never forget: (1) We all sin. (2) Sin has severe and eternal consequences. (3) Christ alone can forgive sin.

We might give only a nod of affirmation to the first truth without experiencing any real disturbance in our hearts. Perhaps especially those who have been in Christ for quite some time are at risk of taking sin too lightly. But pondering the next truth should disquiet any apathetic soul, even a redeemed one. We used to be dead (Ephesians 2:1).

Too often we live in a state of spiritual stupor, brought on by forgetting both the desperation of our sinfulness and the wonder of salvation. This leads us to the third truth—that Christ alone can forgive sin—and the way God works to keep that truth alive in our hearts.

Here, not only was a paralytic man healed, but he and others witnessed the ultimate power of Christ to forgive sin. Whether any of them believed, we do not know, but there is a lesson here for all who do believe: Every work of God we are privileged to witness should serve as a reminder of the greatness of God and His ultimate power to forgive sin.

YOUR LIFE IN ACTION

Be on the lookout today for demonstrations of the power of God. Each time you see it, take a moment to acknowledge, and thank Him, that He alone has the power to forgive sin.

> *Wisdom is shown to be right*
> *by the lives of those who follow it (Luke 7:35 NLT).*

When it comes to Christianity, the world is full of doubters and skeptics. Many question the existence of God; some make room for the possibility that He's out there somewhere. Fewer still accept that Jesus is God who came in the flesh and that "there is salvation in no one else" (Acts 4:12). This belief is so far beyond the realm of human reasoning that God Himself must give us the faith to accept it.

Is there anything you can do to "validate" the gospel and remove at least some of the barriers of resistance and unbelief? Is there some way God can use you to give authentic witness to redemption? Yes.

Your very life as a follower of Christ gives evidence of His saving grace. This does not come about by your "trying to be a better witness," as if you were changing your physical appearance. This validation comes about as your inner growth in Christ becomes outwardly apparent.

Paul put it this way when writing to the Corinthians: "You yourselves are our letter of recommendation, written on our hearts, to be known and read by all. And you show that you are a letter from Christ delivered by us, written not with ink but with the Spirit of the living God" (2 Corinthians 3:2–3). He recognized that the authenticity of their faith would be obvious through the way they conducted themselves.

This did not mean that they (or we) should be silent witnesses who never put the gospel into words. It means that our lives represent not our own claims, but the very claims of Christ.

YOUR LIFE IN ACTION

How was your belief in the gospel influenced by the lives of Christians you knew?

> *Commit your work to the LORD,*
> *and your plans will be established (Proverbs 16:3).*

Do you ever wish God would make the next step so obvious there would be no way for you to miss it? Have you ever been emotionally seized up because you're not confident that what you want to do is what God has for you to do? Or, in a moment of painful honesty, have you ever been reluctant to even seek God's will because you'd already made plans you feared He wouldn't approve?

To *commit* means literally "to roll." It is similar in thought to the word *cast* in Psalm 55:22, "Cast your burden on the LORD, and he will sustain you." As we should be doing with our burdens, we should also be doing with the work our heart is set on undertaking; we should first roll it up to the Lord for clarification and empowerment.

How foolish it is to hide our intentions and desires from God or neglect to learn from Him whether the work is right for us to do. Perhaps He has a different assignment, or a different time or way. At the very least we miss an opportunity to talk with our Father, to interact with Him about something so personal as the plans and desires of our heart. Worse yet, we'll likely find ourselves crawling along under the diminished limitations of our flesh when we could be running and conquering in the Spirit.

God is not out to kill our joy. He wants His children to taste the delicious flavor of success; thus His promise of well-established plans coming *after* we have rolled up to Him our intended and desired work.

YOUR LIFE IN ACTION
When it comes to making decisions, are you in the habit of approaching God first, or of asking Him to bless what you've already decided?

Let your heart therefore be wholly true to the LORD our God,
walking in his statutes and keeping his commandments,
as at this day (1 Kings 8:61).

Most of our struggles with sin do not begin with making wrong decisions, but with failing to make and keep right commitments. Allowing ourselves to get distracted from pursuing God, and neglecting basic spiritual disciplines, brings down our resistance to sin and makes us more likely to stumble.

As an example, consider the basic commitment of having a daily quiet time with God in His Word and prayer. Such a discipline, when faithfully observed over a period of time, can strengthen your spirit in several ways, including:

- guiding your thoughts to where they need to be

- developing your sense of discernment

- making you mindful of God's constant presence

- giving you greater clarity and confidence in making decisions

These are but a few of the ways our spirits can be strengthened through just one area of discipline, and these are all in addition to the reward of building our resistance to sin. So, when we find ourselves in a weakening spiritual state, we would be wise to ask, *What commitments have I set aside that I need to pick up again?*

YOUR LIFE IN ACTION

What commitments have you held on to, related to your spiritual development, that have served you well over the years? Which ones have you abandoned that you need to recover?

Not that I am speaking of being in need, for I have learned in whatever situation I am to be content (Philippians 4:11).

Though our nature pushes us to seek comfort, sometimes even at the expense of relationships, we should know that contentment is better by far. Though elusive, it is as near as God Himself. Paul's words in Philippians 4:11 reveal three truths about contentment:

- Contentment must be learned. It is not in our human nature to be settled and joyful when there are still things we want that we do not have; but when our hearts are turned to God, the switchover to contentment begins. We learn to want what He wants, to accept what He gives, and to reserve our expectations of euphoria for heaven.

- Contentment recognizes circumstances, but does not depend on them. Content people have good days and bad ones. Some content people are wealthy, and some are poor. Paul slept in palaces and dungeons, ate the food of kings and of criminals. Contentment took him to places that comfort would never have gone, and opened up many opportunities for the proclamation of the gospel.

- Contentment makes one generous. Paul wanted the readers of his letter to understand that he was not playing on their sympathies or trying to manipulate them into showering him with gifts and donations. He was verbalizing a truth that had so liberated his life, he hoped they would learn it too. He didn't want what they had; he wanted them to have what he had.

YOUR LIFE IN ACTION

Are you driven by the pursuit of comfort, or are you content? Has God used your various circumstances to give you opportunities for sharing and demonstrating your faith in Christ?

Jesus answered them, "Truly, truly, I say to you, you are seeking me, not because you saw signs, but because you ate your fill of the loaves. Do not work for the food that perishes, but for the food that endures to eternal life, which the Son of Man will give to you. For on him God the Father has set his seal" (John 6:26–27).

Jesus had more fans than He had followers. Some were curious about His unusual teachings, others were fascinated by the miracles He performed, and still others coveted His popularity and hoped to duplicate His capabilities for their own gain.

Receiving good from God and enjoying it does not necessarily mean that a person is a true follower. He or she may want nothing more than . . . *more*, whether that means more bread and fish, or a bigger house and paycheck.

Many are fans, fewer are followers. For them, when the enjoyment ends, so will their discipleship.

Why are you following Jesus? The ultimate truth about Him is this: "There is salvation in no one else, for there is no other name under heaven given among men by which we must be saved" (Acts 4:12).

There are countless benefits and enjoyments that you may experience in this life because you know Jesus, but never lose the wonder of redemption that comes through Him alone.

YOUR LIFE IN ACTION

Take several minutes in prayer, concentrating only on thanking God for salvation through Christ.

After this many of his disciples turned back and no longer walked with him. So Jesus said to the Twelve, "Do you want to go away as well?" Simon Peter answered him, "Lord, to whom shall we go? You have the words of eternal life, and we have believed, and have come to know, that you are the Holy One of God" (John 6:66–69).

For many people, the greatest obstacle to placing their faith in Christ is His claim to be the only way of salvation. This is a difficult truth, and some even find it offensive.

It is an affront to them to think that the other things they have chosen to worship, and even their own perceived goodness, fall short of God's justice. They want to decide what's good enough and determine their own way, or at least have a say in it.

The work Jesus came to earth to accomplish, leading up to His sacrificial death on the cross, was for the purpose of proving that He was the One sent from God. All of His miracles and all of His teaching, indeed everything He said and did testified that He was the "Holy One of God." He was the One sent to save us.

As a Christian, let your heart be stirred to do two things today:

- Humbly thank God for revealing Christ to you so you could call on Him and be saved.

- Pray for those you love who are resisting Christ as the way, truth, and life (see John 14:6).

YOUR LIFE IN ACTION

Pray for your family members and friends who are not believing in Jesus Christ for salvation.

*Humble yourselves, therefore, under the mighty hand of God
so that at the proper time he may exalt you,
casting all your anxieties on him, because he cares for you (1 Peter 5:6–7).*

Offloading our anxieties onto God is sometimes an act of desperation, and it is always an act of humility. When the pain of a certain trial or need begins to dominate our thoughts, we have little strength to do anything but worry. And with whatever energy we may muster, in a state of anxiety, we will likely do or say something that makes matters worse.

Our troubles, whether overwhelming or simply irritating, should drive us first to call on God. In so doing we are humbling ourselves and acknowledging our need for God's care. This is the only reliable exit strategy from our worries.

So if humility takes the pressure off, pride puts—or keeps—the pressure on. The way of the proud man (or woman) grows increasingly difficult throughout his life.

All of us encounter anxiety-producing situations in life, some more threatening than others. Those who humble themselves in the face of these challenges by turning them over to God will endure and grow stronger. But those who try to handle these matters on their own become weak, harsh, and miserable. Pride exacts a higher price than humility ever will.

YOUR LIFE IN ACTION

If you are facing a challenging circumstance in your life right now, have you yet cast your anxieties about this situation onto God? If not, will you take this step of humility today?

*The name of the second he called Ephraim, "For God has made
me fruitful in the land of my affliction" (Genesis 41:52).*

Joseph had gone to Egypt as a prisoner. He was there due to circumstances that could have easily led to a lifetime of bitterness, resentment, and a thirst for revenge. Egypt was a cruel place for him, a place of suffering and injustice.

Things did eventually get better for Joseph, and then they got not just bad again, but worse. After the suffering there was relief, and then more suffering. Sound familiar?

We all have an Egypt experience—a place or time of affliction. Joseph's life is a template, displaying the passing seasons from suffering to relief to suffering to relief and back again. The cycle will not be completely broken until we cross over into heaven.

Yet we can, and should, be like Joseph in that God makes us fruitful in the land of our affliction. We need not live out our days on earth in drudgery, defeat, and barrenness.

We can enjoy the goodness of our Savior through worship and through making disciples. Our heavenly activity now can keep us mindful of our heavenly home that is to come.

YOUR LIFE IN ACTION

What are you planning to do today that has
the imprint of heaven on it?

He told them a parable to the effect that they ought always to pray and not lose heart.... "Nevertheless, when the Son of Man comes, will he find faith on earth?" (Luke 18:1, 8).

People love stories, and Jesus often used parables (stories told for moral/spiritual purposes) to teach things that were new or hard to understand. The problem we sometimes have in reading such parables is that we get so wrapped up in the storyline that we forget the main point. In the case of the parable in Luke 18, the point Jesus made was this: Pray until you get an answer.

The widow in the parable was stubborn in a good way; she was persistent. She appealed to a judge, who was for a long time unwilling to help her, until he gave in and met her request.

Jesus tells this story, His point being clear, and ends by asking, "When the Son of Man comes, will he find faith on earth?" In the context of the parable, Jesus was asking, *When I return, will I find you still stubbornly praying for things that have not yet been answered?*, implying that there are things we will be praying for until our dying day, or until Jesus returns, whichever comes first.

In this way we are to be like the saints described in Hebrews 11:13—"These all died in faith, not having received the things promised, but having seen them and greeted them from afar, and having acknowledged that they were strangers and exiles on the earth."

Are you praying with faith for things you are not certain to personally witness? Be a stubborn pray-er.

YOUR LIFE IN ACTION

What or who should you commit to praying for regularly, knowing that you may be praying for this the rest of your life?

> *Whenever you stand praying, forgive, if you have anything*
> *against anyone, so that your Father also who is in heaven*
> *may forgive you your trespasses (Mark 11:25).*

Holding grudges hinders prayer. While the truth of that statement sinks in, consider a core question: Are you so convinced of the power of prayer that it troubles you when your prayers are hindered?

If not, then prayer has become little more than a symbolic routine. But if keeping a vital prayer life matters to you, put yourself in the place of Gideon's would-be warriors (see Judges 7).

God called Gideon to lead His people in battle. Gideon rallied 32,000 troops and set out to fulfill his duty. Along the way God told Gideon he had too many warriors and began sending some of them back home.

The first 22,000 were relieved of duty because they were afraid. God then had Gideon take the remaining 10,000 through an unusual test that further reduced the number of warriors to a mere 300. Imagine being a disqualified warrior—trained, equipped, sent, and then suspended.

Now imagine being a disqualified pray-er. If you are holding grudges by withholding forgiveness, that is what you are. But this is where you differ from Gideon's would-be warriors. Your calling as a praying man or woman has not been revoked. In fact, God very much wants you praying. He needs intercessors. You can reenlist: *If you have anything against anyone, forgive.*

YOUR LIFE IN ACTION

Is there anyone you need to forgive? Understand that refusing to forgive brings division not only between you and that person, but also between you and God.

"Why are you sleeping?
Rise and pray that you may not enter into temptation" (Luke 22:46).

The enemy is emboldened by our procrastination in prayer, and he will use it to his advantage. The longer we delay praying against temptation, the more likely we are to give in to it.

Of course we should pray when we find ourselves facing temptation. It is appropriate to call out to God in the heat of battle.

But how much better off we would be if we prayed far in advance, even to the point of praying to be spared temptation entirely! This kind of praying raises our awareness of sin's approach, equipping us to recognize sin that can otherwise camouflage itself as harmless and appealing.

It is not wrong to reactively pray. Sin is ever present in our world, and we have a cunning enemy who relentlessly pursues our downfall. But if our praying is always and only reactive in nature, we will lose more battles with temptation than we win.

However, proactive, watchful praying positions us to overcome sin by outmaneuvering the enemy. For this reason, Jesus called on His disciples to rise and pray.

YOUR LIFE IN ACTION

Knowing the ways in which you are weak and likely to be tempted, pray that God will protect you from falling today.

As he passed by, he saw a man blind from birth. And his disciples asked him, "Rabbi, who sinned, this man or his parents, that he was born blind?" Jesus answered, "It was not that this man sinned, or his parents, but that the works of God might be displayed in him" (John 9:1–3).

Incomplete information almost always leads to faulty conclusions. And anytime we leave God out, our information is incomplete.

When the disciples saw a man who had been blind his entire life, their worldview allowed for only one explanation: His deficiency was a punishment for sin. Jesus immediately revealed the hole in their thinking.

There was another explanation that was all about God. A much greater thing was happening: Jesus was being revealed as the Son of God, the promised Messiah. It would be through miracles such as the healing of this man's blindness that Jesus would prove His deity and many would believe in Him.

Have you ever stopped to consider that some of the challenges you or your loved ones face are not really about you or them at all? Could it be that God is displaying His reality through your weakness, even your pain?

God is always doing more than we realize or imagine. In fact, your temporary suffering could become the basis for others to believe in Christ.

YOUR LIFE IN ACTION

If you or a loved one are in a time of suffering, as you pray for comfort and healing, pray also that God will use it for His purposes.

Jesus did many other signs in the presence of the disciples,
which are not written in this book; but these are written so that you may
believe that Jesus is the Christ, the Son of God, and that by believing
you may have life in his name (John 20:30–31).

The reason John gave for writing his gospel account is the same reason we should read it—and all of Scripture—regularly: that we may believe that Jesus is the Christ, the Son of God. We need the reminder.

Jesus is the focal point of the entire storyline of the Bible. The Old Testament, which chronicles the creation of the world, the fall of mankind, and the inability of man to reconnect with God, points ahead to the need of the Savior. The New Testament, which reveals the grand story of redemption, life with Christ, the evangelization of the world, and eternal restoration, exalts the completed work of the Savior.

Yet it is sadly common for believers to sometimes live in a state of spiritual dullness, as if Christ Himself has become weak and irrelevant. It is only in our minds that this could be the case.

Jesus is the same yesterday, today, and forever. He has fully satisfied the demands of God's justice. He has overcome death once and for all. He has not grown weary. He has no less love, wisdom, grace, or mercy today than yesterday. Nor will He tomorrow.

Reading Scripture reminds us of all that Christ is. Strengthen your soul today through the Word of God.

YOUR LIFE IN ACTION

If you do not have a daily Bible reading plan, begin one today.
The Gospels (Matthew, Mark, Luke, and John)
are an excellent place to start.

I will give thanks to the LORD with my whole heart,
in the company of the upright,
in the congregation (Psalm 111:1).

A crowded heart can be a good thing, but only if it's crowded with the right affections. Like gratitude, for instance.

Imagine having a heart so full of gratitude there is no room for grumbling, resentment, anxiety, or revenge. These responses and many others like them are the corrupting temptations that poison our thoughts every day.

However strong our morning resolve might be to resist their grip, by noon—if not before—the memory of some hurt or slight puts us right back under their spell. The anger or fear or shame returns . . . another brief reprieve followed by hours of the same old feelings.

Perhaps today you can try a different approach: Crowd your heart with gratitude. In other words, *give thanks to the LORD with your **whole** heart.*

YOUR LIFE IN ACTION

Pray for several minutes doing nothing but thanking God.
Thank Him for people, provision, etc.

[Jesus] said to them, "Pay attention to what you hear:
with the measure you use, it will be measured to you, and still more will be
added to you. For to the one who has, more will be given, and from the one
who has not, even what he has will be taken away" (Mark 4:24–25).

Having direct access to Jesus didn't guarantee that the disciples would always understand His teaching. On more than one occasion, we find them asking Jesus clarifying questions after the crowds had gone home.

Even when Jesus taught using parables, the disciples didn't necessarily get the point. At least once, described in Mark 4, Jesus used their lack of comprehension to reveal an underlying issue: Their obedience was lagging behind their knowledge. In other words, obeying the truth they knew would increase their capacity to understand more truth, while not acting on the truth they knew would prove a hindrance.

Disobedience—whether in the form of defiance (acting in opposition to God's will) or indifference (taking no action on God's known will)—stunted the disciples' spiritual growth. Does it also stunt yours?

Many times we want to *know* more than we are willing to *do*. Our motive for acquiring biblical knowledge is often for the purpose of making an impression rather than making disciples. We want the reputation of being spiritually mature without doing the real work of our mission: "Go therefore and make disciples of all nations" (Matthew 28:19).

YOUR LIFE IN ACTION

Is your obedience in sync with your biblical knowledge,
or does it lag behind? What do you understand of the truths
in Scripture that you have not yet acted on?

> *Being sent on their way by the church, they passed through both Phoenicia and Samaria, describing in detail the conversion of the Gentiles, and brought great joy to all the brothers (Acts 15:3).*

One of the greatest joys a believer can experience is hearing the news of people being born into the family of God. Our souls are refreshed when we are reminded that the gospel is being actively proclaimed in our own community and throughout the world, and that people of all ages, backgrounds, and nationalities are being delivered from the domain of darkness (Colossians 1:13).

You *need* to hear what God is doing, what grand transformations He is bringing about. If you're not hearing these stories, seek them out.

The advent of modern technology has brought global news into your home, giving ready access to a steady stream of reports from mission agencies, churches, and other organizations God is using to make disciples throughout the world. Pay attention to what God is doing through the witness of your own church and other like-hearted churches in your region.

As you pray for the global witness of the church, listen carefully for the news of what God is doing. Your joy will increase, and your faith will enlarge.

YOUR LIFE IN ACTION

Spend time today seeking out stories of the gospel at work in your community and other places in the world, and thank God for those He is delivering from the domain of darkness.

*From now on, therefore, we regard no one according to the flesh.
Even though we once regarded Christ according to the flesh, we regard him thus
no longer. Therefore, if anyone is in Christ, he is a new creation.
The old has passed away; behold, the new has come (2 Corinthians 5:16–17).*

Christ changes everything, even the way we know each other. Before Christ, we could only know people on a superficial level. Even what might be considered "meaningful" to know about a friend—things like their deepest sadness, highest happiness, or even the history we may have shared with them—comes to an unfulfilling end when we part ways.

But that all changed when we came into Christ. Now there is an eternal significance, or at least the possibility of it, in every relationship. Our "regard" has shifted from the limits of our human love to the limitlessness of Christ's sacrificial love. At the very least, this means:

- You cannot give up praying for the salvation of those you love whose spiritual state you are unsure of.

- You will never close your heart to the hope of reconciliation when conflict has come between you and a brother or sister in Christ.

- You reject any and all demands for revenge, no matter how badly your flesh wants it.

- You rejoice in every demonstration of God's goodness, no matter who benefits from it.

Be glad that you are in Christ today. Let Him live and love through you.

YOUR LIFE IN ACTION

Four items are listed today that characterize the possible
state of various relationships in your life. Take Christlike action
in one of these relationships today.

In Christ Jesus neither circumcision nor uncircumcision
counts for anything, but only faith
working through love (Galatians 5:6).

Some of the harshest people in the world are those who are trying to please God and gain His approval. That was the condition of some Paul wrote to in his letter to the Galatians. They were demanding things of themselves—and therefore expecting the same from those around them—that they assumed would get God's attention and make Him happy. It was (is) a futile attempt to achieve what God has already delivered.

Faith in Jesus Christ finds its expression through loving attitudes and behavior. This is not something a true Christian has to conjure up *(I have faith, so now I must act lovingly)*; it becomes our instinct.

Of course, this is not to say that believers will never again experience conflict; but it does mean that any such obstruction of love between us is concerning, both over the brokenness in the relationship and because of what it says to the world about Jesus. Believers who allow conflict to linger, especially when public, give the enemy grounds to discredit faith in Christ.

Sacrificial, forgiving, longsuffering love is a reliable expression of genuine faith. This is the way Christ loves you. Is it also the way you love others in the body of Christ?

YOUR LIFE IN ACTION

Sometimes we forget that our salvation is complete through Christ, and we start trying to make God love us. Read Galatians 5 today, and everywhere you see the word *freedom,* replace it with the word *rest.*

Rejoice in hope, be patient in tribulation,
be constant in prayer (Romans 12:12).

Look always forward, with the anticipation of eternal rest and glory in the presence of God. This is not naive optimism, because it is coupled to the reality of tribulation and the call to constant prayer. These three—rejoicing in hope, being patient in tribulation, and being constant in prayer—are not easy to do, and we need the reminder today.

Rejoice in hope. More than rejoicing that you have hope, this recognizes the condition that will be true in the future no matter how strongly the circumstances of today argue against it. Sick today? You will be perfectly and eternally whole someday. Burdened today? You will be emptied of sorrow and filled with joy someday, never to be reversed. Weary of wrestling with sin? Someday you'll live where there will never be the slightest hint of sin.

Be patient in tribulation. Rejoicing in hope will put your tribulation in its proper perspective: temporary and fading. No matter how challenging, even agonizing the tribulation of a believer may be, it is dying away and will soon give way to God's glorious restoration brought about through Christ.

Be constant in prayer. How foolish we are to spend a day or an hour without praying to our Father who is in heaven! When we fail in this, we forget that He has all things under control.

YOUR LIFE IN ACTION

Which of these three do you need most today?
Commit this short verse to memory.

Not only has the word of the Lord sounded forth from you in Macedonia and Achaia, but your faith in God has gone forth everywhere, so that we need not say anything. For they themselves report . . . how you turned to God from idols to serve the living and true God, and to wait for his Son from heaven, whom he raised from the dead, Jesus who delivers us from the wrath to come (1 Thessalonians 1:8–10).

If ever there was a true gospel witness, it came through the believers in the region of Thessalonica (present-day Greece). So convincing was their collective witness that Paul declared "we need not say anything." Their witness was proof positive of Christ's redemption.

These believers did not have easy lives. If you read the rest of this letter and 2 Thessalonians, you'll learn they experienced a great deal of persecution and suffering. Yet their faith was undeniable because:

- They turned to God from idols.
- They served God.
- They lived in expectation of Christ's return.

In just a few words, we have an indication of how pagan these people were before they were introduced to Christ. They were in darkness and damned to greater darkness for all eternity.

Yet you and I were no better off in our before-Christ days. We were as dead in our trespasses and sins (Ephesians 2:1) as were these idol worshipers. So should we not share all three of these descriptions with the Thessalonians? Are we serving God and expecting Christ's return?

YOUR LIFE IN ACTION

In what ways is God prompting you to serve Him—
ways that will give evidence that Christ has redeemed you?

Blessed is the man who walks not in the counsel of the wicked,
nor stands in the way of sinners, nor sits in the seat of scoffers;
but his delight is in the law of the LORD,
and on his law he meditates day and night (Psalm 1:1–2).

God desires to bless His children . . . for them to know a deeply rooted and nearly indescribable happiness. Scriptures such as Psalm 1 and Matthew 5 make this clear by presenting the various ways we may encounter His blessing.

However, when happiness (being blessed) is redefined to mean "getting whatever we want" from God, we forfeit the beauty of a truly blessed life. Genuine happiness comes only through the presence of Christ in our lives, especially when He is not having to compete for our affections and satisfaction.

When we have a Philippians 3:7 outlook—"Whatever gain I had, I counted as loss for the sake of Christ"—we exchange short-lived gratification for eternal joy, guilty pleasure for peaceful contentment, the fear of loss for the joy of hope, and the likelihood of disappointment for the assurance of God's intimacy.

Here is true blessing: "You have come to know God, or rather to be known by God" (Galatians 4:9). Within the eternal bonds of this relationship, all happiness can be found.

YOUR LIFE IN ACTION

Think of everything you consider a blessing in your life.
Thank God for each of these; give extra time and attention to
thanking Him for salvation through Jesus!

Blessed is the man who walks not in the counsel of the wicked,
nor stands in the way of sinners, nor sits in the seat of scoffers;
but his delight is in the law of the LORD,
and on his law he meditates day and night (Psalm 1:1–2).

Where do most people look for happiness? Perhaps they seek it through the comfort or prestige of possessions and position. Maybe they look for it in isolation and self-indulgence. Some may pursue it through a schedule filled with activity and outings, or hope to find it within relationships.

These are not all empty pursuits; some can be rewarding and helpful, within reason. But when it comes to relationships, Psalm 1 offers some particular warnings. Because we can all be so greatly influenced by the company we keep, there are certain people we should avoid, including:

- The wicked—the ungodly person who is active in criminal behavior

- The sinner—the person whose reputation is headlined by sin (the most inclusive word used for *sinner*)

- The scoffer—the person who arrogantly mocks and scorns those who do not meet with his approval

To be a truly "blessed" person—one who is experiencing true happiness from God (see yesterday's reading)—you should not allow the wicked, sinner, or scoffer to influence you. Guard yourself from them and their ways.

YOUR LIFE IN ACTION
Prayerfully evaluate your closest friendships.
Are there any ways you are allowing them to be an ungodly influence?
If so, what changes do you need to make?

*Blessed is the man who walks not in the counsel of the wicked,
nor stands in the way of sinners, nor sits in the seat of scoffers; but his delight is
in the law of the LORD, and on his law he meditates day and night.
He is like a tree planted by streams of water that yields its fruit in its season,
and its leaf does not wither. In all that he does, he prospers (Psalm 1:1–3).*

We pick up on the attitudes of those whose influence we allow in. Their outlook becomes a part of ours. This is why we are warned to avoid the wicked, sinner, and scoffer.

It is also why we are given insight into what influences the thoughts and attitudes of the blessed person: "His delight is in the law of the LORD," that is, the Word of God. There is an inseparable link between the genuine and enduring happiness God wants you to know, and the value you place on knowing and living according to His Word.

We must also understand that the blessed life will not be without endurance and suffering. Notice the progressive strength and vitality of the tree described in verse 3, that its fruit is borne "in its season" and not immediately upon planting.

The same pattern is seen in Jesus' teaching (recorded in Matthew 5), where many of those He pronounced "blessed" were at that moment mourning, hungry, thirsty, or persecuted. The promise of blessing does not guarantee a life of little pain. In fact, quite the opposite.

For this reason we must cling to the blessing of God that we know today, and receive it as a mere foretaste of what is to come.

YOUR LIFE IN ACTION

Start today to memorize Psalm 1:1–3.
Make a goal to be able to recite it word for word within a week.

*Nevertheless, we have not made use of this right,
but we endure anything rather than put an obstacle in the way
of the gospel of Christ (1 Corinthians 9:12).*

How much does the gospel mean to you? Imagine loving the gospel so much that you would endure anything—*anything*—to see it spread, bringing the message of eternal life to family members, friends, neighbors, strangers, and yes, even enemies.

Again, how much does the gospel mean to you? To Paul (and others like him), the gospel meant everything. He was willing to set aside every desire and right he had if these proved in any way to be an obstacle to others hearing the good news about Christ.

To a world (and, sadly, often the body of Christ) that elevates the demands and wants of the individual above the call to leading godly, loving lives of service, this sounds strange. And it should, for we are indeed "sojourners and exiles" here (1 Peter 2:11). Our outlook should be firmly set on the advance of the gospel, and that means we will sometimes, perhaps often, need to relinquish our grip on what we want, if getting it would mean the gospel would be hindered.

Our desire and pursuit of all earthly things, even those that are not sinful, and sometimes even those things we rightly deserve (as was true of Paul as described in 1 Corinthians 9), should be seriously and prayerfully thought of alongside the role God has for us in the advance of the gospel to the world. Would prayerful consideration lead us to set any of these aside?

YOUR LIFE IN ACTION

Ask God if there is anything you are pursuing, even something you rightly deserve, that might be an obstacle to those around you hearing and believing the message of the gospel.

*Whether you eat or drink, or whatever you do,
do all to the glory of God (1 Corinthians 10:31).*

The glory of God is beyond our comprehension or description. Yet it is healthy for our souls to grapple with such divine thoughts. It makes us hungry for the presence of God, which is our destiny. To set yourself thinking on the glory of God, consider these two questions: What is the glory of God? How does God display His glory?

Think of the glory of God as the sum total of all His attributes and character on display. Imagine seeing God's love, wrath, mercy, justice, sovereignty, eternality (to name just a few) all working together at the same time. It would be overwhelming, which explains why Moses, Abraham, Isaiah, and others were actually in fear of seeing God. Their humanity could not receive it, nor can ours.

Scripture lays out two primary means by which God displays His glory: through the heavens and earth He created (Psalm 19; 104), and by making mankind to bear His image (Genesis 1:26–28). These showcase His brilliance, beauty, and love, yet they only give a glimpse of all that God is. When we reach the end of our comprehension, the outskirts of His glory are not yet in view.

These thoughts actually lead us to a third question: How do we glorify God? That is, how do we exalt what we do not and cannot know? The answer in part is: *We bring Him glory by doing the most common things for the greatest of purposes.* All of our activities—even those as basic as eating and drinking—should be done with His glory in mind.

YOUR LIFE IN ACTION
Think about some of the common things you do each day
(like eating, resting, talking, and working). How can you
do these things to the glory of God?

The eyes of the LORD run to and fro throughout the whole earth,
to give strong support to those whose heart is blameless toward him.
You have done foolishly in this, for from now on
you will have wars (2 Chronicles 16:9).

Here we have a record of God speaking to Asa (king of Judah) through a prophet. The reason God rebuked Asa so strongly is that Asa, who had repeatedly enjoyed God's help in leading the nation, had instead begun to rely on other kings for assistance. As a result, Asa lost God's help.

As God often does, He had given assignments to Asa that were beyond his ability and capacity. As a humble man, Asa had been in the habit of turning to God for help. He knew that the One who had called him was the One who would provide what was needed.

But on one occasion, when Asa was afraid, the enemy took notice and then took aim. He (the enemy) gave Asa an idea. With no thought of God whatsoever, Asa acted on the idea and brought even more trouble on himself and the nation.

There is a caution here for all servants of the Lord. God's "support" accompanies His call, but there is a certain way—a way that always includes humble dependence on Him—His work is to be done. We must be on guard so that neither pride over our past successes nor fear of our present challenges distracts us from relying on God first and foremost.

YOUR LIFE IN ACTION

Can you recognize any ways that either pride or fear
keep you from relying on God today?
If so, confess that to God and ask Him to help you.

For this reason I bow my knees before the Father, from whom every family in heaven and on earth is named, that according to the riches of his glory he may grant you to be strengthened with power through his Spirit in your inner being, so that Christ may dwell in your hearts through faith— that you, being rooted and grounded in love, may have strength to comprehend with all the saints what is the breadth and length and height and depth, and to know the love of Christ that surpasses knowledge, that you may be filled with all the fullness of God (Ephesians 3:14–19).

Paul prays first that we will know something which cannot be known, and second that we will be filled up with something for which we don't have capacity. Even so, it is in us to try, because the Holy Spirit is within us, giving eternity-focused longings to our time-bound minds. And so we groan with holy discontentment and expectation (Romans 8:23; 2 Corinthians 5:2).

Among the greatest of God's "immeasurables" which our souls long to know is the full expanse of Christ's love. This is a thing (though *thing* is too base a word) which becomes broader, longer, higher, and deeper in our understanding with every thought we give it. The love by which He loves us truly is incomprehensible.

Even believers may sometimes wonder, *Does God really love me?* The answer, of course, is *yes!* Then they may wonder, *But how much does God love me?* and then try to bring His love down to an understandable level.

But approach the same question from the other end, and you will get closer to the right answer. *How much does God love me?* He loves you in an amount that surpasses your capacity to know.

YOUR LIFE IN ACTION

Use the words of Ephesians 3:14–19 to pray for yourself and for your loved ones who are in Christ. Wherever the word *you* appears, replace it with the name of the person you are praying for.

I therefore, a prisoner for the Lord, urge you to walk in a manner worthy of the calling to which you have been called (Ephesians 4:1).

Throughout his Christian journey, Paul could have been given many different titles; but whatever twists and turns his life took, he saw each one against the backdrop of his relationship with Christ. If he sorrowed, he sorrowed in Christ. If he rejoiced, he rejoiced in Christ. Suffering, successful, loved, or abandoned, he was who he was and did what he did for the cause of Christ and the gospel. Even as a prisoner.

Paul personified the strength of keeping a godly perspective in all circumstances. Through his example we learn that trying to figure out the scope, meaning, and purpose of our circumstances, especially the difficult ones, is generally futile. On the other hand, pursuing Christ within all circumstances builds our faith and spiritual stamina.

Though we may at first wonder why a certain trial has come into our life, we can and should move as quickly as possible to the more productive question, *What now?* This gets us to the place of determining how we can best "walk worthy" in the context of our present realities. Our lives are for Christ.

Paul's position as prisoner did not silence or intimidate him. He continued to write, teach, and make disciples from prison. His message only grew in intensity. It was not the fact that he was a prisoner that mattered most to him, but that he was a prisoner *for the Lord*. Circumstances could never change the relationship he had with Christ; they served to reveal and strengthen it.

YOUR LIFE IN ACTION

In what various circumstances has God used you to further His kingdom?

> *I therefore, a prisoner for the Lord, urge you to walk in a manner worthy of the calling to which you have been called (Ephesians 4:1).*

In order to understand what our calling is, we need to overcome two common misunderstandings, regarding:

The Secular vs. The Sacred. To our detriment, we have often compartmentalized the life of a Christian into spiritual pursuits and secular activities. For example, a man may be thought of as a brother in Christ to some, as an engineer or a golfer to others. These may all be true and accurate, but there is a problem with peeling his spiritual identity away from everything else about him.

In reality, our calling which comes from God should encompass every area of our life. We are not secular here and spiritual there; we are spiritual everywhere. We are spiritual beings, and as such should carry our spiritual concerns in our mind and heart always. There should be no boundary between the secular and sacred.

The Call to Salvation vs. The Call to Service. We must also erase the line we've drawn between the call to salvation and the call to service. When God called us to be His children, He also called us to be His servants.

Chapter 4, verse 1 is the great bridge in the letter to the Ephesians, where our position in Christ and the practical living out of our Christianity meet. Interestingly, both are brought together in terms of our "call." Simply put, God did not call any spectators.

YOUR LIFE IN ACTION

In your own words, write out what you understand
your calling to be in Christ.

*O LORD, how long shall I cry for help, and you will not hear? Or cry to you
"Violence!" and you will not save? . . . Though the fig tree should not blossom,
nor fruit be on the vines, the produce of the olive fail and the fields yield
no food, the flock be cut off from the fold and there be no herd in the stalls,
yet I will rejoice in the LORD; I will take joy in the God
of my salvation (Habakkuk 1:2; 3:17–18).*

Habakkuk was agitated by the iniquity and injustice surrounding
him. He pulled no punches when he prayed, *God, I know You see
this, why don't You do something?!*

We can learn a lot about a person by the way they pray when they're
desperate. Habakkuk believed in God, knew God was aware of everything that happened, and felt anguish for those who were suffering.

But just a few chapters later, Habakkuk's tone completely changed.
His desperation gave way to hope. Why? God reminded him that "the
righteous shall live by his faith" (2:4); so what he was seeing, feeling,
and experiencing was not the full and final reality. Relief and joy were
on the way.

From Habakkuk's experience we learn that understanding who God
is and what His eternal purpose is empowers us to pray boldly for
deliverance while also continuing to live by faith. We also learn that
resting in the sovereignty of God gives courage and perspective in the
midst of difficulty.

YOUR LIFE IN ACTION

Habakkuk learned to take joy in God. Give thought today to
the wonder and greatness of God. Worship Him,
perhaps through songs that will restore joy to your soul.

*Though the LORD is high, he regards the lowly,
but the haughty he knows from afar (Psalm 138:6).*

In revival writings and messages, we often read or hear words like *brokenness*, *lowliness*, *humility*, and *contrition*. None of these words sound very appealing, do they? They conjure up images of defeat, shame, and disgrace. But that perception is not in keeping with Scripture.

What is brokenness? While brokenness may come about in significant moments, it is more of an ongoing condition that keeps our hearts attentive to the conviction and leading of the Holy Spirit. This means that before brokenness, there must first be humility (a sustained bowing of our wills to God), and with that humility a true sense of honesty that refuses to hide anything about ourselves from God.

Therefore it is not our heart that God wants to break, but our will. He knows what we, apart from Him, do not . . . that as long as we try to maintain control, we are spiritually weak and barren. On the other hand, joy and victory are found in those whose will has been surrendered to God's good purpose.

Why brokenness? As our flesh loses its dominance through brokenness, we begin to enjoy God's nearness, blessing, peace, and power. We find that brokenness brings about the strengthening of the new nature we've been given in Christ, and we discover the sweetness of fellowshipping with our broken brothers and sisters. These are but a few of the ways our lives are blessed by brokenness.

YOUR LIFE IN ACTION

In what areas of your life are you resisting the work of God,
refusing to submit to Him?

Thus says the One who is high and lifted up, who inhabits eternity, whose name is Holy: "I dwell in the high and holy place, and also with him who is of a contrite and lowly spirit, to revive the spirit of the lowly, and to revive the heart of the contrite" (Isaiah 57:15).

How does God go about breaking us? Often He does so by introducing one of the following into our lives:

- a difficult person
- a traumatic event
- a heightened sense of conviction over personal sin

Do you have any irritating people in your life? Are you willing to accept the possibility that God placed them there for your good, perhaps to teach you to be longsuffering and forgiving?

Have you suffered any trauma to your soul? Can you allow room for God to use that deep hurt to soften your heart and increase your endurance and compassion?

Are you acutely aware of particular sins in your life, even to the point of shame? God may be turning up the heat to make you especially mindful of your need for Him and His sufficiency to deliver you.

Whatever trouble might be in your life, there is generally more at stake than just that issue. Does God want you to make every legitimate effort to love that difficult person? Yes. Does God want you to heal from trauma? Yes. Does God want you free from sin's power? Yes. And through it all God wants to produce in you a humble, contrite spirit.

YOUR LIFE IN ACTION

Take stock of the people and circumstances that are troubling you right now. Ask God to open your heart to the ways He wants to work in your life to make you more like Christ.

Little children, keep yourselves from idols (1 John 5:21).

You probably don't have a graven image in your house—a hand-made object that is a god to you and your family. However, you may be keeping idols in closer proximity than you realize.

The people to whom John wrote lived in an idol-saturated culture. Nearly any drive or desire they had could be expressed by showing allegiance to one god or another. Idol worship was pervasive, and John knew that a profession of faith in Christ would not ensure that the bonds were broken.

Some would give up on the invisible God to return to something they could see and feel. Others would grow jealous of their idolatrous neighbors and rejoin them in immediate carnal pleasure, thereby forsaking the promise of fullness of joy that would come at a later time.

Idols are as appealing now as they were then, regardless what form they may take. Our society is not known for its graven images, but it is as populated with God-replacements as any civilization in history.

For this reason we must be vigilant to keep ourselves from idols—that is, from giving to anything or anyone that which belongs to God Himself: the greatest of our love, loyalty, and worship.

YOUR LIFE IN ACTION

Can you think of any possession, activity, person, or desire
in your life that competes with your true heart devotion to God?
What changes do you need to make to keep yourself from idols?

> *[Uzziah's] fame spread far, for he was marvelously helped,*
> *till he was strong. But when he was strong, he grew proud, to his destruction.*
> *For he was unfaithful to the LORD his God and entered the temple of*
> *the LORD to burn incense on the altar of incense (2 Chronicles 26:15–16).*

Uzziah's legacy is sad. He is one of many leaders whose glorious life is overshadowed by an inglorious death . . . another entry in the encyclopedia of those who started well but ended poorly.

Uzziah (a.k.a. Azariah) became the king of Judah at the age of sixteen, and he reigned for fifty-two years. Under him the kingdom grew prosperous and enjoyed military dominance. His years of rule were, for the most part, marked by affluence and peace.

For a long while he was successful and respected, but later his pride took him down when he presumed to take on duties that God had given only to the priests. When given the opportunity to repent, Uzziah remained defiant. God struck him with leprosy, and he lived his last years in isolation.

If we derail, most of us will derail at the same place Uzziah did: the place of self-sufficiency. When God's assignments become familiar and natural to us, we tend to marginalize God and rely mostly on ourselves, forgetting that it was God who called us in the first place. Many a man or a woman has faltered when he or she became self-reliant and felt little need for God.

YOUR LIFE IN ACTION

You are writing your legacy every day. If the final chapter were written today, would it tell of one who glorified God to the very end, or of one who became proudly self-reliant and finished poorly?

> *In the year that King Uzziah died I saw the Lord sitting upon a throne, high and lifted up; and the train of his robe filled the temple (Isaiah 6:1).*

Walter Price, pastor of Fellowship in the Pass Church in Beaumont, California, observed: "Circumstances matter. No one encounters God in a vacuum."

The prophet Isaiah once described having a vision of God that was so overwhelming he thought it might literally kill him (Isaiah 6:5), and he connected that heavenly encounter to a personal circumstance: the death of his king.

We tend to make more of our circumstances than we should for all the wrong reasons. We sometimes embellish in hopes of drawing attention and sympathy, or exaggerate in an attempt to make ourselves a hero or a victim. On the other hand, we may downplay our circumstances—or outright deny them—in hopes of burying the shame they are likely to bring.

To be sure, circumstances are not of utmost importance, yet they are the backdrop of every encounter we have with God in this life. This is why it is important that we face our circumstances truthfully and with faith, knowing that even unfavorable circumstances present favorable conditions to encounter God and to lean more fully into His mercy and grace.

YOUR LIFE IN ACTION

In a sentence, describe the prevailing circumstance(s) of your life right now. What are you learning about God and His ways as a result?

In the year that King Uzziah died I saw the Lord sitting upon a throne, high and lifted up; and the train of his robe filled the temple (Isaiah 6:1).

The death of his king framed for Isaiah the conditions of a significant encounter with God; significant because he "saw the Lord" (can you imagine?), and it shaped the future of how Isaiah related to God and how he served Him.

When we look back over the circumstances of our life, there are usually a few that stand out. These landmark circumstances show times when God seemed to be working on us and shaping us with heightened intensity. We remember certain dates or periods of time, certain people, certain places, certain truths God was impressing on us with great emphasis.

We remember changes that came into our lives, whether through joy or sorrow, and we can see now that God was working all along. God was (is) in our circumstances. Things don't just happen. Life is not a string of random, senseless events. God is at work.

It is good to revisit these landmarks from time to time and to recapture the depth and intensity of those days. For example, in the Old Testament God often reminded Israel of their bondage and of His delivering them. That was a landmark He wanted them never to forget.

What does God want you to never forget?

YOUR LIFE IN ACTION

Revisit your landmarks. Make a quick list of two or three significant seasons in your life when God deepened your walk with Him. Spend some time thanking God for those personal landmarks.

> *It is God who works in you, both to will and to work*
> *for his good pleasure (Philippians 2:13).*

Let's first of all agree that God does indeed use people, and then let's quickly jettison the notion that He uses people in the same way *people* use people. The two cannot be compared on any level.

Man is, by nature, selfish. His desires and motives are generally linked to his own comfort and ego.

God, on the other hand, never detaches His acts from His character of divine love, holiness, and righteousness. In other words, all that God purposes to do, He does ultimately to exalt His own glory, and His glory always encompasses the good of His children, even if they momentarily suffer (2 Corinthians 4:16–18).

We gain through everything God does. It is good for us when God's purposes are accomplished.

To be used by people can sometimes prove hurtful, but to be used by God is honorable. To people we might respond in disgust, "You *used* me!" and by that recognize they were thinking *only* of themselves. To God we would say, "You used *me*" and with humility affirm the honor of being involved in His mission.

YOUR LIFE IN ACTION

In what ways has God used you?
In what ways did His using you prove to be a blessing?

> *Oh give thanks to the LORD; call upon his name;*
> *make known his deeds among the peoples!*
> *Sing to him, sing praises to him; tell of all his wondrous works! . . .*
> *When he summoned a famine on the land*
> *and broke all supply of bread, he had sent a man ahead of them,*
> *Joseph, who was sold as a slave (Psalm 105:1–2, 16–17).*

Joseph was a man God used. Though his journey brought seasons of hardship, pain, and rejection, never once was Joseph out of God's care.

To understand the purpose in Joseph's harsh circumstances, and the good that came from them, we must look beyond Joseph himself. We need to see him as part of a group picture, not as an individual portrait.

Psalm 105 celebrates the "deeds" and "wondrous works" of God. Joseph's life—including the low points—was a high point in God's dealings with His people.

Joseph was sent ahead to deliver God's people from famine and starvation. God inserted him in just the right place at just the right time to accomplish His will.

Like Joseph, if your life is given over to God, you are connected to all the saints of God and joined to all the purposes of God. You will know the struggle of endurance as well as the sacredness of a high calling.

YOUR LIFE IN ACTION

Imagine yourself in a group portrait with saints from history and today. How does the reality of being connected to these brothers and sisters challenge you to fulfill God's plan for you?

*By faith Joseph, at the end of his life, made mention of the exodus
of the Israelites and gave directions concerning his bones (Hebrews 11:22).*

If Joseph was part of a group picture in Psalm 105, his individual portrait comes out in Hebrews 11, where the focus is on his faith (see also Exodus 13:19).

The last wishes of a dying person reveal much. In Joseph's case we see a faith in God so full that it touched a nation.

In death, Joseph clung to God, believing He would yet accomplish His promise to deliver the people of Israel from Egypt and settle them in their own land. Joseph realized he would not live to see it, so he told his countrymen, *When you head for the promised land, take my bones with you.*

Matthew 6 presents a thought by which we can imitate Joseph's faith: "Do not lay up for yourselves treasures on earth . . . but lay up for yourselves treasures in heaven. . . . For where your treasure is, there your heart will be also" (vv. 19–21).

Our someday exodus from earth is as certain as the nation of Israel departing Egypt. Like them, we have never seen our promised land, but it is, even now, prepared for us.

Joseph believed God so fully that he made plans based not on present realities but on the future fulfillment of God's promise. We should do the same.

YOUR LIFE IN ACTION

What does it mean to lay up treasures in heaven?
What should you be doing to accomplish this?

> *Then Midianite traders passed by. And [his brothers] drew Joseph up and lifted him out of the pit, and sold him to the Ishmaelites for twenty shekels of silver. They took Joseph to Egypt (Genesis 37:28).*

The pit is one of many ways the life and times of Joseph foreshadow Jesus and the gospel.

- Both Joseph and Jesus left their father's house and were sent to a foreign land. "I have come down from heaven, not to do my own will but the will of him who sent me" (John 6:38).

- Both suffered in innocence. "For our sake he made him to be sin who knew no sin, so that in him we might become the righteousness of God" (2 Corinthians 5:21).

- Both were betrayed and sold. "Then one of the twelve, whose name was Judas Iscariot, went to the chief priests and said, 'What will you give me if I deliver him over to you?' And they paid him thirty pieces of silver" (Matthew 26:14–15).

- Both were rejected by those they loved. "O Jerusalem, Jerusalem . . . ! How often would I have gathered your children together as a hen gathers her brood under her wings, and you were not willing!" (Matthew 23:37).

- The personal sufferings of both brought about the deliverance of many. "If many died through one man's [Adam's] trespass, much more have the grace of God and the free gift by the grace of that one man Jesus Christ abounded for many" (Romans 5:15).

YOUR LIFE IN ACTION

Give thanks to God for salvation through Jesus Christ.
Pray through each of the above verses, taking time with
each one to praise and thank your Savior.

> *The LORD was with Joseph, and he became a successful man,*
> *and he was in the house of his Egyptian master. His master saw that the LORD*
> *was with him and that the LORD caused all that he did to succeed in his hands. . . .*
> *The keeper of the prison paid no attention to anything that was in Joseph's charge,*
> *because the LORD was with him. And whatever he did,*
> *the LORD made it succeed (Genesis 39:2–3, 23).*

Within a matter of hours, a great deal changed about the outward circumstances of Joseph's life. But there was also a great constant: The Lord was with him.

Paul's experiences with ups and downs were similar to Joseph's, and brought him to the contentment of knowing both "how to be brought low" as well as "how to abound" (Philippians 4:12). In fact, the closing of his letter to the Philippians reads like a thank-you note, which is startling because he wrote it while incarcerated.

How can a man in prison have such a full and grateful heart? And, you many wonder, would you have the same joyful perspective if you were to be "relocated" from a palace to a prison, from great supply to barely getting by?

To set our experiences or our emotions as a metric of God's love is to leave our hearts vulnerable to doubts, fear, and anger. We must instead learn to rest in the great constant: The Lord is with us.

YOUR LIFE IN ACTION

What changes in your outlook come about when you
ponder the truth that God is with you?

> *Yet the chief cupbearer did not remember Joseph,*
> *but forgot him (Genesis 40:23).*

Being forgotten is insulting, especially when the one who forgets is a person you served well. Such was the case with Joseph and the cupbearer.

Because we have the benefit of knowing how the story ends, we can easily overlook this event as a mere setback; but for Joseph it could have been the breaking point. God was in the setback, though. He was making Joseph into a man of perseverance.

When we encounter hardship, our first response is often: *Get me out of here, now!* This is the cry of a hurting soul, an understandable reaction to pain. Left unchecked, though, that cry can morph into resentment and even revenge.

However, when a person is assured by faith that God is in control, his response to the same hardship is: *Get me out of here whenever You choose.* This is the beginning of patience.

There is another level of trusting in God that requires more than patience; it demands perseverance. The persevering soul says, *Get me out of here whenever You choose, if ever You choose.* This is the spiritual condition of one who accepts that he may be lashed to his burden until Christ Himself removes it, knowing that the way he carries his burden displays God's grace.

YOUR LIFE IN ACTION

Even persevering ones can be encouraged by friends.
Who do you know that, though carrying their burden graciously
for a long time, could benefit from your words of love today?

The wicked flee when no one pursues,
but the righteous are bold as a lion (Proverbs 28:1).

Joseph's brothers held on to their sin for a long time, well beyond the day Joseph forgave them (Genesis 45). We see this in the anxiety and defensiveness of their behavior as they:

- tried to explain what had happened in Egypt
- bargained with their father when he wanted them to return to Egypt
- pleaded with Joseph's house steward to accept their explanation about the missing payment
- continued to lie about Joseph being killed—even repeating that lie, unknowingly, to Joseph's face
- assumed that Joseph would retaliate after their father died

Guilt lodged in their hearts, and they continued to live as unforgiven men. Imagine the wasted years!

Perhaps you don't have to imagine, because you are well acquainted with the heavy burden of guilt. Be assured that this is not how God wants you to live.

If your guilt is legitimate because you have sinned against Him and have done wrong to another person, be quick to confess and, if appropriate, make restitution. But if yours is a phantom guilt, stalking you even though God has forgiven you, remind the enemy—and yourself—that Jesus paid it *all*.

YOUR LIFE IN ACTION
Meditate on Psalm 32.

DIRTY FEET

*Jesus said to him, "The one who has bathed does not need to wash,
except for his feet, but is completely clean. And you are clean,
but not every one of you" (John 13:10).*

In Christ we are forgiven and free, never again under the threat of sin's penalty. Even so, we are often in need of God's forgiveness. Why? Because we still sin.

Some theologians describe God's forgiveness in two categories: judicial and parental.

The first is expressed in Romans 8:1, "There is therefore now no condemnation for those who are in Christ Jesus," meaning that as our Judge, God has accepted Christ's death on our behalf and offered us a full pardon.

The second, parental, is depicted by the disciples' dirty feet (John 13). Jesus explained that if they had already bathed—that is, they had received Christ's atonement for their sins—they need only wash away the dirt of the day. These sins did not indicate the absence of salvation but the fact that they, like we, would still sin (see Ecclesiastes 7:20) and need correction from the Father.

As we grow in Christ, even though we will still sin, the frequency of it should decrease, and our sensitivity to it should increase. As the love between a parent and child is affirmed when that child has to be corrected, so receiving forgiveness from our Father—having our dirty feet washed—brings to light once again the matchless and eternal love that He has lavished on us.

YOUR LIFE IN ACTION

Are there any "outstanding" sin issues between you and God today? Don't delay in confessing your sin and experiencing His cleansing. Praise God for His forgiveness, both judicial and parental.

Surely there is a future,
and your hope will not be cut off (Proverbs 23:18).

In Christ we will never experience a truly hopeless moment; yet we will *feel* the sting of disappointment from time to time. None are immune to having their reality come short of their hope. When this happens, there is one thing we will do and two things we should do.

The one thing we will do is hurt. It is a mistake to deny pain (even if we have brought it on ourselves), because it is dishonest to do so. Psalm 55:22 tells us, "Cast your burden on the LORD, and he will sustain you." We cannot give over (cast) to God that which we deny having. The hurt that accompanies our disappointment does us the good service of turning our thoughts to God, so do not deny it.

The two things we should do are pray and give thanks. Remember this about the Savior when your disappointment drives you to prayer: "We do not have a high priest who is unable to sympathize with our weaknesses" (Hebrews 4:15). Is it not amazing and comforting to know that Christ has empathy for you? God's is not a long distance love; He is "near to the brokenhearted" (Psalm 34:18).

Finally, recognize that disappointment is included in the "giving thanks always and for everything" directive of Ephesians 5:20. Expressing thanks to God directs our thoughts to the goodness of God and brings sunlight into every valley.

YOUR LIFE IN ACTION

Is disappointment robbing you of the joy of the Lord?
Are you being honest with God about it?
Have you prayed? Are you thanking Him?

The LORD is my shepherd; I shall not want.
He makes me lie down in green pastures.
He leads me beside still waters.
He restores my soul.
He leads me in paths of righteousness for his name's sake (Psalm 23:1–3).

Grief, deep disappointment, or any form of significant life setback makes realists of us all. We want straight talk rather than platitude; we want to hear the truth of what we're in for as far as it can be known.

So here it is in a nutshell: The journey of soul restoration is rarely short, and we are wise not to be in a rush.

While it is true that there are no shortcuts, there is indeed a way out of the pain; or, more accurately, a way *through* it.

Many who have traveled a difficult road emerge to say it was one of the richest times of God-awareness and God-nearness they ever experienced. And so it can be for you if do not rush . . . if you give time to taking in the green pastures and still waters.

When your soul hurts, when you have no fight left in you so you *must* be still, listen to your Shepherd. Learn of Him. He is the way through.

YOUR LIFE IN ACTION
Meditate on Psalm 23.

*Open my eyes, that I may behold wondrous things
out of your law (Psalm 119:18).*

The natural man—he or she who does not have the Holy Spirit—cannot accept or understand spiritual things. They are nonsense to him; his nature opposes spiritual truth.

With that in mind, the reading and understanding of God's Word is an amazing thing that we must never take for granted. We should approach it as an honorable habit through which God Himself teaches, reproves, corrects, and trains us (2 Timothy 3:16). We should both invite and welcome the Spirit into this daily sacred hour.

Martin Luther said, "The Bible cannot be understood simply by study or talent; you must count only on the influence of the Holy Spirit." John Calvin wrote, "The testimony of the Spirit is superior to reason. For . . . these words will not obtain full credit in the hearts of men until they are sealed by the inward testimony of the Spirit."

He who is spiritual—he who has been born of the Spirit (John 3:6)—has the resident divine Truth Teacher to enlighten him about the things of God. That man is not limited to his best observations or thoughts. The Holy Spirit will take God's Word, the Word which He has inspired and revealed, and illuminate it for all those in whom He dwells.

YOUR LIFE IN ACTION

Think highly of any time you give to reading God's Word or listening to others teach from it. Acknowledge the Holy Spirit within you, who will give you understanding.

We have spoken freely to you, Corinthians;
our heart is wide open (2 Corinthians 6:11).

Paul said that his heart was "wide open" to the Corinthians. What does it mean to have a wide open heart?

A wide open heart is **selfless**. This person has his love priorities right: God, others, self (Matthew 22:35–40). He has plenty of room to show genuine concern for those in need. He prioritizes love over comfort.

A wide open heart is **humble**. In the words of C. S. Lewis, "True humility is not thinking less of yourself; it is thinking of yourself less." Humility is a nearly constant fixation on God's mercy, expressing itself through attitudes and activities that exalt God and draw attention to Him.

A wide open heart is **authentic**. This person walks in the light (1 John 1:7). He is honest about his spiritual state—not taking credit for God's work, not hiding his struggle against sin, not showcasing his works, and never forgetting that apart from Christ he can do nothing (John 15:5).

How open is your heart?

YOUR LIFE IN ACTION

If *selfless*, *humble*, and *authentic* do not describe your heart,
what words do?

We have spoken freely to you, Corinthians; our heart is wide open.
You are not restricted by us, but you are restricted in your own affections.
In return (I speak as to children)
widen your hearts also (2 Corinthians 6:11–13).

The New Testament contains two letters Paul wrote to the Corinthian church. Between the first and the second, some false teachers had brought confusion to the Christians there and had tried to undermine Paul's credibility.

But there was much more at stake than a good man's reputation, as important as that may be. In this case Paul wrote a partial defense (what we know as 2 Corinthians) because it was really the gospel that was under attack. He knew that if these false teachers could put him in a bad light, the people would not listen to his message.

As it turned out, however, Paul's reputation did serve to reopen hearts that were on the verge of closing. He appealed to the Corinthians to remember that throughout his past ministry he had opened his heart to them. This means he had conducted himself with love, compassion, generosity, and integrity. They had no reason to mistrust him then, nor did they now. Based on that, Paul urged them to keep listening to his message, and God used the credibility of his character to affect the spread of the gospel.

We cannot contribute to our own salvation, nor can we coerce others to believe. However, our character and conduct can be either a hindrance or a help to the message of the gospel. Which are you?

YOUR LIFE IN ACTION

In what ways is your life affecting the gospel
in your extended family and community?

Behold, you delight in truth in the inward being,
and you teach me wisdom in the secret heart (Psalm 51:6).

Broken people have open hearts. Having faced their own sinfulness, shortcomings, and God's amazing grace, broken people are stripped of pretense. Life is no longer about impressing others or fearing rejection. They have reached the bottom and met God.

David's brokenness came through intense conviction over sin. After giving in to adultery and attempting to cover it up through murder, David lived a public lie for months. When confronted with his guilt (remember his encounter with Nathan the prophet?), David finally came clean and repented. He eventually became known as "a man after [God's] heart" (Acts 13:22).

Hannah's brokenness came through the deep disappointment of unfulfilled desire. She longed to be a mother, but could not conceive. She turned to God in desperation time after time, and He eventually blessed her with a son named Samuel. She and her husband dedicated him to the service of God, and Samuel grew up to be the spiritual leader of his people.

When God so works in your life to bring you to an end of your striving and resisting Him like David, or pursuing Him like Hannah, see this as discipline and not punishment. Through the breaking He is loving you, changing your life, opening your heart.

YOUR LIFE IN ACTION

Are you resisting God's work in your life today? Are you still pursuing Him, though weary and disappointed? Recognize the work God is doing in your heart, and by faith thank Him for it.

The purpose in a man's heart is like deep water,
but a man of understanding will draw it out (Proverbs 20:5).

If we were to write a table of contents for the human heart, we might list such categories as: hopes, fears, dreams, regrets, beliefs, friends, enemies, questions I have for God.

Now think of the risk a person takes when he opens his heart to you. He is telling on himself, revealing his deepest thoughts, surrendering the so-called safety of secrecy.

We should never take such trust lightly; it is a crucial part of disciple making. As we set out to minister to people, we hope they will open their heart to us (how can we truly help them if they don't?), as a means of moving them toward Christ.

We must understand the sacredness of that moment when they choose to become more open than they have in the past. The deep water is being disturbed; a heart is opening, awakening.

This is your call to pray, to become an intercessor for a soul coming out of darkness and into light, or (in the case of one who already knows Christ) a soul coming out of slumber and into revived life.

Be sensitive to the Holy Spirit in every conversation. Be alert to God at work, opening a heart. Be prayerful. Be ready.

YOUR LIFE IN ACTION

Ask God to give you discernment as you talk with people.
When a conversation goes unusually deep, acknowledge that God
may be at work, and be ready for Him to use you in that person's life.

You also must help us by prayer, so that many will give thanks on our behalf for the blessing granted us through the prayers of many (2 Corinthians 1:11).

Prayer is a grand opportunity for us to be involved in the work of God on earth. We may never know all that is accomplished through prayer, but we do know of two constant results.

Prayer brings intimacy with God. It brings us into a heightened awareness of God's presence.

In the Old Testament, prayer is likened to seeking the face of God (2 Chronicles 7:14–16). In the New Testament, in response to the disciples' request that Jesus teach them to pray, He began by saying, "When you pray, go into your room and shut the door and pray to your Father who is in secret [private]" (Matthew 6:6). If we neglect the private aspect of prayer, we forfeit the joy that comes simply from being in His presence.

Prayer brings thanksgiving to God. Naturally, we will thank God when He answers our prayers in the way we hope He will, giving us what we ask.

Even so, have you ever considered that this thanksgiving is truer to the purpose of prayer than receiving is? The more people who pray, especially in united prayer over a certain need (as in the case of 2 Corinthians 1), the more God will be thanked when He brings the answer.

YOUR LIFE IN ACTION

Make this a personal thanksgiving day. Throughout the day, thank God for every answer to prayer He brings to your memory, no matter how long ago He answered.

Trust in the LORD, and do good;
dwell in the land and befriend faithfulness.
Delight yourself in the LORD,
and he will give you the desires of your heart (Psalm 37:3–4).

We should pray until we either get what we want or we want what we get. Both are answers, and both are good.

The first question in the Westminster Larger Catechism is: "What is the chief and highest end of man?" The answer is: "To glorify God, and fully to enjoy Him forever."

John Piper observed that this statement could rightly be adjusted to say, "To glorify God *by enjoying* Him forever."

As it relates to prayer, the joy we find in God is less about getting what we want from Him and more about wanting what we get—that is, a greater understanding of His desires for us.

God is not fickle; His ways do not change. He does not respond to the prayers of His children through mood swings or on-again-off-again affection.

His ways are right, just, good, and steady. And even if our prayer is met with an answer we do not understand or, if we're honest, appreciate at first, we can be sure that His answer will prove to be best.

YOUR LIFE IN ACTION

Have you ever asked God for something and become glad that He did not give what you asked? What did you learn about Him and His ways through that experience?

POWER IN WEAKNESS

I was with you in weakness and in fear and much trembling,
and my speech and my message were not in plausible words of wisdom,
but in demonstration of the Spirit and of power, so that your faith might not rest
in the wisdom of men but in the power of God (1 Corinthians 2:3–5).

In his book *Loving God,* Chuck Colson described his thoughts while waiting to speak at a prison chapel service:

> As I sat on the platform, waiting my turn at the pulpit, my mind began to drift back in time . . . to scholarships and honors earned, cases argued and won, great decisions made from lofty government offices. My life had been the perfect success story, the great American dream fulfilled. But all at once I realized that it was not my success God had used to enable me to help those in this prison, or in hundreds of others just like it. . . . No, the real legacy of my life was my biggest failure—that I was an ex-convict. My greatest humiliation . . . was the beginning of God's greatest use of my life; He chose the one experience in which I could not glory for His glory.

Colson went on to observe that "God doesn't want our success; He wants us." Certainly our failures are a large part of who we are, and God is not surprised at this.

The failures that bring us low and drive us to seek God's mercy become a display case for His restorative grace. In our weakness He shows Himself strong.

YOUR LIFE IN ACTION

Reflect on people you know whose lives you have seen God restore and revive. How has the display of God's power through them affected you?

> *He said to me, "My grace is sufficient for you, for my power is made perfect*
> *in weakness." Therefore I will boast all the more gladly of my weaknesses,*
> *so that the power of Christ may rest upon me. For the sake of Christ, then,*
> *I am content with weaknesses, insults, hardships, persecutions, and calamities.*
> *For when I am weak, then I am strong (2 Corinthians 12:9–10).*

Do you like being weak? Paul did, eventually. Paul had a weakness that was clearly very troubling to him. He begged God to take it away, and God said no.

From God's view Paul needed that weakness. Through it the power of Christ was highly visible, and because of it Paul lived with a sustained awareness of God's grace. So God kept the weakness in place.

At some point Paul moved beyond accepting his weakness, not by learning to cope with it but by prizing the sufficiency of God's grace because of it. Through him and others like him, we learn that weak men depend on God, seek God, know God, love God, and exalt God.

Weak men realize that if they weren't so weak, they wouldn't seek God so much, so they come to be happy about being weak. And others look at weak men and say, "Look how great God is!"

God is glorified and weak men rejoice, not in their weakness but in God's strength.

YOUR LIFE IN ACTION
How is God displaying His strength to you and others
through your weakness?

He said to me, "My grace is sufficient for you, for my power is made perfect in weakness." Therefore I will boast all the more gladly of my weaknesses, so that the power of Christ may rest upon me (2 Corinthians 12:9).

By chaining three key words together from this passage, we see a beautiful picture of how God wants to work through His children.

Power: This means an inherent power, a power that resides in a person by virtue of his nature. He—in this case, God—didn't *become* strong; He *is* strong.

Perfect: This means to carry through completely, to accomplish, to finish, to make something full that was lacking fullness.

Weakness: This means to have inherent weakness and frailty, to lack both strength and capacity. It is the absence of power and the constant state of imperfection.

God, the all-powerful One, looks on one who has neither power nor the capacity for power. God wants to accomplish a certain thing, and He has arranged so that the thing He wants to accomplish must be done through the one who has no power.

God determines to infuse some of His power into the powerless one (generally after the powerless one admits he is powerless). When this happens, the infusion begins, and the impossible is accomplished. And if all ends as it should, the powerless one admits, *God did it!*

YOUR LIFE IN ACTION

God has given you spiritual gifts by which to serve Him.
Spend some time in prayer surrendering those gifts to God and
asking Him to help you serve by His power, not your own.

He said to me, "My grace is sufficient for you, for my power is made perfect in weakness." Therefore I will boast all the more gladly of my weaknesses, so that the power of Christ may rest upon me (2 Corinthians 12:9).

In his book *Prayer: Basic Training*, Warren Wiersbe describes what happens to us when God makes His power perfect in our weakness. He calls this the "principle of transformation," using John 16:21 to illustrate:

"When a woman is giving birth, she has sorrow because her hour has come, but when she has delivered the baby, she no longer remembers the anguish, for joy that a human being has been born into the world." Wiersbe writes,

> This is a perfect illustration of joy that comes through transformation, not through substitution. The same baby that causes the pain also causes the joy. Jesus did not say, "Your sorrow will be replaced by joy." He said, "Your sorrow will be turned to joy." This is transformation. The very thing that brings sorrow to our lives, God transforms to bring joy. The world cannot bring about this kind of spiritual transformation, so the world depends on substitution.

He ends by saying, "Sorrows transformed into joys cannot be snatched from us." The same can be said for weakness and power. God's transformations will not be undone.

YOUR LIFE IN ACTION

Describe the differences between transformation and substitution. In what ways have you settled for substitution in your own life?

*The kingdom of God does not consist in talk
but in power (1 Corinthians 4:20).*

Talking is necessary, even for proclaiming the gospel, but our words often get in the way of God's message. Agreed?

What if you were not able to speak for even a few days? What would your life communicate then?

Would people know of God merely by observing the non-talking you? Would God be glorified in your silence?

If we serve God in word only, we are not serving Him well. Our lives should demonstrate God's power.

Our walk shouldn't just equal our talk—it should surpass it. As important and influential as words are, the visible power of God flowing through us is of supremely greater value, because "the kingdom of God does not consist in words but in power."

Effective ministry is not about what we know or how well we can express ideas and concepts. We should not concern ourselves with being eloquent, but rather with living by faith so that God's work is seen in and through us.

YOUR LIFE IN ACTION

Determine today that you will speak carefully and prayerfully . . .
that you will be intentional about what you say. Pray that your life will
demonstrate God's power, both in speech and in silence.

The LORD has done great things for us; we are glad.
Restore our fortunes, O LORD, like streams in the Negeb! (Psalm 126:3–4).

Three times each year, the faithful journeyed to Jerusalem to observe feasts and celebrate God's goodness. As they climbed the hill to the city and the temple, they would sing what we know as the *Songs of Ascent* (Psalms 120–134).

Two verses of Psalm 126 give insight as to how God's people worshiped Him then and should now. Worship encompasses the past ("The LORD has done great things for us"), the present ("We are glad"), and the future ("Restore our fortunes").

It should be noted that these were anxious times for the Jews; they lived under the threat of attack. Regardless of the threat, and perhaps because of it, they constantly remembered God's past deliverances, collectively proclaimed their gladness in Him, and corporately asked God to do again what He had done before. (Quite often worship begins by simply telling one another what God has done.)

Today, we are on a bridge called *Now*. From it we look toward the unknown in tomorrow and back to the goodness of God in yesterday. We should let our hearts be glad because of what God has done, celebrate Him by telling others, and trust Him for what is to come.

YOUR LIFE IN ACTION

Sometime in the next few days, look for an opportunity
to share your gladness over God's goodness by telling of a way
He has helped you in the past.

> *Restore our fortunes, O LORD, like streams in the Negeb!*
> *Those who sow in tears shall reap with shouts of joy!*
> *He who goes out weeping, bearing the seed for sowing,*
> *shall come home with shouts of joy,*
> *bringing his sheaves with him (Psalm 126:4–6).*

Eugene Peterson wrote that Psalm 126 tells of people "whose lives are bordered on the one side by a memory of God's acts and the other by hope in God's promises" (from *A Long Obedience in the Same Direction*). While celebrating God's goodness of the past, the people pray that He will restore them again. In this particular prayer, the psalmist makes use of two images: dry stream beds and grain sacks.

"Streams in the Negeb" are actually ditches in the desert. For most of the year they are dry, but in the rainy season they fill quickly and overflow. This image illustrates that God's deliverance sometimes overtakes us without warning. It happens rapidly and takes us by surprise.

The image of a farmer sowing seed and then later returning with sheaves of harvested grain illustrates that God's deliverance sometimes comes slowly, only after certain things have been done or conditions met. In this scenario, the people of God endure in their labor and wait.

In either case God delivers, and in that we rejoice. Though the waiting is often longer than we would wish, "shouts of joy" are in our future.

YOUR LIFE IN ACTION

Describe a "quick answer" to prayer that you or someone close to you experienced. Now recall a "slow answer" you have experienced.

Behold, how good and pleasant it is when brothers dwell in unity!
It is like the precious oil on the head, running down on the beard,
on the beard of Aaron, running down on the collar of his robes!
It is like the dew of Hermon, which falls on the mountains of Zion!
For there the LORD has commanded the blessing, life forevermore (Psalm 133).

We do not create unity. We can only preserve it. God created unity, and it is to be the normal state of His family.

In Ephesians 4, Paul states that maintaining "the unity of the Spirit in the bond of peace" is essential to living in "a manner worthy of the calling to which you have been called" (vv. 1–3). Biblical unity has much deeper meaning than being with people who share your worldview and Christian convictions.

Biblical unity is heart-level fellowship marked by love, forgiveness, service, and sacrifice. It is loving one another as Christ loves us. C. H. Spurgeon once said that in "dwelling together in love we have begun the enjoyments of eternity."

Our human nature will never achieve this type of unity, and rarely would it want to. It would cost *self* too much. But our redeemed nature longs for it, so we must guard against those attitudes that corrode it—resentment, jealousy, anger, and the like.

YOUR LIFE IN ACTION

What are you doing to maintain the unity of the Spirit in the bond of peace? What attitudes are you harboring that corrode unity within God's family?

Where shall I go from your Spirit?
Or where shall I flee from your presence?
If I ascend to heaven, you are there! If I make my bed in Sheol, you are there!
If I take the wings of the morning and dwell in the uttermost parts of the sea,
even there your hand shall lead me,
and your right hand shall hold me (Psalm 139:7–10).

God is everywhere all the time. We cannot escape Him. He is fully aware of our every thought, word, and action.

There are two reactions we may have to this truth. One would be to fear God, and the other would be to rest in Him. Both are appropriate.

We fear God because He is the only being that is omnipresent. There is none greater than Him.

We also fear because this omnipresence means it is impossible for us to hide our sin, no matter how quick, quiet, or clever we try to be. God always knows. He doesn't *find out*; He *knows*. Fearing God provokes us to obey Him.

At the same time, we take comfort from the security of God being here, being there, and being everywhere. Never are we away from Him. His care is constant.

YOUR LIFE IN ACTION

God is everywhere all the time.
In what ways does this truth cause you to fear Him?
In what ways does it cause you to rest in Him?

*You formed my inward parts; you knitted me together in my
mother's womb. I praise you, for I am fearfully and wonderfully made.
Wonderful are your works; my soul knows it very well (Psalm 139:13–14).*

John MacArthur summarized the message of Psalm 139 by saying, "God knows us perfectly, but we can know Him now only imperfectly." To that we could add: One day we will know Him perfectly.

Job said, "Behold, these are but the outskirts of his ways, and how small a whisper do we hear of him!" (Job 26:14).

Paul made a similar statement: "Now we see in a mirror dimly, but then face to face. Now I know in part; then I shall know fully, even as I have been fully known" (1 Corinthians 13:12).

There is nothing about us God does not know; some day we will know Him fully as well. This is the great reason our spirits groan for heaven.

We have in us more than a desire to escape this earth and this life. God has given us a longing for His presence—a longing to know Him perfectly.

YOUR LIFE IN ACTION

Read Psalm 139, and meditate on what it will mean to be in the perfect presence of God, to know Him even as He knows us.

"I will multiply your offspring as the stars of heaven and will give to your offspring all these lands. And in your offspring all the nations of the earth shall be blessed, because Abraham obeyed my voice and kept my charge, my commandments, my statutes, and my laws" (Genesis 26:4–5).

In this passage, God spoke of three generations: Abraham, Isaac, and Isaac's offspring. To Isaac He promised a lineage of blessing ("your offspring") because of his ancestry of obedience ("Abraham obeyed my voice").

The faithfulness of one man set the spiritual course for multiple generations. The same can be true of you.

Do not minimize the choices you make today. You already know that the choice to obey God in one thing makes it more likely that you will choose to obey Him in the next.

But you must also think beyond yourself, taking your children and grandchildren (both physical and spiritual) into account. They will be largely shaped by your legacy—a legacy you are building one day at a time, one choice at a time.

YOUR LIFE IN ACTION

In one or two sentences, describe the legacy you want to leave to the coming generations.

> *Jacob said, "O God of my father Abraham and*
> *God of my father Isaac . . ." (Genesis 32:9).*

Jacob prayed to the one true God, acknowledging Him as the same God his father and grandfather worshiped. "God of my father" was an honorable way for Jacob to address God, because his heritage, though blemished here and there by sin, was God-centric. He was a third-generation patriarch, intent on carrying on the same spiritual formation he had received.

Even so, it was not the men who were meant to be exalted in this prayer, but the God of these men. In addressing God as he did, Jacob was essentially proclaiming that God had never changed and never would.

God was exactly the same in Isaac's day as He was in Abraham's, and as Jacob found Him to be in his own. This was a great hope and encouragement to him, as it should be to us.

Psalm 102 has been called "The Prayer of the Afflicted." It emphasizes the eternal and unchanging nature of God:

> Of old you laid the foundation of the earth, and the heavens are the work of your hands. They will perish, but you will remain; they will all wear out like a garment. You will change them like a robe, and they will pass away, but you are the same, and your years have no end (vv. 25–27).

YOUR LIFE IN ACTION

Pray through the above verses, worshiping God because He is who He has always been and always will be.

The people believed; and when they heard that the LORD had visited
the people of Israel and that he had seen their affliction,
they bowed their heads and worshiped (Exodus 4:31).

See if you can relate: The people of Israel were at an extremely low point. They were captives and slaves in the land of Egypt. A pervasive sense of hopelessness afflicted them. It seemed God had forgotten them.

Sometimes we just need to know that God hasn't forgotten us . . . that He sees and knows. Our faith tells us that if God sees and knows, He will deliver. We take comfort in knowing that His help is on the way, even if it doesn't come as quickly as we'd like.

Long before God actually delivered the people of Israel from captivity, He let them know, through Moses and Aaron, that He was going to. Though they would still face some battles with impatience and resistance, and their faith would falter, the news that deliverance was on the horizon brought them great joy. And they worshiped God.

You see the point, right? Today you live in a land of captivity, and you mourn over it. Yet you also know that God has promised deliverance.

Let this be your assurance then, that God sees and knows. He has not forgotten you!

YOUR LIFE IN ACTION

Worship the Lord today for the promise of His return,
for the coming glory of His eternal presence, for the hope that
all of your hardships will be put behind you.

John came to you in the way of righteousness, and you did not believe him, but the tax collectors and the prostitutes believed him. And even when you saw it, you did not afterward change your minds and believe him (Matthew 21:32).

How attentive are you to the ways God is working in the lives of the people around you? Are you aware that He is drawing people to Himself, igniting believing faith in their hearts and calling them to salvation?

Do you see God letting people come to the end of their own efforts and finally surrender to Him? Do you observe self-righteous people hardening their hearts, and broken ones turning to Christ?

God is at work in the world around us. People in Christ-denying nations are being born again, knowing that if the news of their faith becomes public, their lives are in grave danger.

Men and women in prison are owning up to their depravity, repenting, and believing the gospel. The grossest of sinners are falling on grace and being transferred from the kingdom of darkness to the kingdom of light.

What a shame and horror it would be to see all that God is doing and still not believe in Him. Do you know of God's works? Are you making them known?

YOUR LIFE IN ACTION

Pray that God's works would be known, and that the news of His works would become a light to draw others out of spiritual darkness.

Set your minds on things that are above,
not on things that are on the earth (Colossians 3:2).

S*et your minds.* These three little words deliver great power. What do they mean?

To *set our minds* means more than redirecting our thoughts when our minds wander off course. In fact, we are encouraged to do the opposite rather than allowing our minds to wander, we should be *telling* them where to go. We should be aiming our thoughts with as much concentration as a sniper aims his rifle.

Some people believe they cannot be held responsible for what they think. Perhaps you've believed that too.

But the Bible would not tell us to set our minds if it were not possible to do so. In setting our minds, we are taking control of our thoughts.

This is important because our thoughts are what put our actions and even our attitudes into play. Before we do something, or feel a certain way about a person or circumstance, we think about it. Our thoughts always lead the way.

Who controls your thoughts?

YOUR LIFE IN ACTION

Give extra attention to your thoughts today; be intentional with them. Purpose to pray for people and situations that might normally annoy you or make you anxious. Align your thoughts with truth.

Set your minds on things that are above,
not on things that are on the earth (Colossians 3:2).

Set your minds—three powerful little words. One clear way we can point our thoughts in a God-honoring direction is by the habit of giving thanks.

For instance, on a typical day, if nine things go well for you but one does not, are you grateful for the nine or angered by the one? Do you become so angry that you all but forget the nine, and perhaps even begin to doubt God's love? This can easily happen when we neglect to *set our minds* as the Bible instructs.

What if, at the beginning of your day, you set your mind on gratitude? You determine to watch for things to be grateful for and even to say a silent *thank You* to God each time you see Him at work.

Would that guarantee that nothing bad will happen? No. But won't you handle difficulty better if your mind has been set in the right direction to begin with?

A mind set on God is not easily disturbed.

YOUR LIFE IN ACTION

Start your habit of thanksgiving right now. Before you do anything else, think back through today (or yesterday) and thank God for specific things He did that showed His love for you.

*Let no one despise you for your youth, but set the believers an example
in speech, in conduct, in love, in faith, in purity (1 Timothy 4:12).*

Many see youth as a time to learn, explore, and maybe make a few mistakes (on purpose). Most people don't place a lot of value on youth and have low expectations of preteens and teens.

But what if there's a different way to look at youth? A better way?

Paul, the older gentleman who wrote the above Scripture as part of a letter, encouraged Timothy, the younger man to whom he wrote, to treat his youthfulness responsibly.

Essentially he was saying, "If you despise your youth—if you waste and devalue it—others will treat it that way as well. But if you embrace your young years by living them for godly purposes, others will follow your example. Not only will they show you more respect, they will also be influenced by you. You will be the one casting the shadow rather than the one walking in it."

If your youth is well behind you, that doesn't mean you are exempt from the teaching of this passage. The question for you is, what are you doing to support and encourage the young ones in your life?

YOUR LIFE IN ACTION
Think about the young men and women in your family, church,
and community. Take time to pray for them by name,
using the words of 1 Timothy 4:12 to guide your prayer.

> *Moses said to Pharaoh, "Be pleased to command me when I am
> to plead for you and for your servants and for your people, that the frogs
> be cut off from you and your houses and be left only in the Nile."
> And [Pharaoh] said, "Tomorrow" (Exodus 8:9–10).*

What could Pharaoh have been thinking? If presented with the same decision (set a time for the plague of frogs to be lifted), wouldn't you have said, *"Now!"*? Why would anyone want to wait one more day?

The natural reaction to Pharaoh's odd choice is to shake our heads in bewilderment, and perhaps even to laugh at his foolishness. Tomorrow? Really?

It's not a laughing matter, however, when a person responds to God's conviction by putting it off to a more convenient time (see Acts 24:25). Nor is it wise to get in the habit of spiritualized procrastination: *I'll obey starting tomorrow.*

The point of the saying that "delayed obedience is disobedience" is that "later" means the same as "no." Our hearts grow harder each time we say no to God, meaning we are no wiser than Pharaoh and his love for frogs.

YOUR LIFE IN ACTION

Have you adopted an attitude of spiritualized procrastination toward God in any area of your life? Will you say *yes* to God today?

Jesus answered, "Were not ten cleansed? Where are the nine? Was no one found to return and give praise to God except this foreigner?" And he said to him, "Rise and go your way; your faith has made you well" (Luke 17:17–19).

Artist Robert Doares included "The Grateful Leper" in his *Immanuel* series, which depicts various events in the life of Christ. In this drawing you can see nine men off in the distance, obviously overjoyed by the fact that Jesus has just healed them of leprosy. The focal point of the picture is a kneeling man, his face unseen, bowing at the feet of Jesus.

What is striking about the picture is the variance of distance. Nine of the ten are far away from Jesus, as if they had gotten all they wanted from Him and had moved on.

One man, however, overwhelmed by Christ's compassion, stayed close. He was the only one to return to Jesus and give Him thanks. And Jesus, seeing in this gratitude an awakening of faith, pronounced the man "well" (an indication that the man believed in Christ and was born again).

The attitude of gratitude and the habit of giving thanks to God will help keep us close to Him. May we never overlook or take for granted any act of God on our behalf. May we always gives thanks.

YOUR LIFE IN ACTION

Have you been neglectful of thanksgiving in your life?
Make time today to be alone with Jesus and give Him thanks
for all that He does for you, beginning with salvation.

> *Continue steadfastly in prayer, being watchful in it*
> *with thanksgiving (Colossians 4:2).*

What is the usual condition of your heart when you pray? Are you often fearful? Angry? Discontent? Hurried?

We know that we should pray, and even that we should continue in prayer—that is, be always ready to pray.

But being ready to pray means more than having a willingness; it also means maintaining our core. The value of a lifeguard isn't found in his willingness, but in his readiness, and that comes through his faithfulness to keep in shape.

Are you ready to pray? According to Colossians 4:2, readiness in prayer ("being watchful") comes through the faithful habit of thanksgiving. This maintains our spiritual core, because it keeps us in the habit of seeing and acknowledging God and His works.

Keep yourself praying and ready to pray by maintaining an attitude of gratefulness for what God is doing in and around you. Be steadfast in prayer by being watchful in thanksgiving.

YOUR LIFE IN ACTION

Before you ask God for anything today, think of ten things you are thankful for, and specifically express your thanks to God for each one.

We will not hide them from their children,
but tell to the coming generation the glorious deeds of the LORD,
and his might, and the wonders that he has done (Psalm 78:4).

Faith and joy can be contagious. All it takes is one believer telling another about the way he or she has personally experienced the work of God.

Have you ever been the hearer? Or the teller?

Think about some of the encounters with God in your life. Do you recall a time when He met a financial need that had you deeply concerned? Were you ever rejected by a friend, estranged for a long time and later reconciled by God's doing?

Have you or a loved one been deathly ill, and God healed? Or have you ever been drawn so low by grief that only God could lift you out, and He did?

Have you ever told anyone about it, especially someone younger (at least younger in the faith)? You need to tell others about the glorious deeds of the Lord. They need to hear it, and you need to tell it.

YOUR LIFE IN ACTION

What can you tell today?
Who can you tell today? Go and tell!

> *Be watchful, stand firm in the faith, act like men, be strong.*
> *Let all that you do be done in love (1 Corinthians 16:13–14).*

What does it mean to "act like men"? For the moment, set aside any ideas you may have of what a real man is or does, and consider only the description of manhood given in this passage. See what an honorable and duty-bound calling it should be.

A man is watchful. All God's men should live with the same vigilance that a law enforcement officer has when a BOLO (be on the lookout) is broadcast for a suspect or missing person. Even though he has other duties to perform, that officer will watch closely for anyone who matches the given description.

This is an example of how a man of God should live. As he goes about fulfilling his obligations at home and on the job, he is watchful, looking out for three things in particular: (1) anything that would hinder him from doing the will of God, (2) any opportunity to bring honor to God through his words or actions, and (3) the approach of any threat to those under his care.

A man stands firm in the faith. To place his faith in Jesus Christ means that a man is relying on Christ alone for salvation. He has recognized that nothing he could ever do or accomplish would qualify him for heaven. Yet he also recognizes that his faith is not just about future fulfillment—an eternity secured with God when he dies—but is the center and foundation of his life every day. Faith in God for the future is lived out through absolute trust in Him each day.

YOUR LIFE IN ACTION

If you are a man, pray that God will make these biblical descriptions true of you. If you are a woman, pray these things for the men in your life (husband, father, sons, brothers, etc.).

> *Be watchful, stand firm in the faith, act like men, be strong.*
> *Let all that you do be done in love (1 Corinthians 16:13–14).*

What does it mean to "act like men"? It is important to our culture and to every home to seek a biblical answer to that question.

A man is strong. The language here implies two important points: (1) It refers to more than physical strength, and (2) it describes the activity of continuing to become strong.

Therefore, a man should be growing and developing all of his life in all sorts of ways. He should always be maturing, which only happens to those who maintain a true sense of humility and a willingness to learn. A godly man's strength is seen not in being satisfied with the status quo, but in his humble pursuit to learn more about God and His ways each and every day of his life.

A man is loving. Some are reluctant to attribute too much love to manhood, because they think of love as soft and tame. This is to misunderstand both manhood and love, for love is boldly sacrificial.

One need think only of Jesus Christ to see a clear display of love, and there is nothing soft about it: "Greater love has no one than this, that someone lay down his life for his friends" (John 15:13).

YOUR LIFE IN ACTION

If you are a man, pray that God will make these biblical descriptions true of you. If you are a woman, pray these things for the men in your life (husband, father, sons, brothers, etc.).

The LORD said to Moses, "Why do you cry to me?
Tell the people of Israel to go forward" (Exodus 14:15).

Sometimes God tells His people to stop loitering in prayer and start taking action. This is not the same as telling them to stop praying, but rather commanding them to act on what He has already made clear regarding His will.

God said a similar thing to Joshua when he was mourning excessively over the recent defeat at the city of Ai. God wanted him to instead deal with the sin that caused the defeat: "The LORD said to Joshua, 'Get up! Why have you fallen on your face?'" (Joshua 7:10).

We wait in prayer when we aren't sure what God wants us to do, or when. Even then our waiting is not passive, however.

Waiting prayer is driven by the willingness and faith to move when God says to. But loitering prayer is a different matter, and most often results from fear, unbelief, or perhaps even defiance.

Are you loitering in prayer? Has God given you clear direction regarding some aspect of His will, and yet you are either afraid or unwilling to take action? Even if it is a challenging thing God is calling you to do, has He not proven Himself worthy of your trust and obedience?

YOUR LIFE IN ACTION

Think through the concerns you have been praying about.
Are you waiting in prayer or loitering in prayer? If you are loitering,
purpose to trust God and obey Him without further delay.

Whoever believes in the Son has eternal life;
whoever does not obey the Son shall not see life,
but the wrath of God remains on him (John 3:36).

In his book *Stop Asking Jesus Into Your Heart*, author J. D. Greear observed, "The apostle John almost always talks about 'believing' in the present tense because it is something we do continually, not something we did once in the past. . . . The posture [of believing] begins at a moment, but it persists for a lifetime."

For those who battle doubts regarding salvation, it is better to ask *Am I believing in Christ?* than *Have I believed in Christ?*

Are you believing, this very moment, completely in Christ for salvation? Is your soul fully accepting that "there is salvation in no one else" (Acts 4:12), and even your very best efforts cannot earn God's redemption? ("This is not your own doing; it is the gift of God, not a result of works, so that no one may boast," Ephesians 2:8-9 says.)

It is good to ponder salvation and prayerfully consider the state of our believing. If doing so brings doubt and uncertainty, then there is nothing of greater importance than settling that matter before the Lord. If it brings assurance, which we pray it does, then there is no greater joy our hearts can know today.

YOUR LIFE IN ACTION

Read John 3 and Ephesians 2:1–10. Read prayerfully, asking God to give you understanding as you read.

All have sinned and fall short of the glory of God, and are justified by his grace as a gift, through the redemption that is in Christ Jesus, whom God put forward as a propitiation by his blood, to be received by faith (Romans 3:23–25).

We may describe grace using many terms: amazing, abundant, lavish, and so on. But the one word we must never use is *free*, for the cost of grace was enormous. (Words fail.)

When we believe in Jesus Christ through the message of the gospel, we are granted a pardon. Our sentence is canceled, and our record of guilt is expunged.

That is *our* experience, but we must never forget that this pardon did not come cheaply, and it certainly wasn't free.

We were *guilty*, even "dead in the trespasses and sins in which [we] once walked . . . and were by nature children of wrath" (Ephesians 2:1, 3). The verdict of our guilt was not set aside; God demanded that it be met. And in Christ it was. So salvation is a matter of both pardon and redemption, of the Innocent paying the debt of the guilty.

Each day—not just weekly on Sunday or annually on Easter—we should recall the high cost of grace . . . and thank God that He paid it!

YOUR LIFE IN ACTION

Read one of the biblical accounts of the crucifixion and resurrection of Jesus (Matthew 27:24–28:10; Mark 15:1–16:8; Luke 23:18–24:12; John 19:1–20:10).

ARE YOU A COMPLAINER?

*In the morning you shall see the glory of the LORD,
because he has heard your grumbling against the LORD.
For what are we, that you grumble against us? (Exodus 16:7).*

The New Living Translation says God "has heard your complaints, which are against the LORD and not against us." Moses' point was clear: The people's grievance wasn't with him and Aaron, it was with God. Until they saw their complaining in light of that reality, nothing could be resolved. The people would continue in shortsighted faith, brought on by forgotten blessing.

Only a few days had passed since God had delivered them from captivity, and even fewer days since He had provided water in the desert. Yet they faced their new challenge as if God had done neither of those things.

Forgetfulness often leads to complaining. Our human hearts are prone to doubt God. Each new emergency seems to overwrite our memories of God's strength. And even when we do remember, we may still doubt.

But God is not like us. His feelings toward us are not fickle, His love does not waver, He does not grow weary. He never changes.

Are you a complainer? If so, you are likely also a forgetter. You've allowed your current circumstances to overwrite your memories of what God has done in the past, replacing them with fears, uncertainty, and perhaps discontentment. Recognize that your grievance is with God, and return to Him.

YOUR LIFE IN ACTION

If that last paragraph describes you, admit your thoughts and feelings to God. Thank Him for how He has proven His love and power to you in the past, and trust Him to work in your current circumstances.

As by the one man's disobedience the many were made sinners, so by the one man's obedience the many will be made righteous. Now the law came in to increase the trespass, but where sin increased, grace abounded all the more, so that, as sin reigned in death, grace also might reign through righteousness leading to eternal life through Jesus Christ our Lord (Romans 5:19–21).

Sin reigned in death. Don't let the gravity of those words escape you. The nature of sin has not changed, even for those who have been delivered from its penalty through believing in Jesus Christ.

Sin is still destructive. It is still bad for you.

Our culture broadly accepts sin, even pushing for its advance while applauding those who flaunt their defiance of any truth that contradicts their wants and wishes.

But how accepting are we of sin on a personal level—sin that we tolerate for ourselves because our flesh likes it? Is the nature of that sin any different than the nature of the sin we detest and protest in others? No, it is not.

Jerry Bridges wrote, "Our sin is a burden that afflicts us rather than a pleasure that delights us."

This is the true nature of sin, the biblical way to see it. Is this how you see *your* sin?

YOUR LIFE IN ACTION

What sin have you been tolerating and accepting in your own life? Confess it to God today, and turn from it with His help.

As you received from us how you ought to walk and to please God, just as you are doing, that you do so more and more. . . . Now concerning brotherly love you have no need for anyone to write to you, for you yourselves have been taught by God to love one another, for that indeed is what you are doing. . . . But we urge you, brothers, to do this more and more (1 Thessalonians 4:1, 9–10).

Some people waste years trying to find some secret that will pick up the pace of their spiritual maturing. They hope that by uncovering this mystery they will shift into warp speed, becoming ultra-wise and immune to temptation.

While this is not really a selfish ambition (though it may be for some), it is most certainly an unrealistic one. The path of spiritual formation is long.

Long, yes . . . but not really all that mysterious. In fact, Paul sums up the simplicity of it in the phrase "more and more" (1 Thessalonians 4:1, 10). Paul told the Thessalonians that they already knew what to do, they just needed to continue doing it. They needed to stay on the path, not look for a different or shorter one.

It is not unusual for us to get impatient with our spiritual progress. We may even begin to wonder if we've missed some teaching that would suddenly bring new understanding.

Certainly we need to continue to grow and, with prayerful wisdom and discernment, learn. But there is also a great chance that what you need most is to continue doing "more and more" of what you're already doing.

YOUR LIFE IN ACTION

List the habits and disciplines that are a regular part of your current spiritual formation. Share your list with a godly friend, and ask them to pray with you that you will remain faithful.

The aim of our charge is love that issues from a pure heart
and a good conscience and a sincere faith (1 Timothy 1:5).

Are you ever asked for advice on life issues? Do friends or family members seek you out because they think of you as one who lives wisely and with understanding? If so, be careful that the counsel you give is biblical.

When someone we love is in pain, we want them out of it as soon as possible. And that can cause our compassion to get in the way. Well-intentioned people sometimes give unbiblical advice.

This is why Paul spoke of a "sincere" faith when he instructed Timothy about ministry. A sincere faith is authentic, real, and reliable, not just well-intentioned.

When it comes to counseling people to walk in the ways of God, especially when they are weakened and harassed by some harsh circumstance, it is tempting to want to give them an easy answer. But easy answers are rarely sincere (in the true sense of the word). We must never set aside or soft-pedal biblical truth under the guise of compassion.

To counsel someone in accordance with "sincere faith" means telling them the truth. And that could mean they will suffer a little longer or have to take some hard initiative like forgiving or seeking forgiveness. But in the end, truth delivers.

YOUR LIFE IN ACTION

Can you think of a time when someone gave you an easy answer, and you later regretted that you had not been told the biblical truth about how you should handle your situation?

Trust in the LORD with all your heart,
and do not lean on your own understanding.
In all your ways acknowledge him,
and he will make straight your paths (Proverbs 3:5–6).

There should be nothing casual about our relationship with God. This point is clearly made and emphasized in one of the most well-known passages in the Bible, Proverbs 3:5–6.

Notice these word choices in particular: trust God with "all your heart," and acknowledge Him in "all your ways." Both phrases imply a hold-nothing-back way of giving ourselves continually over to God.

We sometimes use this passage as a sort of medicine, partaking of it when we are confused or unsure.

While there is nothing wrong with this approach per se, it does diminish the enlightenment we could get from it at all other times. It is not only in seasons of difficulty that we need God to make our paths straight—we need His guidance each moment of every day.

To "acknowledge" God does not mean to give Him a casual nod, indicating that you know who He is. It means to know Him with an intimacy that is always deepening. To paraphrase verse 6: *In everything you do, get to know God more and more, and He will always guide you.*

YOUR LIFE IN ACTION

What are you learning about God
through your current circumstances?

Why are you cast down, O my soul,
and why are you in turmoil within me?
Hope in God; for I shall again praise him,
my salvation and my God (Psalm 42:5–6).

Do you ever talk to yourself? It's really not that unusual; most people carry on internal conversations from time to time.

There is a risk in doing this, however, and it's the same risk we face when we converse with another person: We sometimes tell lies.

The psalmist faced down discouragement by telling himself the truth: Present realities are not permanent realities; I will praise God again.

This is the same God-focused mindset Joseph displayed when he named his second son Ephraim (which means "making fruitful") because, he said, "God has made me fruitful in the land of my affliction" (Genesis 41:52).

This was Joseph's way of reminding himself that God protects, provides, and restores because that is His nature. Circumstances are seasonal, but God is everlasting.

When you do talk to yourself, make certain you tell yourself the truth. God has not changed, and He has not turned away. Set your hope on Him.

YOUR LIFE IN ACTION

What truth about God do you need reminded of today?
Acknowledge that truth to God in prayer, and then
remind yourself of it throughout the day.

Oh, the depth of the riches and wisdom and knowledge of God!
How unsearchable are his judgments
and how inscrutable his ways! (Romans 11:33).

In the study *Experiencing God*, Henry Blackaby and Claude King introduced seven realities of experiencing God, the first one being, "God is always at work around you."

It is important that Christians recognize this, because it puts us in the position of joining God in what He intends rather than establishing our own cause and asking God to support us in our plans.

To add a thought from Romans 11:33, not only is God always at work around us, He is always doing more than we could possibly understand. We must never limit our trust in God to what our physical senses can take in or what our human mind can comprehend.

Combine everything you know with everything you feel, and then add everything you think; it all adds up to partial truth. God is doing *more*.

Second Corinthians 5:7 reminds us that "we walk by faith, not by sight." We cannot always see what God is doing, but we can be sure that He is always working to accomplish His will.

YOUR LIFE IN ACTION

Is it difficult for you to believe that God is working in certain situations right now? Tell Him you accept by faith that He is working. Activate your faith by acknowledging what is true.

Whoever has despised the day of small things
shall rejoice (Zechariah 4:10).

We are so accustomed to quantifying what we have and what we do, even in the church, that we walk shamefully close to spiritual snobbery on one side or spiritual indifference on the other. When we allow ourselves to be driven by the assumption that big numbers indicate God's pleasure more than small ones do, we miss the significance of what God is doing here and now.

We might trivialize a passing conversation with a neighbor. But what if God is stirring in that neighbor's heart, and he or she has been looking for a believing friend?

We might begrudge our limited ability to give. But what if an additional $20 per month is all that is needed for a missionary to be able to report for duty?

These are not small things. They are God-given opportunities to make Him known.

Do not belittle what God has assigned to you, as if it will not matter whether you obey. Remember what Jesus said: "Whoever gives one of these little ones even a cup of cold water because he is a disciple, truly, I say to you, he will by no means lose his reward" (Matthew 10:42).

YOUR LIFE IN ACTION

Do you look at how you're serving the Lord and feel inferior or superior to others? Ask God to change your outlook, and commit to be faithful to Him in whatever He assigns you.

*As we have opportunity, let us do good to everyone,
and especially to those who are of the household of faith (Galatians 6:10).*

The church sometimes attempts to reduce biblical instruction to slogans and sound bites. We're particularly fond of "They will know we are Christians by our love," based on John 13:35.

Who doesn't want to be thought of as loving? Yet we often want the reputation without putting in the work to earn it.

Within the instruction to "do good to everyone," we are told to prioritize our fellow believers ("the household of faith"). The challenge in doing this comes because of our over-familiarity with each other; human nature tends to treat the familiar with contempt, or at least disregard.

For example, we're less likely to show compassion to a person we believe to be harsh, or we're reluctant to help someone whose money management has put them in a bind in the past. In both cases, our knowledge of their past—our familiarity—lowers our desire to "do good" to them.

We need to change our view, however, and understand that the great benefit of doing good to one another in the household of faith is that it causes us to also fulfill the command to love one another. This is the "do the right thing" kind of love that the body of Christ is called to observe, where to love one another (do good) is to love God.

YOUR LIFE IN ACTION

Is God prompting you to do good for someone
in the household of faith? What is it? Will you do it?

This is the love of God, that we keep his commandments.
And his commandments are not burdensome (1 John 5:3).

Whenever we're feeling that the cost of obedience is too high and too hard, we need to remember that the cost of *disobedience* is much greater.

The commandments of God are not burdensome. We may find them difficult because we have to fight our old nature, but God's commands add no weight whatsoever to our burden.

God is not your rival, and life with Him is not a game you can either win or lose. In Christ your eternity with God is secured.

Rather than making the time between earth and heaven difficult for you, His commands are meant to keep you aware of His holiness (which your obedience could never achieve) and His grace (by which He has pronounced you righteous). His commandments showcase His love.

Obedience to God does not earn salvation, but it does give proof of it. Those who know Him, and who are growing in their obedience toward Him, are increasingly convinced of His love. This lightens any burden and increases every joy.

YOUR LIFE IN ACTION

Think of a time when you chose to disobey God rather than obey Him. Did you find the cost of disobedience higher than obedience would have been?

There is great gain in godliness with contentment,
for we brought nothing into the world,
and we cannot take anything out of the world (1 Timothy 6:6–7).

There may be things you want, but if having them means a slow-down in your spiritual growth, you should reconsider. Wanting "stuff" gets in the way of pursuing God.

In 1 Timothy 6, Paul strongly warns us to avoid those who teach anything that competes with our godliness. He specifically warned against any teaching that equates godliness with material gain. The longing for more possessions reveals a discontented heart, and a discontented heart is spiritually stagnant.

One of the best ways to monitor your level of contentment is to look toward the end of your life—"we brought nothing into the world, and we cannot take anything out." On your very last day, you will measure true riches in terms of their spiritual value, so you should start looking at them that way now. That outlook will put your focus where it ought to be: growing in godliness.

There is a day coming—God has already determined when—for you to give an account of your life to God (Romans 14:12). On that day it will not matter how full your closets are. Therefore, it should not matter today.

YOUR LIFE IN ACTION

If God were to ask you what really matters most to you,
acquiring things or growing in godliness,
what would your answer be?

[Cast] all your anxieties on him,
because he cares for you (1 Peter 5:7).

Did you know there is a way anxiety can actually help us? We understand that worry is not good for us, and not something God wants in our lives (Isaiah 41:10; Matthew 6:25; Philippians 4:6).

It is best for us to live with the abiding awareness of God being in control. Our hearts can rest in Him only because this is true.

However, worry sometimes outflanks our resolve to trust God, and the doubts come flying in. It is at this point, when anxiety is invading and trying to take control, that we can initiate a counterattack through prayer.

Rather than giving in to anxiety and watching our confidence in God fade away, we can do the very thing the Bible commands: cast our anxieties on God. This becomes a divine encounter—an intimate moment with our Lord—because we cannot cast our anxieties on Him without openly acknowledging how desperately we need Him and how steadfast is His love to deliver us.

Worry serves a good purpose, then, but only if it pushes us nearer to God.

YOUR LIFE IN ACTION

One by one, specifically bring each anxiety to God in prayer.
Visualize yourself casting them on Him. Do not pick them up again.
Listen to God's reassurance, and follow His instruction.

> *In all toil there is profit,*
> *but mere talk tends only to poverty (Proverbs 14:23).*

Talking about doing something isn't the same as doing it. In fact, talking is often a misguided attempt to get out of the doing. We can rationalize that as long as we're talking about it we're accomplishing it, but that's just not the case.

Of course, we're not thinking here in terms of planning or counting costs (the Bible favorably addresses both), but of idle conversation. This is what a person does to keep up appearances. He wants others to think he has understanding he does not truly possess, or ambitions he does not honestly plan to execute. "Mere talk" is the sound of intention and the illusion of progress.

This is not just an on-the-job concern. We can just as easily falsify our intentions at home or in regard to our own spiritual development through the idleness of talk, talk, talk.

It is not what we intend to do, or what we talk about doing, that will make any difference. "We must work the works of him who sent me while it is day; night is coming, when no one can work" (John 9:4).

YOUR LIFE IN ACTION

Are there things you've been talking about doing
instead of doing them? What action does God want you to take?

Remember therefore from where you have fallen;
repent, and do the works you did at first.
If not, I will come to you and remove your lampstand from its place,
unless you repent (Revelation 2:5).

By grace the penalty of sin is removed, but not necessarily the consequences. Believers still sin and therefore encounter the loving and corrective discipline of their Father (Hebrews 12:3–11).

As long as we defy God by ignoring the plea of His Holy Spirit calling us to repent, we remove ourselves from the spiritual disciplines that were helping us keep on track. Sin weakens and hardens us.

There is a way out of the spiritual wasteland of sin, and that is to return to the "works" (spiritual habits and disciplines) you once observed. Start praying again. Return to the fellowship of the church. Return to daily reading and meditating on Scripture.

Begin to do once again those things that strengthened your spirit in the past. Do them not as a means of impressing God, but to activate repentance that will bear fruit.

Throughout Scripture we are warned against delayed repentance. It may be your intention to repent at some time later on, but your intent serves no real purpose other than to keep you in the wasteland of sin for another day. Or longer.

YOUR LIFE IN ACTION

What are some of the works you did in the past that you need to make part of your spiritual habits once again?

We also, when we were children, were enslaved to the elementary principles
of the world. But when the fullness of time had come, God sent forth his Son,
born of woman, born under the law, to redeem those who were under the law,
so that we might receive adoption as sons. And because you are sons,
God has sent the Spirit of his Son into our hearts, crying, "Abba! Father!"
So you are no longer a slave, but a son,
and if a son, then an heir through God (Galatians 4:3–7).

The nature of our relationship with God can be described in three words: *slave, son,* and *heir.* As slaves, we were constrained either by sin or the empty promises of religion, perhaps both.

God rescued us "when the fullness of time had come" and made us sons. (How great is our God, that He did not keep us as His slaves, but made us His sons instead!)

Yet the joy that is ours today as His sons and daughters cannot compare to what we will know when we receive the inheritance God has promised to all His heirs (Romans 8:18–25).

You may have never been a "bad" sinner in the ways we often (mistakenly) measure sin. Even still, you were dead in your trespasses and sins, a child of wrath, separated from Christ, and without God in the world (Ephesians 2:1–12). You had no buying power with God, no claim to His love. He had to give it.

And because He did, you are no longer a slave. You are a son and an heir. There is no grander story than yours—from slave to son to heir.

YOUR LIFE IN ACTION

List some things that are true of you now that you are a son
and an heir of God that were not true of you before.

I consider that the sufferings of this present time are not worth comparing with the glory that is to be revealed to us. . . . For in this hope we were saved. Now hope that is seen is not hope. For who hopes for what he sees? But if we hope for what we do not see, we wait for it with patience (Romans 8:18, 24–25).

Assurance in the present rests in the security of the future. Everything about this life, even suffering, must yield to the glory that is ahead.

At the moment you became a believer in Jesus, you began a metamorphosis from glory to glory (2 Corinthians 3:18). You began looking ahead.

You have started to shed the grave clothes of what you once thought made life precious but eventually knew them as weights and sins that so easily entangle (Hebrews 12:1). You are being sanctified.

God is at work in you. This is a precious promise, a glorious reality. He is preparing a place for you, and preparing you for a place (His place). Look ahead!

YOUR LIFE IN ACTION

In what ways has God been sanctifying and transforming you, that is, making you more and more like Jesus Christ?

Have nothing to do with irreverent, silly myths.
Rather train yourself for godliness; for while bodily training is of some value,
godliness is of value in every way, as it holds promise for the present life
and also for the life to come (1 Timothy 4:7–8).

The godly do not become so through passivity. They are as devoted to spiritual strengthening as a world-class athlete is to his or her sport. All of life centers on that pursuit.

Physical training is a potent illustration of growing in godliness, for both the athlete and the believer focus on what lies ahead. Neither is satisfied with current conditions; they are always pressing forward.

Like every word picture, though, this one falls short of representing the whole truth. Believers are not competing against one another, nor are we on a course to win or lose.

Yet the work we put into growing in godliness is valuable in "every way," meaning that all of life is enriched when we are growing spiritually stronger. Our focus on godly development benefits us in this life and also rewards us in the next.

Knowing that God "rewards those who seek him" (Hebrews 11:6), let us continue to train for godliness without distraction.

YOUR LIFE IN ACTION

In what ways do you benefit in this life by growing in godliness?
What does the Bible teach about heavenly rewards?

Am I now seeking the approval of man, or of God?
Or am I trying to please man? If I were still trying to please man,
I would not be a servant of Christ (Galatians 1:10).

Knowing that we are accepted by God through Jesus Christ should put to rest every anxiety we have about what others think of us.

If God has given us His approval, what more could possibly be gained through the approval of man?

We sometimes—perhaps often—forget the immeasurable riches of God's grace toward us; and when we do, our insecurities cut in line.

We return to approval-seeking mode and try to give people a reason to like us, only to find sin crouching at the door. We go where we shouldn't, say more than we should, and hide our light under a basket (Matthew 5:15), all in the hunt for what we already had in abundance.

Those who are at rest in the love and approval of God are the best at giving love. They have nothing to prove.

YOUR LIFE IN ACTION

Do you often find yourself trying to gain the approval
and acceptance of others? Spend time reading verses that
reassure you of God's love. Begin with Romans 8:31–39.

TRUST, PURE AND SIMPLE

They cried out to God in the battle, and he granted their urgent plea
because they trusted in him (1 Chronicles 5:20).

The response Peter gave to Jesus' question was beautiful. Several disciples had just abandoned Jesus, and He asked the twelve remaining, "Do you want to go away as well?"

Peter replied, "Lord, to whom shall we go? You have the words of eternal life, and we have believed, and have come to know, that you are the Holy One of God" (John 6:67–69).

Peter's words revealed a heart of pure trust. He knew that it would be absolute foolishness to leave Jesus, because no one else had the words of eternal life. Leaving Jesus would mean losing everything.

Trust was also what God heard in the prayers of the Israelite warriors when He gave them victory (1 Chronicles 5).

Trust is what God looks for in your heart and listens for in your prayer. Do you trust Him, acknowledging with Peter that there is no one else to whom you could possibly turn?

YOUR LIFE IN ACTION

Write a description of what it means to have
absolute trust in another person. Now, add to that description
the ways God exceeds your description.

He said to them, "You give them something to eat" (Luke 9:13).

It's one thing to see the need. It's another thing to meet it. Love is displayed through acts of compassion. Like the disciples, we may become keenly aware that there are people within our reach who are hungry—or lonely, frightened, discouraged, wounded . . .

We may mourn for them, and legitimately pray for their restoration. And then we will very likely feel compelled to send them away, hoping they will find the help they need.

But what if Jesus would speak to you as He spoke to His disciples? *You feed them.*

Will your compassion, your love, take you that far? Are you willing to engage with them deeply, even to the point of sacrifice? Or would you take the easy path and send them away?

Jesus Himself fed over 5,000 souls that day, and He did so through sending the disciples out into the crowd at least three times (to seat them, to serve them, and to collect leftovers). This is a great picture of what happens each time you choose to help meet a need; you serve up what God Himself provides, and you touch lives repeatedly.

YOUR LIFE IN ACTION

Have you been on the receiving end of compassion?
Thank God for a particular time He met your need. Also consider thanking the one(s) through whom He reached out to you.

*Just as you once presented your members as slaves to impurity
and to lawlessness leading to more lawlessness, so now present your members
as slaves to righteousness leading to sanctification (Romans 6:19).*

Each sin we commit makes it easier to commit another, and then another. It is the nature of sin to never be satisfied; sin demands regular feeding.

Jerry Bridges wrote, "Sin tends to cloud our reason, dull our consciences, stimulate our sinful desires, and weaken our wills."

These are but a few of the weights sin lays upon our lives. What awful costs we willingly pay!

There is an equal and opposite effect that comes through obedience. Each *no* to self and *yes* to God strengthens our spirit and positions us to make the wise choice the next time.

This is the way of sanctification, of knowing God more richly and enjoying Him more fully. This is His will for us, and it is what is best for us in every way.

YOUR LIFE IN ACTION

Ask God to show you the areas where you are
walking in disobedience. Confess the sin He reveals,
accept His forgiveness, and ask Him for the wisdom to obey.

> *A friend loves at all times,*
> *and a brother is born for adversity (Proverbs 17:17).*
> *He who withholds kindness from a friend*
> *forsakes the fear of the Almighty (Job 6:14).*

Maybe Job's friends should get partial credit. They at least cared enough to show up.

Being the well-known and influential man that he was, Job surely had more than four friends. Still, only these few came to his side in the days of adversity.

True, their silence was more helpful than their words, but again, they were present. Let's give them that.

The biblical standard of true friendship is high and all too rarely seen. "A friend loves at all times"—*all* times. Convenience makes no difference; love overrides convenience.

No situation is too dreadful to keep a friend away. Love responds to need, not to appearance.

The human part of your nature will now ask, *Do I have any such friends?* But the Christ part will ask, *Am I such a friend?*

YOUR LIFE IN ACTION

Are you a friend who loves at all times?
Ask God to show His love through you at all times.

*"There are devoted things in your midst, O Israel.
You cannot stand before your enemies until you take away
the devoted things from among you" (Joshua 7:13).*

Israel had a sin problem, and it was costing them dearly. They had already lost one battle because of it, and God warned them that the losses—and the sufferings—would continue until the sin was dealt with.

You may be familiar with the story. In their first advance toward conquering and inhabiting the Promised Land, Israel had defeated the city kingdom of Jericho with little resistance. But one man (later revealed to be a man named Achan) had violated God's command by keeping some of the spoils for himself.

This hidden sin resulted in the death of 36 soldiers in the next battle. God made it clear: They would never defeat their enemies unless and until the sin was dealt with.

The nature of sin has not changed. It sill limits us to lesser things than God desires for us. We weaken ourselves by the sins we ignore, but we will find our strength renewed when we deal with our sin God's way.

YOUR LIFE IN ACTION

Are you tolerating any sin in your life? Deal with it aggressively and immediately. Confess it to God, receive His forgiveness, and leave this sin behind you.

THERE'S WORK FOR YOU TO DO

We are his workmanship, created in Christ Jesus for good works,
which God prepared beforehand, that we should walk in them (Ephesians 2:10).

As a Christian, you belong to God. You have found your identity, and now you are learning and accomplishing your purpose—which is ultimately His purpose.

On a personal level, the implications of this truth are staggering. Both your birth and your rebirth were initiated by God, and His intent is to insert you into His divine work.

Your work in His kingdom is not a matter of random selection; God has "prepared [it] beforehand." You were made for it, and it was made for you.

Todd Adkins wrote, "God doesn't just want to save our souls; He wants to bring every area of our life into a godly wisdom and usefulness." You are not biding your time here. At the moment you believed in Jesus, you joined heaven's workforce on earth.

This does not necessarily mean God will have you move or change jobs, although He may. In many New Testament instances, Christ sent those He saved back to where they came from so they would testify of Him there. He gave them new purpose, not a new address.

Trusting that God has you where He does for His purposes, what are you doing to make Him known there?

YOUR LIFE IN ACTION

Pray through Ephesians 2:10, making it personal. Acknowledge to God that He created you, saved you, and prepared good works for you to do. Trust Him to direct you in fulfilling His purposes for you.

*The wise of heart is called discerning,
and sweetness of speech increases persuasiveness (Proverbs 16:21).*

The book of Proverbs has many recurring themes of wisdom. One of the more dominant is this: The mouth is connected to the heart. Eventually, the words we speak give us away, revealing our true selves.

Therefore, our best approach to taming our tongue (James 3) is to guard our heart (Proverbs 4:23–24). More than learning to watch what we say, we need to be careful what we treasure.

The ability to communicate with each other is a gift. What would life be if we could feel love but not express it, or if we had knowledge that could save a friend but could not give it?

How would we pass along ideas, warnings, news, and encouragement were it not for the gift of speech? How would we share the gospel?

Yet we all know that words can be as abusive as they can be helpful. They can destroy a life as easily as they can build one up.

This is where the heart comes in, why the things you love and nurture in your soul make all the difference. "Out of the abundance of the heart [your] mouth speaks" (Luke 6:45).

YOUR LIFE IN ACTION
In what ways does your heart need to change
so that your speech is persuasive in a God-pleasing manner?

> *When a man's folly brings his way to ruin,*
> *his heart rages against the LORD (Proverbs 19:3).*

A lot of people misdirect their anger toward others, and some even toward God. What they fail to see—or perhaps see but refuse to admit—is that their own folly is to blame. They're merely suffering the consequences of their own decisions.

Quite often the guilt we rightly feel leads us to rage and blame. By nature we are uncomfortable with guilt and want to evict it almost as soon as we are aware of its presence.

However, guilt, although it no longer holds us under a curse, can still serve a purpose. And it is because of that purpose that we don't want to be too quick about sending guilt away.

Dismissing guilt too soon only adds to the folly that invited it to begin with. Sometimes we *feel* guilty because we *are* guilty. In this case we have committed some sin that has jammed the flow of love and peace that should be ours in Christ. And it is precisely because of the guilt we *feel* that we *know* there is a problem.

This is when we may choose to rage (as Proverbs 19:3 suggests) or blame others, but the better course is to humble ourselves and admit that the fault is ours. With that confession, guilt has served its purpose and should then—and only then—be dismissed.

YOUR LIFE IN ACTION

Is there any legitimate guilt in your soul right now?
Let it drive you to confess your sin to God. Then, having been forgiven,
thank God that the guilt is gone.

I am the vine; you are the branches. Whoever abides in me and I in him,
he it is that bears much fruit, for apart from me you can do nothing (John 15:5).

We are all on life support; we depend on the sustenance we receive from outside ourselves, whether that is oxygen, food, or love. Something outside of us keeps us alive. This is especially true in a spiritual sense; the case for saying so is made in the three facts and one promise of John 15.

Fact #1: Jesus is the vine; He is life and the giver of life. There is no end to Him. Unlike mankind that weakens and dies, Christ is as alive and vibrant as He ever was, and He always will be.

Fact #2: We are branches. We have to be connected to a source of life in order to live. As humans, we cannot generate or sustain life. To live we must have a relationship with God. Our very existence—physical and spiritual—comes from Him.

Promise: Those who believe in Jesus Christ move from death to life (John 5:24) and begin to abide in—to constantly draw their life from—the vine. This is a new kind of life that far exceeds the physical life of air, food, and water. It is an abundant and fruit-bearing life that does not end.

Fact #3: It is impossible to obtain the promise apart from Christ. There is salvation (real life) in no other (Acts 4:12).

YOUR LIFE IN ACTION

Are you abiding in the vine? If yes, praise Him for life.
If you are unsure, talk to someone today who can help you be certain.

The word of God is living and active, sharper than any two-edged sword, piercing to the division of soul and of spirit, of joints and of marrow, and discerning the thoughts and intentions of the heart (Hebrews 4:12).

Sometimes we surprise ourselves, and not in a good way. We accept the fact that others will misunderstand us on occasion, but when we are a stranger to ourselves, bewildered by our own desires, moods, and behavior, it is time to bring our unsettled thoughts before God. We need truth, not speculation.

One of the most precious qualities of the Word of God is its certainty. It reveals what is true about us, not what might be or what we wish for. We can absolutely rely on what God's Word says; it leaves no margin for maybes.

As you practice the habit of regular intake of God's Word, you will know what is true of yourself and become more certain about what you need to be doing. You will discover "thoughts and intentions" that may have been hidden even from yourself.

Approach God's Word as a student, not as a teacher. Come to hear counsel, not to argue your case. Come with the resolve to do what God says, not to consider it against other options.

YOUR LIFE IN ACTION

As you have been spending time in God's Word, has God been convicting you of something, or prompting you to make some sort of change, or take a certain action? Will you obey Him today?

In the morning sow your seed, and at evening withhold not your hand,
for you do not know which will prosper, this or that,
or whether both alike will be good (Ecclesiastes 11:6).

It is easy to spiritualize our idleness. A great deal of important works gets left undone under the guise of "waiting on the Lord." Sometimes we just need to get busy.

To be clear, this is not to suggest that being busy is the hallmark of spiritual maturity. There is certainly a time for counting cost and seeking counsel before taking on important jobs (Luke 14:28–33). Yet that in itself is commendable labor.

What the Bible opposes is the idleness of laziness and indifference. This is the posture of those who argue for *later* over *now* (Proverbs 26:13–16), and sometimes their arguments sound reasonable.

This is not God's way, however. He is sending laborers into His fields and asking those very workers to pray that others will join them.

Night is coming, He warns us, and the time for work will be done. So we must all report for duty. Now.

YOUR LIFE IN ACTION

If you are not actively engaged in serving the Lord in some way, dare to ask Him to lead you to a place of service.

I know that nothing good dwells in me, that is, in my flesh. For I have the desire to do what is right, but not the ability to carry it out. For I do not do the good I want, but the evil I do not want is what I keep on doing (Romans 7:18–19).

In a message to congress, U.S. Naval Commodore Oliver Perry wrote, "We have met the enemy and they are ours." Years later, cartoonist Walt Kelly famously paraphrased this to read: "We have met the enemy and he is us" (proving that truth can be found in the funniest places).

When it comes to obedience and growing in Christ, we are often our own enemy. We choose to do the very things we want to quit doing—things that set us back. Psychologists call it self-destructive behavior; the Bible calls it sin (Romans 8:20), and we must deal with it as such.

Sadly, many Christians seem to think that dealing with their sin appropriately means feeling guilty about it for a long time. But this extended stay in guilt only leads to regret, which leads to shame, which leads to frustration, which leads to . . . more sin. What are they (we) missing? Forgiveness!

Dealing with sin means receiving and accepting God's forgiveness, not looking for ways to prolong our guilt. True, there may be additional actions we need to take, like asking forgiveness from someone we've hurt or making restitution, but we must never devalue God's mercy by wallowing in guilt over sin He has already forgiven.

YOUR LIFE IN ACTION

Are you enjoying the freedom of God's mercy, or are you needlessly nurturing guilt? By faith, thank Him for His forgiveness, and ask Him to help you move forward in it.

Have you not known? Have you not heard? The LORD is the everlasting God,
the Creator of the ends of the earth. He does not faint or grow weary;
His understanding is unsearchable. He gives power to the faint,
and to him who has no might he increases strength (Isaiah 40:28–29).

In his book *Introverts in the Church*, Adam McHugh wrote, "Our healing prescription begins not in exploring the nature of our introversion, as important as that is; our healing comes in probing the depths of God's nature."

Personalize this observation by replacing the word *introversion* with whatever your own struggle(s) might be, and you'll come to the same conclusion: The answer to every problem and shortcoming is found in God.

Problems are real; we humans are frail, fallible, and fallen. We are deficient in more ways than we know. Even those with redeemed souls need to face up to the truth of their condition.

However, we should, as has been said, "glance at our need and gaze at our God." We must become students of the character and nature of God, seeking to know Him rather than nurturing an infatuation with ourselves.

When you look for answers and reasons for the challenges in life, begin and end your search with God Himself. Ask Him, and trust Him, to make Himself better known to you through these circumstances.

YOUR LIFE IN ACTION

What are you learning about the nature and ways of God
through the challenges of your life?

*Thus says the LORD: "Let not the wise man boast in his wisdom,
let not the mighty man boast in his might, let not the rich man boast in his riches,
but let him who boasts boast in this, that he understands and knows me,
that I am the LORD who practices steadfast love,
justice, and righteousness in the earth.
For in these things I delight, declares the LORD" (Jeremiah 9:23–24).*

In *The Knowledge of the Holy*, A. W. Tozer said, "What comes into our minds when we think about God is the most important thing about us." Interesting, and more than a little convicting.

How well you know God has a great deal to do with how often you think about Him, but it has even more to do with who or what you allow to influence your thoughts about Him. This is why Scripture emphasizes that seeking God is an active pursuit of truth rather than a passive aggregating of opinions (see Proverbs 1:7; Acts 17:11; 2 Corinthians 10:5).

If you are careless regarding whose teaching and influence you allow in, you are likely to be deceived in your understanding of God and thereby weakened in your faith.

The converse is equally true and perhaps more convicting: Someone may be shaping their thoughts about God based on *your* influence. All the more reason to "grow in the grace and knowledge of our Lord and Savior Jesus Christ" every day (2 Peter 3:18).

YOUR LIFE IN ACTION

Write out a list of some of the basic thoughts you have about God.
Add Scripture references where you can.

It is better to go to the house of mourning
than to go to the house of feasting,
for this is the end of all mankind,
and the living will lay it to heart (Ecclesiastes 7:2).

Have you ever listened—*really* listened—to the words of a broken-hearted person? Sometimes this is when they are at their wisest.

The loss they have encountered has stripped them of pretense and given them a clearer view of the end of life. This provides clarity for both how they want to live and what legacy they want to leave.

The Bible says we should avail ourselves of the wisdom of the sad, even to the point of learning from their circumstances to "number our days that we may get a heart of wisdom" (Psalm 90:12).

We need to be reminded that earthly life is brief and that every day should be given over to God and His will for us, to be about doing the works He has prepared for us (Ephesians 2:10).

Some people go so far as to say that they make all of their big decisions in a cemetery, because of the perspective it brings. That may seem a bit morbid, but there certainly is wisdom in remembering that God has numbered our days.

YOUR LIFE IN ACTION

Have you ever considered what you desire your spiritual legacy to be?
Describe it in two or three sentences.

[Jesus] would withdraw to desolate places and pray (Luke 5:16).

No one has ever dealt with more demands than Jesus did. People pressed themselves into His personal space every day. Still, He would *withdraw* and *pray*.

You may not be able to do this every day, but you really should find ways and set times to withdraw. Your soul needs it, and those who depend on you need your soul to be strong.

But simply withdrawing is not enough. You must do so for the greater purpose of praying.

Even if you pray regularly throughout your days, try to add special times of withdrawing for extended prayer. Have a long conversation with God.

YOUR LIFE IN ACTION

Schedule a time to withdraw for prayer. Make whatever arrangements you need so that you are not likely to be interrupted.

Faith is the assurance of things hoped for,
the conviction of things not seen (Hebrews 11:1).

Hope takes on new meaning when it becomes coupled to faith in Christ. *Before* Christ, "to hope" means little more than "to wish." *With* Christ, however, wishful thinking is replaced with confident anticipation.

Hope is no longer a matter of wishing that someday such and such might happen. Now it's about knowing that a day *is* coming when certain things that cannot yet be seen *will be* seen.

This is the kind of hope God wants His children to carry in their heart. This is the kind of hope that makes it possible to endure present sufferings and not to overreact to insults and slights.

This is the kind of hope that makes it possible to forgive and to love our enemies. This is the kind of hope that helps us keep our promises and "not love the world or the things in the world" (1 John 2:15).

Are you in need of hope today—not of fantasy or wishes, but of truth and certainty? Then look ahead . . . to what you cannot yet see, knowing that one day you will see it. Live in the assurance of things hope for.

YOUR LIFE IN ACTION

In your own words, write out a definition for biblically based hope.

*We know that for those who love God all things work together for good,
for those who are called according to his purpose. For those whom he foreknew
he also predestined to be conformed to the image of his Son, in order that
he might be the firstborn among many brothers (Romans 8:28–29).*

Let's be careful never to separate the familiar verse 28 from the less familiar verse 29. If we separate them, we'll reach an incomplete deduction that emphasizes our personal comfort over God's purpose.

It is true that God makes all things work together for good; but we must understand that what is *good* is our being conformed to the image of Jesus Christ.

As we all know, the conforming process is sometimes a difficult one, and it's easy to lose proper perspective when we're in the midst of it.

Theologian Wayne Grudem offers an excellent reminder: "Every day of our lives, we may quiet our discouragement with the comfort that comes from the knowledge of God's infinite wisdom: if we are his children, we can know that he is working wisely in our lives, even today, to bring us into greater conformity into the image of Christ."

God is more committed to your growth in Christ than you are. His work in you is constant, and it is *good*.

YOUR LIFE IN ACTION

Write out the words to Romans 8:28–29 as a way of
settling them into your heart.

---

*Many Samaritans from that town believed in him because of
the woman's testimony, "He told me all that I ever did" (John 4:39).*

Anumber of things happen when Jesus sets a soul free. Here are
four of them:

1. We celebrate (oh, that there were an even happier and
   brighter word!) not having to pretend any longer. This
   is the beautiful essence of freedom, isn't it? That which
   has shamed us, and which we knew would probably be
   forced out into the light someday, has lost its threat.

2. We discover that we really aren't beyond the reach of
   God's mercy. Even though Scripture had assured us all
   along that God would forgive, the inner voice of condemnation had long been telling us that we were the
   one exception. Now that voice has gone silent.

3. Christ captivates our thoughts and our conversation.
   When your soul has been set free, it's hard to talk about
   anyone more than the One who freed it.

4. Others are awakened. To witness the transformation of
   a soul is to catch a glimpse of heaven. That is an unfor-
   gettable sight.

Next time you are privileged to see a rebirth, ponder the holy significance. And pray for others to be awakened.

YOUR LIFE IN ACTION

Think of the last person you know who believed in Jesus Christ.
Rejoice for that person, and pray that God will use
his or her salvation to awaken others.

Put on then, as God's chosen ones, holy and beloved, compassionate hearts,
kindness, humility, meekness, and patience, bearing with one another and,
if one has a complaint against another, forgiving each other;
as the Lord has forgiven you, so you also must forgive.
And above all these put on love, which binds
everything together in perfect harmony (Colossians 3:12–14).

As you prepare for the day, what thought do you give to how your mind and heart are dressed? In choosing your clothing, you've probably considered several things, including the weather, what activities you'll be doing, and who you'll be spending time with. Should you not be equally thoughtful about how you clothe your heart? The Bible says to "put on" such things as:

Compassion – Are you ready to hear, see, and if it is within your power, meet the needs of friends and strangers today?

Kindness – Will you encourage people today, and try to lighten the weight of their burden?

Humility – Will you think of yourself less and of God and others more?

Meekness – You will face some difficulties today. Are you prepared to keep anger in check and instead use your God-given strength to make peace?

Patience – Are you willing to wait when God says wait?

YOUR LIFE IN ACTION

Pray through the list above, and ask God to
clothe your heart with each of these attributes.

. . . praying at all times in the Spirit, with all prayer and supplication.
To that end keep alert with all perseverance, making supplication
for all the saints (Ephesians 6:18).

In the book *Dispatches from the Front*, Tim Keesee wrote about a church he worshiped with in one of the world's difficult places: "The congregation here numbers nearly four hundred, but they have no more than a couple dozen Bibles among them."

Our prayers should span the globe. When we pray "for all the saints," this includes brothers and sisters we've never met, and probably won't meet in this life. Keesee's quote above points out just one way we need to pray—that the Scriptures will be translated and made available to these hungry-hearted saints.

Be encouraged to know that the gospel is advancing, even in the hardest places of the world, to the very threshold of hell. We must pray for our brothers and sisters who live in these dangerous and oppressive lands. Pray for their most basic needs of food and shelter to be provided, for proper medical care, for physical protection, for their faith to remain strong, for their faithful witness, and so on.

When you pray for the body of Christ, think beyond your own experience and culture. Pray for those "from every nation, from all tribes and peoples and languages, [who will be] standing before the throne and before the Lamb" (Revelation 7:9).

YOUR LIFE IN ACTION

Many online and printed resources tell of the advance of the gospel throughout the world and recommend specific areas where prayer is needed. Include one of these sources in your prayer times.

They said to each other, "Did not our hearts burn within us while he talked to us on the road, while he opened to us the Scriptures?" (Luke 24:32).

On the day Jesus rose from the dead, two disciples were walking to the village of Emmaus. As they walked, they discussed the events of the preceding days, especially the crucifixion of their Lord. Suddenly they were joined by a man they did not recognize who began to explain something they had failed to grasp until that day: the Scriptures all point to the Christ.

When Jesus later revealed His identity to them, the two understood why their hearts "burned within" them when He had opened the Scriptures. Even as disciples, they had just begun to understand the width, height, and depth of the Word of God.

May our findings in Scripture be the same today as theirs, and may we marvel just as they did. For while the Bible has many things to teach us about life, its ultimate purpose is to point us again and again to our Savior.

So let us seek for more than understanding, or even encouragement (as much as we may need those things today). Let us seek Christ in the Scriptures.

YOUR LIFE IN ACTION

As you continue your daily Bible reading, make note of what various passages and books teach about Jesus Christ. Some references are more obscure than others, especially in the Old Testament.

He heals the brokenhearted and binds up their wounds.
He determines the number of the stars; he gives to all of them their names.
Great is our Lord, and abundant in power;
his understanding is beyond measure (Psalm 147:3–5).

A clear and starry night sky reveals God's power and declares His majesty. Far beyond knowing how many stars are there, God determines how many there will be. And He names them. This is the work of our great God.

If He is powerful enough to determine the number of the stars (Psalm 147:4), create the heavens and the earth (Genesis 1:1), number the hairs on your head (Luke 12:7), cast out demons (Luke 11:20), raise people from the dead (Hebrews 11:35), walk on water (Matthew 14:25), stop a storm (Mark 4:39), and make the sun stand still (Joshua 10:13) . . .

Can you trust Him to give you eternal life (John 10:28), make all grace abound to you (2 Corinthians 9:8), deliver you from temptation (1 Corinthians 10:13), comfort you in your affliction (2 Corinthians 1:4), and know what you need and then supply it (Philippians 4:19)?

Yes, you can.

YOUR LIFE IN ACTION

Worship God by telling Him of ways you see His power displayed through creation. Then take several minutes to worship Him for ways He has personally displayed His power in your life.

Do not love the world or the things in the world. If anyone loves the world, the love of the Father is not in him. For all that is in the world—the desires of the flesh and the desires of the eyes and pride in possessions—is not from the Father but is from the world (1 John 2:15–16).

As the children of Israel were preparing to inhabit their promised land, God gave clear commands regarding the enemies they would encounter: "They shall not dwell in your land, lest they make you sin against me; for if you serve their gods, it will surely be a snare to you" (Exodus 23:33).

We should be equally stalwart when it comes to our personal intolerance of sin. Even though sin can no longer separate believers from the love and mercy of God, it can still do a great deal of damage by destroying relationships, undermining our witness, and disqualifying us from certain kinds of service.

Sin has no rightful claim on you, so why give it any space in your affections? Love God with your *whole* heart. Get serious about ridding your heart of any degree of love for sin.

YOUR LIFE IN ACTION

Israel's warriors fought together to drive the enemies from their land. Perhaps you need some fellow warriors to fight alongside you. Consider recruiting a few prayer partners you can pray with.

The people of Israel did what was evil in the sight of the LORD.
They forgot the LORD their God and served the Baals and the Asheroth.
Therefore the anger of the LORD was kindled against Israel, and he sold them
into the hand of Cushan-rishathaim king of Mesopotamia. And the people
of Israel served Cushan-rishathaim eight years (Judges 3:7–8).

There is a harsh lesson to be learned from the book of Judges (besides trying to pronounce odd names). The lesson is this: God's people like to sin. The proof of this is seen in how long they (we) are willing to put up with the consequences of sin even though they (we) know how to get out from under those consequences.

The book of Judges presents a cycle of peace-rebellion-judgment-repentance-deliverance-peace. This cycle is repeated numerous times, with the rebellion season lasting for years each time (eight, eighteen, twenty, and so on). What a long time to endure self-inflicted suffering!

Yet we cannot claim moral superiority, because we enjoy our sin too. Sometimes for a long time, even when the way of repentance and peace is clear to us. The delay is on our part, not God's, for "The LORD is merciful and gracious, slow to anger and abounding in steadfast love" (Psalm 103:8).

YOUR LIFE IN ACTION

Give thanks to God for His patience and mercy. If there is any long-standing sin in your life, why go on another day in hardness of heart? Confess, repent, and receive God's forgiveness.

The angel of the Lord appeared to him and said to him,
"The Lord is with you, O mighty man of valor" (Judges 6:12).

Gideon was not chosen because he had what it took to get the job done. He wasn't displaying any real courage when the angel of the Lord called him a "mighty man of valor." In fact, he was living in fear and already had an escape plan in place if his enemies attacked.

To be fair, Gideon was living and acting like everyone else. He was probably no more fearful than the rest of his countrymen, yet God called him to be a deliverer. In addressing Gideon as a mighty man of valor, the angel described not who he was but who God would make him.

There are things that will be true of you that aren't yet true of you. Let your heart take courage in knowing that you are not limited to being only who you are or who you have been. God is at work in you "to work for his good pleasure" (Philippians 2:13), and His work never ceases.

Gideon did indeed become a mighty man of valor, but not because he was a self-made man. He was a God-made man. Like you.

YOUR LIFE IN ACTION

Read the story of how God worked through Gideon (Judges 6–7).

> *All who saw it said, "Such a thing has never happened or been seen*
> *from the day that the people of Israel came up out of the land of Egypt*
> *until this day; consider it, take counsel, and speak" (Judges 19:30).*

Judges 19 is one of the most bizarre sections of the Bible. The story it tells is shocking—actual events that reveal the wickedness of individuals and an entire culture. The sin mankind is capable of is revolting.

Quite often believers prefer to lead sanitized lives of naiveté, blocking out the wickedness that surrounds us.

While there is some solid footing for this approach—"to keep oneself unstained from the world" (James 1:27)—we cannot close ourselves off from the terrifying need of the gospel. Being unstained does not mean being indifferent.

The darkness of our world beckons the light. As a believer, you have that light. Don't hide it.

YOUR LIFE IN ACTION

Have you ever stopped to consider what your response to the wickedness of the world should be? What is God calling you to do?

As a deer pants for flowing streams, so pants my soul for you, O God.
My soul thirsts for God, for the living God.
When shall I come and appear before God? (Psalm 42:1–2).

People who are lonely need more than companionship; they need intimacy. And that's why they need to pray.

This is not a superficial piece of advice that means, "If you're lonely, pray about it" (*it* being your loneliness), but rather a recognition of the true nature of prayer and how profoundly a prayer life can change us.

Prayer is a means of deepening our intimacy with God; some would even say prayer is the truest indicator of our intimacy with God. Prayer brings the wonder of God into clearer view, and reminds us that we are fully dependent on His grace.

Prayer brings our thoughts into alignment with truth, and focuses them on God. As our prayer life develops, the roots of worship spread into every segment of our lives. We grow in our awareness of God's presence. We enjoy Him. We love Him. We rest in Him.

So, what should the lonely do? They should pray. And so should the happy, sad, content, hungry, rich, poor, peaceful, agitated, young, and old—from every tribe and nation. Let them "draw near with a true heart in full assurance of faith" (Hebrews 10:22).

YOUR LIFE IN ACTION
If you don't have a time set aside each day for uninterrupted prayer, begin the habit today.

*He did evil, for he did not set his heart to
seek the LORD (2 Chronicles 12:14).*

The history books of the Old Testament tell of the lives of kings, both good and evil. This one-sentence summarization of King Rehoboam's reign should alert all people—not just leaders—to the dangers of carefree living.

Be warned: The human heart is naturally inclined to take the easy and evil way.

If you give no thought or take no action to seek the Lord today—or to guard your heart, take your thoughts captive to obey Christ, set your mind on things above, limit your words, or any other such thing the Scripture instructs—you will no doubt come into the evening with many regrets and having committed a great deal of sin.

You will have lived a Rehoboam-like day because you did not set your heart to seek the Lord. You approached life passively and let the day take you in whatever direction an unguarded heart may wish to go.

Perhaps you've had several Rehoboam-like days in a row . . . or several weeks, or . . . Why not break that pattern today?

Set your heart to seek the Lord. Be intentional about growing in Christ today.

YOUR LIFE IN ACTION

What three things can you do today, and every day,
to set your heart to seek the Lord?

> *Let another praise you, and not your own mouth;*
> *a stranger, and not your own lips (Proverbs 27:2).*

Have you ever been in one of those awkward conversations where a person keeps making himself the topic?

Some people are masters at this, capitalizing on every turn of the discussion to tell a tale of their own heroism, intelligence, or suffering. They can never hear themselves say enough about themselves.

Now you may be wondering, *Am I that person?*

Our words eventually give us away. If we have pride in our hearts, and think more of ourselves than we ought to, sooner or later we will talk in ways that make that obvious.

Boasting is just one way pride comes out, which also means that if you "put off" boasting (in the spirit of Colossians 3:8–10), you deprive pride of some of its oxygen.

A good principle to live by: When there are good things to be said about you, let others say them. And if these good things are never said, embrace the humility of your obscurity and be content with God's approval alone.

YOUR LIFE IN ACTION

Describe why it means more to be praised by others
than to praise yourself.

> *Do nothing from selfish ambition or conceit, but in humility count others more significant than yourselves (Philippians 2:3).*

Here are a few lessons from this straightforward verse.

1. Motive matters to God, and therefore it should matter to us.

2. Ambition is not condemned, but selfish ambition is. The difference between the two is obvious, and our hearts know it.

3. Conceit, or the vanity of self-admiration, will make a person a failure even if his plan succeeds. The conceited person can never be satisfied with the admiration others give him, because there is no respect in their admiration.

4. Counting others more significant means:

    *   Humility is the posture of love.
    *   In humility I will make do with less so others can have more.
    *   Through my humility others should experience God's love.

Humility is not supposed to be a characteristic that some within the body of Christ have and others do not. Humility should mark us all.

YOUR LIFE IN ACTION
In what ways has God used the humility of others
to show His love to you?

---

*Jesus answered them, "Truly, truly, I say to you,
everyone who practices sin is a slave to sin" (John 8:34).*

Time after time, the Bible reminds us how hopeless we were (or are) without Christ. Our situation was worse than we knew, and nearly impossible for us to grasp even now—dead in trespasses and sins (Ephesians 2:1), having no hope (2:12), alienated and hostile in mind (Colossians 1:21), and slaves to sin (John 8:34).

The nature of sin is to overpower and imprison us. Sin confounds and confuses, causing us to love the very thing that is destroying us. We want out of it while wanting more of it.

As someone once said, "Sin will take you further than you want to go, cost you more than you want to pay, and keep you longer than you want to stay." Sin is stronger than we are, and it was (past tense intentional) a very real threat.

The only thing surer than sin's power, however, is sin's defeat. Jesus has overcome it!

He is our emancipator. In Him we are no longer slaves to sin (Romans 6:18–22), but "fellow citizens with the saints and members of the household of God" (Ephesians 2:19).

YOUR LIFE IN ACTION

Praise God today for defeating sin
and freeing you from its enslavement.

Then she said, "I have found favor in your eyes, my lord,
for you have comforted me and spoken kindly to your servant,
though I am not one of your servants" (Ruth 2:13).

Here we drop in on a conversation between two remarkable people who, unlike many in their culture, knew, feared, and worshiped the one true God.

Ruth was a young widow whose loving loyalty compelled her to take care of her grief-stricken mother-in-law. Boaz was a kind and compassionate landowner who was willing to go the extra mile in providing for the needy.

In Ruth we see ourselves, and in Boaz we see Christ. Redemption is the macro lesson of the book of Ruth; there are many micro lessons as well. For example, 2:13 presents a lesson in the power of kind and timely words and the reviving comfort such words can bring to a restless soul.

Ruth and her mother-in-law, Naomi, were barely getting by. They had lived through much suffering (famine) and the pain of multiple deaths in their immediate family. They were well acquainted with grief. The two women returned to Naomi's homeland, hoping to rebuild some semblance of a life.

Though they continued in their sorrow for a while longer, at just the right time God spoke through Boaz, who affirmed Ruth for her virtuous perseverance. These kind words brought comfort to Ruth and reminded her that God would take care of her.

YOUR LIFE IN ACTION

Our words have great power, when they are backed up with truth, sincerity, and a commitment to help. Who needs to hear a word of comfort and hope from you today?

> *"Watch and pray that you may not enter into temptation.*
> *The spirit indeed is willing,*
> *but the flesh is weak" (Matthew 26:41).*

Temptation is common among all Christians. This is not to say that *most* deal with it, but that *all* deal with it.

Every believer is tempted, though not by the same sins. Even so, there is a great difference between being tempted and entering into temptation.

We know that our enemy is aware of our particular weaknesses, and these are the temptations he will be sure to put in our path. James 1:14–15 describes his pattern: "Each person is tempted when he is lured and enticed by his own desire. Then desire when it has conceived gives birth to sin."

The devil knows what the "own desire" is for each person. He crafts temptations around our individual vulnerabilities and lets nature take its course.

Many will pray in the moment of temptation. That is good, and much needed. However, it is better to pray *before* temptation comes. This preparing of the soul makes us more watchful of the devil's schemes, and decreases the threat of temptation getting the upper hand.

YOUR LIFE IN ACTION

Pray, at the beginning of your day and throughout,
that you will not enter into temptation.

Hezekiah received the letter from the hand of the messengers,
and read it; and Hezekiah went up to the house of the LORD,
and spread it before the LORD (Isaiah 37:14).

Hezekiah did literally what we should do figuratively with all our needs, anxieties, and complaints—he spread them out before God in prayer. With his kingdom and his life under threat, Hezekiah ran to the front line of prayer.

What would it mean for us to spread our concerns before the Lord?

It would mean much the same as it meant for Hezekiah. We would be refusing to take matters into our own hands, because we recognize there is no way to have the right perspective on any situation until we first take it to God.

It would also mean we will not attempt to withhold any information from God (as if that were possible), but will place every fear, every need, and every request before Him while also admitting to every failed effort we have made in our own strength. This is praying with absolute honesty—hiding nothing and surrendering everything.

What can be accomplished by praying as Hezekiah did, spreading all things out before the Lord? More than we can imagine.

YOUR LIFE IN ACTION

Are you honest in prayer, fully revealing your soul before the Lord?
If not, what keeps you from approaching God in this way?

The people refused to obey the voice of Samuel. And they said, "No!
But there shall be a king over us, that we also may be like all the nations,
and that our king may judge us and go out before us
and fight our battles" (1 Samuel 8:19–20).

Do you have any envy in your heart, a desire to have what others have and seem to enjoy?

What if God were to "give in" and let you have what you envy? Would you be any more satisfied than you are now?

Would you finally be content? Would you have joy? Would you be any better off (in ways that really matter)?

Envy is an indication of a restless heart, always pursuing something more or something else. Envy also reveals a divided heart, willing to say with the lips that God is good while not really believing that God is enough.

At the least, envy is distracting; at the worst, it is dangerous. This is the lesson the nation of Israel learned when they demanded a king.

Be careful what you envy and what you demand of God. He just might give it to you.

YOUR LIFE IN ACTION

What examples can you think of where a person or group of people received what they demanded and it ended up hurting them?

The people refused to obey the voice of Samuel. And they said, "No!
But there shall be a king over us, that we also may be like all the nations,
and that our king may judge us and go out before us
and fight our battles" (1 Samuel 8:19–20).

What do the Old Testament nation of Israel and the sinking of the *Titanic* have in common? Both are tragic stories of warnings that were ignored.

In one case people perished because warnings were either withheld from the proper people or not taken seriously. In the other case people perished because they got what they asked for.

The human heart is foolish. It is so foolish, in fact, that even when warned of the danger that lies in its path, it often rejects the offer of God's correction and continues on its chosen way.

God warned the people of Israel, speaking through the prophet Samuel, that the king they demanded would bring them servitude and suffering, and still they refused to change course. The heart wants what the heart wants, even if it hurts. Again, the human heart is foolish.

God warns us through His Word, by promptings of the Holy Spirit, in the loving confrontation of godly friends, in blocking our way . . . and still we head toward the iceberg. Our heart cannot be trusted, but God can.

YOUR LIFE IN ACTION
Is God sending you warnings about the choices you are making
or the direction you're heading? Listen to Him.
This is His loving way of correcting and protecting you.

Hear my cry, O God, listen to my prayer;
from the end of the earth I call to you when my heart is faint.
Lead me to the rock that is higher than I,
for you have been my refuge,
a strong tower against the enemy (Psalm 61:1–3).

Life can be overwhelming, which is why we cringe when we hear statements like, "God will never give you more than you can handle." We know by experience this is not true. (And let's be honest, not everything we're trying to handle is from God.)

There is something more that we know, and it is of the greatest importance: God is a rock that is higher, a refuge, a strong tower. In Him we are safe even when the tumult goes on and on.

Paul knew this, and so he survived imprisonments, beatings, shipwrecks, and more (2 Corinthians 11:23–33). Each of the things he listed was beyond his coping capacity.

Believers should be realists. In this world we will have many trials and sorrows. This is a reality, but only a temporary one.

Here is a permanent reality: "Take heart; I [Jesus] have overcome the world" (John 16:33).

YOUR LIFE IN ACTION

Write out the words of Psalm 61:1–3 and Colossians 3:2–3.
What do these verses teach you about the refuge you have in Christ?

David said, "The LORD who delivered me from the paw of the lion and from the paw of the bear will deliver me from the hand of this Philistine." And Saul said to David, "Go, and the LORD be with you!" (1 Samuel 17:37).

David was a man of great confidence. The showdown with Goliath was not his first encounter with a deadly foe—one that by all appearances (and statistics) should have pulverized him.

Where did David's confidence come from? It wasn't past experience, even though he had killed the lion and the bear. (Shepherding is not for the cowardly.) David tells us plainly that it was God, not his own strength or skill, that made him victorious.

So, is the lesson here that we shouldn't trouble ourselves with skill training, but just rely on God to take care of us in the moment?

No. We should invest in our God-given talents, not bury them.

The lesson is that even highly skilled people with winning records (David – 2 / Wild Beasts – 0) should recognize and openly acknowledge that God is the source of their strength. This is their motto; let it be yours: "Some trust in chariots and some in horses, but we trust in the name of the LORD our God" (Psalm 20:7).

YOUR LIFE IN ACTION
Be intentional today about acknowledging God.
Do not attempt to take credit for what He does through you.

There came out from the camp of the Philistines a champion named
Goliath of Gath, whose height was six cubits and a span (1 Samuel 17:4).

By our reasoning, Goliath should have won. He was bigger than David and more experienced. He was outfitted with the best custom-made weaponry. Goliath clearly had the upper hand in the intimidation category, having kept the army of Israel off the field for forty days and counting.

Then, God triggered the faith of a ruddy young shepherd, and the giant died. As it turned out, the battle didn't belong to Goliath, or really even to David. This battle belonged to God. And so does the battle you fight today.

In spiritual terms, more battles are lost through surrender than through defeat. When we believe only what our eyes see and our ears hear, we forget that God is the *almighty* God, and our faith is depleted.

So we run away from trouble, give in to temptation, or settle for the status quo. The battle that could have proven to be a turning point in our lives instead becomes one more resignation.

This is a pattern that, by God's grace and because of His forgiveness, you *can* break. Stop focusing on the size of your struggle, and concentrate instead on the greatness of God. "Be strong in the Lord and in the strength of his might" (Ephesians 6:10).

YOUR LIFE IN ACTION
Read Ephesians 6:10–18, and pray through each phrase.

*David said to Saul, "I cannot go with these, for I have not tested them."
So David put them off. Then he took his staff in his hand and chose five smooth
stones from the brook and put them in his shepherd's pouch. His sling was
in his hand, and he approached the Philistine (1 Samuel 17:39–40).*

David refused Saul's armor because it was unfamiliar to him. He knew what it was to fight with the agility that a sling allowed him; Saul's armor would have slowed him down and made him vulnerable.

It would have been dangerous to go into battle with what another man said should be good enough. To David, hand-me-down weapons were no more useful than borrowed bravery.

We are wise to keep company with those who love God deeply and have great faith in Him. We can learn much from their lives and the wisdom they have gained by walking with the Lord.

Yet the time comes when we will face challenges—and responsibilities—that require personal faith. Robert Murray M'Cheyne once said, "A man is what he is on his knees before God, and nothing more."

We must certainly worship with our brothers and sisters in Christ, and we should be faithful to "stir up one another to love and good works" (Hebrews 10:24) Yet we must also be faithful to strengthen ourselves in the Lord and not depend on the faith of others to make us strong.

YOUR LIFE IN ACTION

Are you taking responsibility to grow stronger in the Lord?
What are you doing to grow?

David said to the Philistine, "You come to me with a sword and with a spear and with a javelin, but I come to you in the name of the LORD of hosts, the God of the armies of Israel, whom you have defied" (1 Samuel 17:45).

David was approximately seventeen years old at the time of his encounter with Goliath. Even at that young age he was already known by many within King Saul's court. (He had also been privately anointed to be successor to the throne.)

Had it not been for his great love for God, David could have been flooded with arrogance and taken every opportunity to promote himself. Fighting a giant would have been a huge lift to his ego and notoriety.

But this is David we're talking about—a man after God's own heart (1 Samuel 13:14). In his mind, none of what would happen that day in the Valley of Elah was about him. He cared only that the reputation of God was under attack.

There was no guarantee David would survive, and he certainly could not count on backup. But he had already made his choice to live and serve for the pleasure of God, knowing that death was always a possibility. He had counted the costs beforehand; his life was not his own.

You may never encounter the danger that David did, or that others do in the name of Christ. Still, every believer should come to terms with the facts that their life is no longer their own, and some giants need to die.

YOUR LIFE IN ACTION

Think about what it means to live for the glory of God's reputation and not for your own. How would this outlook change the way you handle conflict and difficulty?

---

*We do not have a high priest who is unable to sympathize with our weaknesses,
but one who in every respect has been tempted as we are, yet without sin.
Let us then with confidence draw near to the throne of grace, that we may
receive mercy and find grace to help in time of need (Hebrews 4:15–16).*

The dual nature of Jesus Christ—that He was both God and human at the same time—is beyond our ability to fully grasp. Yet we acknowledge this truth each time we petition God in prayer, especially "in time of need."

We are trusting His power to give what we ask because we believe He is divine; we're also acknowledging His empathy for our neediness because He "became flesh and dwelt among us" (John 1:14). Our Savior suffered *for* us, and He also suffered *with* us.

The devil likes to make us think we are bothering God when we pray about troubling issues, as if God views us with disdain on account of our humanness. We are too little to matter, and God is too great to care.

But in truth Christ is well acquainted with our sufferings, and He sympathizes with our weaknesses. He does not begrudge giving mercy and grace.

Jesus didn't observe our condition from a distance; He lived it. He knows. He understands. And because He lived for years on earth as a man—without sinning—we can approach God with confidence. Our sympathetic Savior grants unlimited access to the Father.

YOUR LIFE IN ACTION

When you find yourself in a time of need,
does it reassure you to know that Christ sympathizes with you?
How does this help?

To this end we always pray for you, that our God may make you worthy of his calling and may fulfill every resolve for good and every work of faith by his power, so that the name of our Lord Jesus may be glorified in you, and you in him, according to the grace of our God and the Lord Jesus Christ (2 Thessalonians 1:11–12).

P aul was a man of prayer. He prayed for those who served with him in the gospel ministry, and he prayed for those in the churches where he served.

In his prayers, we can find a pattern for praying for our brothers and sisters in the Lord. Using the words of 2 Thessalonians 1:11–12, pray for the saints in your church today and for those who are proclaiming the gospel throughout the world.

- Pray that God will make them "worthy of his calling," that they will not give up, turn back, or give priority to any lesser cause.

- Pray that God will "fulfill every resolve for good and every work of faith by his power." Pray that they will never rely on themselves or any scheme to accomplish the work only God can do. Pray that their faith in God will become stronger and stronger.

- Pray that Christ will be glorified through them. Pray that God will protect them from any temptation to make a name for themselves or take credit for God's work.

YOUR LIFE IN ACTION

Pray through this passage, using the above prayer points, for those God puts on your heart today. Pray for these people by name.

I urge that supplications, prayers, intercessions, and thanksgivings be made for all people, for kings and all who are in high positions, that we may lead a peaceful and quiet life, godly and dignified in every way. This is good, and it is pleasing in the sight of God our Savior, who desires all people to be saved and to come to the knowledge of the truth (1 Timothy 2:1–4).

The Bible places great emphasis on the role of prayer in the church. For the body of Christ to be healthy, and indeed for any member of the body to be healthy, prayer is non-optional.

We are instructed to pray about many things that pertain to our own lives, but in this passage the prayers are targeted toward others, especially those in authority.

Interestingly, the promise of a peaceful and quiet heart (which is quite a thing to have in our noisy, angry world) is made to those who intercede in this manner.

We might rationalize not praying for certain persons or leaders because we don't like them or agree with them. But we must not see prayer as something we have the right to withhold or as something we restrict to those we deem worthy of our prayer.

Our prayer is to "be made for all people." We dare not draw a line where God hasn't.

YOUR LIFE IN ACTION

Pray today for the leaders in your church, workplace, community, state, and nation.

Samuel said to Saul, "You have done foolishly. You have not kept the command
of the LORD your God, with which he commanded you. For then the LORD
would have established your kingdom over Israel forever. But now your
kingdom shall not continue. The LORD has sought out a man after his own heart,
and the LORD has commanded him to be prince over his people, because you
have not kept what the LORD commanded you" (1 Samuel 13:13–14).

Saul's sin cost him the throne of Israel. More specifically, Saul's sin of impatience cost him the throne.

The command was clear: "Seven days you shall wait, until I [Samuel] come to you and show you what you shall do" (10:8). Because these instructions came through the prophet Samuel, they were from God.

Saul waited not a minute longer and then took matters into his own hands. His impatience revealed a heart that had strayed from God, one that was willing to rationalize and improvise based on appearances. In the heat of the moment, he would rely on what he thought best, not on what God had made clear.

What would you have done? We'd like to think we would have remained faithful, obeying God no matter what circumstances seemed to indicate. But we also have our own history of impatience, don't we?

YOUR LIFE IN ACTION

Can you recall a time when you moved forward in impatience rather than trusting God and obeying Him? What happened as a result?

David said to [Mephibosheth], "Do not fear, for I will show you kindness for the sake of your father Jonathan, and I will restore to you all the land of Saul your father, and you shall eat at my table always" (2 Samuel 9:7).

We are drawn to the story of Mephibosheth for a couple of reasons. The first is because of the love it reveals coming from the heart of one of the greatest men who ever lived.

David showed a surprising depth of grace to Mephibosheth. One would hardly expect a king to associate with a man that society would have likely considered second class at best.

David did more than associate with him, though. David made him a member of his household. Grace upon grace!

The second reason we are drawn to this story is because *we* are Mephibosheth. Through the grace of our King, we have been plucked from obscurity and given a permanent seat at His table.

Just as Mephibosheth came to David's house by way of David's love for Jonathan, so we have come to God's house by way of His love for Jesus. We are in, not because we deserve to be, but because of grace.

YOUR LIFE IN ACTION
Read Ephesians 2:1–10.
Thank God for His grace shown to you.

If one gives an answer before he hears,
it is his folly and shame (Proverbs 18:13).

How many misunderstandings could we have avoided if we had listened a little longer, and listened with the intent to understand rather than retort?

The facts are, we increase our level of understanding through listening, and we raise the likelihood of conflict by talking.

> When words are many, transgression is not lacking, but whoever restrains his lips is prudent (Proverbs 10:19).

> Whoever is slow to anger has great understanding, but he who has a hasty temper exalts folly (Proverbs 14:29).

> Whoever restrains his words has knowledge, and he who has a cool spirit is a man of understanding (Proverbs 17:27).

Of course, talking is necessary for communication to occur, but so is listening. The Bible makes it clear in the verses cited here, and in many others, that the words you speak will be enriched by the understanding you gain through listening.

YOUR LIFE IN ACTION
Purpose to be a good listener today.

When the mourning was over, David sent and brought her to his house,
and she became his wife and bore him a son.
But the thing that David had done displeased the LORD (2 Samuel 11:27).

David's plunge into adultery shows us how the enemy works against us, little by little, setting a trap of temptation. Learn from David's errors in judgment, and pray that you will not enter into temptation.

- David was not in the best place. It had been his custom to accompany his troops into battle, but for some reason David chose to stay home this time. This break in what had proven to be good leadership practice cracked the door for sinful choices. An easy choice led to an evil choice.

- David stared when he should have looked away. The sight of a beautiful woman who was another man's wife, especially when she was unclothed, should have prompted David to look away and walk away. Instead, he let his eyes linger.

- David inquired about her. This means that what he had allowed himself to stare at, David was making room for in his affections. He was already far down the path of sin; he was making plans.

Do you find yourself inching toward giving in to temptation today?

YOUR LIFE IN ACTION

If your answer to the above question is *yes*, stop. Admit to God where you are, and ask Him to deliver you from this temptation. Perhaps call a godly friend to pray with you.

RESPECT AND FEAR

*David said to Abishai, "Do not destroy him, for who can put out his hand
against the LORD's anointed and be guiltless?" And David said, "As the
LORD lives, the LORD will strike him, or his day will come to die, or he will go
down into battle and perish. The LORD forbid that I should put out my hand
against the LORD's anointed" (1 Samuel 26:9–11).*

This was the second time David spared Saul's life. Most of David's
advisors urged him to kill Saul, saying it would be a justified act
of revenge.

Yet David refused to act, on the basis of two convictions:

- He had a respect for the king that was based in the fear of
  the Lord. Saul was more than a man, and more than a king.
  He was "the LORD's anointed." God alone had the right to
  end Saul's life.

- He recognized that vengeance belongs only to God. Even
  though his advisors made a rational argument for taking
  Saul's life, David knew that vengeance is a divine matter,
  not a human one.

This part of David's story gives us a larger-than-life example for those
occasions when we may rationalize taking actions that are severe and
irreversible. What matters most is not how we feel about it, or even
how many agree with us. What matters is: Is it right?

YOUR LIFE IN ACTION

Are you facing any severe and irreversible decisions?
Have you prayed and asked God, with an open heart, what His will is?

Nathan said to David, "You are the man!" . . .
David said to Nathan, "I have sinned against the LORD."
And Nathan said to David,
"The LORD also has put away your sin;
you shall not die" (2 Samuel 12:7, 13).

In one of the most widely known confrontations of Scripture, Nathan the prophet let David know that his sin of adultery was not hidden. David had been "found out."

Being found out is dreadful. Having one's darkest secrets exposed feels like a fatal end to the life we've worked so hard to protect and conceal. Now, that life is over.

Though it cost him dearly, David would tell us it was a good thing when that life was over for him.

Within the instant of Nathan's rebuke (or, as we experience it, the conviction of the Holy Spirit), grace made an opening, and David took it. He had been in deep sin for a long time, but he chose not to stay in it one second longer.

YOUR LIFE IN ACTION

If God is dealing with you about a sin you have been hiding, respond to His conviction. Repent, and trust Him to cleanse you by His grace.

If possible, so far as it depends on you,
live peaceably with all (Romans 12:18).

It's just not possible to be at peace with everyone; we all know this. However, let's not use that as an excuse for coddling our anger. "So far as it depends on you" reaches further than we realize.

- Can you learn to refrain from lying, gossiping, slandering, and other such sins of the tongue?

- Can you trust God for the humility to go to those you have wronged, admit what you've done, and seek their forgiveness?

- Can you, being steeped in God's mercy yourself, bring that mercy into your hurts and offenses, and forgive "as God in Christ forgave you" (Ephesians 4:32)?

Speaking with kindness, living in humility, walking in the mercy of God—these are all enablers of peace that we can choose. Or not.

YOUR LIFE IN ACTION

Pray through today's list, asking God to search your heart as you do. Are you doing all that you rightly can to live peaceably with others?

"This Moses, whom they rejected, saying, 'Who made you a ruler and a judge?'—this man God sent as both ruler and redeemer by the hand of the angel who appeared to him in the bush" (Acts 7:35).

Perhaps there is some truth in the saying "People can't change," if by that we mean that people can't change themselves.

But we know for certain that people can *be changed*. Likely, you are an example of this yourself. So is Moses.

Remember the burning bush experience Moses had in the wilderness, which proved to be an encounter with God? As a result, Moses became a changed man (perhaps *changing* is a better word).

God had given him a purpose, but only after taking him through a long season of obscurity. Don't forget that the burning bush experience came after forty years of wilderness living.

Burning bush experiences appeal to us. They are dramatic, and frankly, hard to overlook.

The long anonymity of wilderness living is another matter, though. We'd rather speed through this, or avoid it if possible. But both are filled with the presence of God.

YOUR LIFE IN ACTION

What lessons has God taught you in your wilderness years
that prepared your heart to serve Him?

Finally, my brothers, rejoice in the Lord (Philippians 3:1).

In his letter, Paul instructed the Philippians about many important things they needed to keep in mind and heart as they lived out their faith. Yet this one thing was primary: *Rejoice in the Lord.*

From this short phrase we should remember:

- Joy should be a significant part of the believer's life, both in intensity and in frequency. We should rejoice exuberantly, and we should rejoice often. We should set our hearts to rejoice, making it a proactive approach to life rather than an afterthought to occurrences.

- Our joy should be centered on Christ. We should, as some say, "make much of Jesus." Our hearts should be filled with Him; and when they are not, we should take responsibility to refill them. Think on Christ Jesus, on His love, on His sacrifice, on His beauty and His perfection. Tell others of His goodness to you, of His eternal love and how He made you His.

Are you rejoicing in the Lord now?

YOUR LIFE IN ACTION
Tell the Lord how He gives you joy.
Perhaps make a list and read it to Him.

> *I give thanks to my God always for you because of the grace of God*
> *that was given you in Christ Jesus, that in every way you were enriched*
> *in him in all speech and all knowledge—even as the testimony about*
> *Christ was confirmed among you (1 Corinthians 1:4–6).*

Praying for your church is not a matter of praying for *them*, it is a matter of praying for *us*. You cannot separate yourself from its condition.

The Corinthian church was racked with problems and was well populated with sin-loving people. Through his letter, Paul rebuked and corrected them about issues as severe as incest and prostitution and their collective willingness to overlook such unholy practices.

Your church may not be facing those types of issues, though perhaps it is, but you can be sure that sin is present and destroying lives. And so you must pray, even as Paul prayed.

Before, during, and after writing this letter, Paul carried these people in his heart. We should follow his example.

Here, as seen in the opening verses of this letter, is the place to begin praying: Thank God that He has given you and all the believers in your church His grace in salvation. Pray now that the testimony of Christ will be confirmed through the life of your fellow believers and by others coming to faith in your community. Ask God to make your church healthy enough to reproduce.

YOUR LIFE IN ACTION

Do you regularly pray for your church, or do you prefer to complain or gossip about it? If you're not in the habit of praying for your church, start today. And remember, it's *us*, not *them*.

What then is Apollos? What is Paul? Servants through whom you believed,
as the Lord assigned to each. I planted, Apollos watered, but God gave the growth.
So neither he who plants nor he who waters is anything, but only God who gives
the growth. He who plants and he who waters are one, and each will receive
his wages according to his labor. For we are God's fellow workers.
You are God's field, God's building (1 Corinthians 3:5–9).

Christian celebrity is a contradiction in terms. The work of the kingdom belongs to God, and so do the workers.

There is no place for boasting, and seeking the praise of others only lifts us up for a longer fall. Haughtiness in God's servants clouds His glory. People are distracted and sometimes misled by the very ones they look to for instruction in godliness.

There is an equally obstructive hazard coming from the opposite direction. When we see our role as too unimportant to matter, our indifference to the work of God impedes it. Many believers embrace a sort of pseudo-humility where *I'm not worthy* really means *I'm not willing*. They need to be reminded that "not to think more highly of himself than he ought to think" is preceded by "present your bodies as a living sacrifice" (Romans 12:1, 3).

What matters in all of this is that God has work to be done, and His plan includes our involvement. We should report for duty, but when the praise begins, let us be a praise-giver, not a praise-taker.

YOUR LIFE IN ACTION
Do you find yourself either taking credit for God's work or backing away from it due to a false sense of humility? If so, how do you need to respond to God today?

I urge you, then, be imitators of me (1 Corinthians 4:16).

If all we'd ever heard or read of Paul's teachings were these four words—be imitators of me—we would surely have the wrong idea about him and, more importantly, about walking with Christ.

But we know that Paul wasn't claiming to be perfect, nor was he planning to hide his imperfections for the sake of appearance. Paul was talking about the importance of building one's whole life on the foundation of Jesus Christ.

From the moment Jesus Himself called out to Paul on the road to Damascus, *everything* in his life came under the ownership of God. Paul therefore urged the same lifestyle on all those he "fathered" in the faith.

It is good to follow the example of the godly, remembering that they are human and will fall short of God's will at times.

Hopefully there are people in your life whose overall direction is worthy of being imitated. Hopefully you are worthy of being imitated as well.

YOUR LIFE IN ACTION

Whose life do you find worthy of imitating?
What would a person's life look like
if they were imitating you?

> *Truly, truly, I say to you, whoever hears my word and believes*
> *him who sent me has eternal life. He does not come into judgment,*
> *but has passed from death to life (John 5:24).*

We often hear the terms "passed on" or "passed away" used in reference to someone who has died. Perhaps some find this a softer way to say a difficult thing, that a loved one has departed from this life. In a literal and truer sense, the moment one believes in Christ, he or she passes on from this life—not from life to death, but from dying to living.

Wuest's *The New Testament: An Expanded Translation* helps preserve the meaning and flow of the Greek language in which the New Testament was originally written; it renders the latter part of the verse above: "and into judgment he does not come, but has been permanently transferred out from the sphere of death into the life."

If you are a Christian, the truth Jesus taught in John 5:24 should thrill your soul. You have already "passed on."

There is nothing beyond death for you but life, and that life includes no judgment of guilt, no clearing of debts, no qualifying of your worthiness. In Christ you have been "permanently transferred out from the sphere of death."

YOUR LIFE IN ACTION

Read John 5:19–29.

> *He said, "Do not be afraid, for those who are with us are more than those who are with them." Then Elisha prayed and said, "O LORD, please open his eyes that he may see." So the LORD opened the eyes of the young man, and he saw, and behold, the mountain was full of horses and chariots of fire all around Elisha (2 Kings 6:16–17).*

Elisha the prophet was a man of mighty faith. Through him God repeatedly warned the nation of Israel of invading armies and spared them of attack. This happened so many times that one particular king decided that the only way to conquer Israel was to take Elisha captive.

One morning, Elisha's servant awoke and found that they were surrounded by an enemy army. He was terrified, but Elisha was not.

Why? Because Elisha could see something more, a portion of reality that could only be taken in by faith: "Those who are with us are more than those who are with [the enemy]."

Do you feel overwhelmed today, perhaps even afraid? Remember this: "He who is in you is greater than he who is in the world" (1 John 4:4). In order for you to be defeated, the enemy doesn't have to be stronger than you, he has to be stronger than God.

YOUR LIFE IN ACTION

Take each specific issue that makes you afraid or worried, and acknowledge in prayer that God is greater.

Where jealousy and selfish ambition exist,
there will be disorder and every vile practice (James 3:16).

Of all the things that can block intimacy with God—and one another—none is more formidable than our own selfish heart. Instinctively, we think of ourselves first. And that gets in the way of love.

In his classic tale *A Christmas Carol*, author Charles Dickens painted a sad picture of selfishness through the character Ebenezer Scrooge. Although his heart was eventually won over through the kindness of his nephew and a frightening look at where his selfish ways were taking him, Scrooge wasted years blocking the love that was daily at arm's length. Imagine the loneliness of a heart so consumed with self!

Perhaps you don't have to imagine at all.

At the very least, selfishness brings confusion and unrest. Furthermore, selfishness can wear away our peacefulness, causing us to pull away from people and they from us.

Eventually we find that by putting ourselves first, we have lost far more than we've gained. Rather than deepening intimacy and knowing more and more love, we find ourselves very much on our own—even in a crowd.

YOUR LIFE IN ACTION

How would you define selfishness?
What contributes to selfishness, and what takes it away?

The beginning of strife is like letting out water,
so quit before the quarrel breaks out (Proverbs 17:14).

There are two simple rules that can protect us from a great deal of heartache:

1. Never start an argument.
2. Never join an argument.

The Bible tells us that "the anger of man does not produce the righteousness of God" (James 1:20). This means that the closer we get to anger, the further we are from godliness.

For this reason we must beware that arguing only releases the anger, turning a trickle—that could have been fixed—into a flood that cannot be stopped.

Sadly, we live in an angry culture, where many seem to be looking for a place—or a person—on which to release their indignation. This torrent of anger is sweeping our nation, our communities, and even our churches and families far out into the depths of overwhelming darkness.

May the strength of our peace, found only in Christ, become their salvation.

YOUR LIFE IN ACTION

Do you contribute to the anger or to the peace in your home, church, and community? What personal changes do you need to make in order to become a man or woman of true peace?

*Do nothing from selfish ambition or conceit, but in humility
count others more significant than yourselves. Let each of you look not only to
his own interests, but also to the interests of others (Philippians 2:3–4).*

Followers of Christ are servants—people who care for others by giving them a place of greater importance than our own and displaying that care in both action and attitude. Nowhere is this disposition of greater importance than within the family unit where each member, regardless of age, rank, or role, should elevate the giving of love over the receiving of it.

But because our family knows us best, we may be reluctant servants at home. It is often easier for us to serve a stranger than it is our family members because we are ashamed of not consistently doing so before, we're afraid we won't be able to keep it up, or we're waiting for someone else to do the right thing first.

Encourage yourself into action by thinking of the transformation serving one another can bring to your family dynamic. Rivalry, pride, jealousy, and such divisive behaviors are overpowered by true humility. Serving, when done for love's sake rather than for personal gain, keeps a Christlike example ever visible to your children, your spouse, and your guests.

Do not wait to feel like serving; your flesh will resist and make all sorts of arguments against it. Yet there is one reason for serving, and it tops every excuse: "If I then, your Lord and Teacher, have washed your feet, you also ought to wash one another's feet. For I have given you an example, that you also should do just as I have done to you" (John 13:14–15).

YOUR LIFE IN ACTION

What can you do to serve the members of your family this week?

THE GRASSHOPPER COMPLEX

The men who had gone up with [Caleb] said, "We are not able to go up against the people, for they are stronger than we are." So they brought to the people of Israel a bad report of the land that they had spied out, saying, "The land, through which we have gone to spy it out, is a land that devours its inhabitants, and all the people that we saw in it are of great height. And . . . we seemed to ourselves like grasshoppers, and so we seemed to them" (Numbers 13:31–33).

The spies' report was factual but not truthful. There really were inhabitants in the land that stood taller than they; that was a fact.

Even so, the spies couldn't really have known what these largish people thought of them; that was all in their faith-deprived heads. Of far greater consequence was their forgetting that God had promised to give them the land—this is where their report was short on truth.

How easy it is to forget God when all we see are problems "of great height." All that God has promised, and most of what He has done, flees from our memories and our hearts. We begin to think that all we have to fight with is our own strength, and perhaps the help of a few like-minded friends.

That will never be enough, we reason. And we are right.

But even if we are grasshoppers and our problems are giants, God is God. And He is enough.

YOUR LIFE IN ACTION

Spend some time meditating on the greatness and power of God.
After that, bring your needs and concerns to Him in prayer.

> *Paul and Barnabas remained in Antioch, teaching and preaching the word of the Lord, with many others also (Acts 15:35).*

Some names never make it into the history books. Some who do great things will remain anonymous, or will be grouped among the unnamed "many others"—which is the case in Acts 15—for all time. But when it comes to the work of God's kingdom, it is never about who is named and who is not or who gets credit and who does not, because . . .

- What is being done is the issue, not who is doing it. This work is eternal; the souls of men and women are at stake. Worrying over notoriety is a distraction and can lead to jealousy and conflict. Those who seek credit serve themselves, not God.

- Who is being served is of supreme importance. How much more effective believers would be in living out and proclaiming the gospel if each one were to embrace the attitude of John the Baptist—"I'm not even worthy to be his slave and untie the straps of his sandal" (John 1:27 NLT).

- God will reward what man overlooks. To be forgotten by man is nothing; you can be sure that God sees, knows, and will not forget.

YOUR LIFE IN ACTION

Can you be content with anonymity, with not getting credit or mention for the work you do in the name of Christ? In light of eternity, what value is there in earthly notoriety?

. . . testifying both to Jews and to Greeks of repentance toward God and of faith in our Lord Jesus Christ (Acts 20:21).

That which unites us is greater than the sum of all that divides us. This is a spiritual truth, not a commentary on the culture.

In his farewell to the elders of the church at Ephesus, Paul relived the *what* and *why* of his life since Christ had saved him. Since that time, his whole purpose centered on one message, and it was the same message he delivered (from God) to Jew and Gentile alike: Believe on the Lord Jesus Christ.

Regardless of our heritage, socio-economic status, or family and personal history, we too should live with the gospel as our center.

Never should we forget our plight before we believed, never should we forget the Savior who gave His life for our sins, and never should we think ourselves more deserving of grace than anyone else.

Remember the gospel. Remember Jesus. Pray for, love, and reach out to those who need Him—just as you do.

YOUR LIFE IN ACTION

In your own words, describe what it means to
live a gospel-centered life.

*I did not shrink from declaring to you
the whole counsel of God (Acts 20:27).*

Pastor Bill Elliff once led his church in an unusual exercise—he had each person write their own obituary. "What is it that you will leave?" he asked. "Think of what you want God to have accomplished through your life."

Paul may not have been writing his obituary, but he was thinking intently about what he would leave. And what he wanted was to leave men and women who had believed in Christ. To that end he had been, and would continue to be, fearless. He would concentrate on doing God's will with boldness.

This doesn't mean he was unkind, but he certainly wasn't wishy-washy, either. Paul was motivated by eternal matters; his life reached beyond the outer boundaries of what most count as success.

What will you leave? Is it what God wants to accomplish through you?

YOUR LIFE IN ACTION

Try writing a draft of your obituary, asking yourself,
"What do I want to be true of my life at the end?"

You then, my child, be strengthened by the grace that is in Christ Jesus, and what you have heard from me in the presence of many witnesses entrust to faithful men who will be able to teach others also (2 Timothy 2:1–2).

Pastor Crawford Loritts noted, "Church work tends to burn people out, but the work of the church—making disciples—brings life, hope, and purpose." His observation should bring us to ask, *Are we busy doing the right things?*

Just before ascending back to heaven, Jesus gave what is known as the Great Commission: "Go therefore and make disciples of all nations" (Matthew 28:19).

This is the work of the church and the work of *every* Christian. This divine purpose should be the nucleus of all our work and prayer.

Nothing is of greater consequence than making disciples, yet there is a compelling simplicity to it—tell others what you have learned about Christ. This will keep you learning, telling, growing, and obeying.

YOUR LIFE IN ACTION

What have you learned about Christ that you should be passing on to others?

As we share abundantly in Christ's sufferings, so through Christ we share abundantly in comfort too (2 Corinthians 1:5).

Are you more prone to speak of your sufferings or of the comfort Christ has given?

If you have suffered, you surely know that never once did Christ take His eyes off you or withhold His love. He is a God who draws nearer and nearer to those in pain, as He has for you.

When you have occasion to share the part of your story that includes your suffering, or even when you are recalling these times in the privacy of your own memories, never leave out the part about how Christ comforted you.

In fact, emphasize that part. Dwell on it. Bring it to the front.

"This light momentary affliction is preparing for [you] an eternal weight of glory beyond all comparison" (2 Corinthians 4:17).

To remember only our suffering is to forget the goodness of God.

YOUR LIFE IN ACTION

How would you describe the comfort you have received from God to someone who is in need of His comfort today?

*Anyone whom you forgive, I also forgive. Indeed, what I have forgiven,
if I have forgiven anything, has been for your sake in the presence of Christ,
so that we would not be outwitted by Satan; for we are not ignorant
of his designs (2 Corinthians 2:10–11).*

If forgiveness brings the power to restore, unforgiveness carries an equal power of destruction.

Where sin has been confronted, confessed, and repented of (as seems to have been the case in point here), forgiveness is next on the agenda. But when it is not offered, the fallout can be even greater and more widespread than what occurred with the sin that set the whole mess in motion.

As repentance frees the sinner, and the giving of mercy frees the offended, so unforgiveness can stop restoration in its tracks.

When we forgive, we yield all rights to vengeance. Furthermore, we slam the door on Satan's plans to use the offense for any further destruction and division.

Forgiveness is our holy stance in an unholy war. Do not be ignorant of his designs; when Satan can't keep an offender from repenting, he's just as happy—and victorious—to keep the offended from forgiving.

YOUR LIFE IN ACTION

Are you up to date on repenting?
Are you up to date on forgiving?

---

*You yourselves are our letter of recommendation, written on our hearts,
to be known and read by all (2 Corinthians 3:2).*

A letter of recommendation tells the truth and sets a level of expectation about the person to whom it refers. If a person falls short of what the letter implies, the integrity of both the recommended and the recommender are called into question.

In this case, however, the "letters" were people—men and women Paul had discipled. Their lives bore the imprint of his, as his life bore the imprint of Christ. He wasn't out to make them Paul-like, but Christlike.

It would be rare if you were not an influence on someone's life. More than likely your imprint is on the soul of your spouse, your children (and grandchildren), a neighbor, your friends, and perhaps others.

How Christlike is that imprint? This is the question that should most concern you in terms of discipleship, because these lives, these "letters," are being read by others in turn. Those you influence are themselves being an influence.

Do not conceal your devotion to Christ or keep the ways He is transforming you to yourself. Be an intentional letter writer.

YOUR LIFE IN ACTION

In what ways do you most influence those closest to you?
What would they be most likely to say are the
major lessons they learn from you?

We want you to know, brothers, about the grace of God that has been given among the churches of Macedonia, for in a severe test of affliction, their abundance of joy and their extreme poverty have overflowed in a wealth of generosity on their part (2 Corinthians 8:1–2).

God can overcome the contrary nature of things to bring about an unexpected result. How else could "a severe test of affliction" and "extreme poverty" coexist with an "abundance of joy"?

Furthermore, how could a group of people living within this mixed bag of circumstances look outward and put the needs of others ahead of their own?

God does amazing things within the human heart. It is pure joy to watch His love and life being expressed through those who might otherwise be expected to stay on the sidelines or offer excuses for not getting involved.

But God has called no spectators. His grace that transforms us on the inside calls us to join His work, even when we're in the midst of challenges.

The Macedonians did, and so should we.

YOUR LIFE IN ACTION

Regardless of your limitations or current challenges,
ask God how He wants you to serve Him today.
Don't delay your obedience to a time of greater convenience.

Yet for the sake of David your father I will not do it in your days, but I will tear it out of the hand of your son (1 Kings 11:12).

Solomon did not make it easy for his children to walk in the ways of God. Sadly, this man that we often associate with wisdom sinned so grievously that God removed the larger portion of the kingdom from his heir.

The kingdom that had grown so strong under David (Generation 1) and continued to increase under Solomon (Generation 2), diminished under Rehoboam (Generation 3). But the decline began under Solomon, who chose lust for women over love for God.

It is easy to be disgusted by Solomon's choices. He was wise, wealthy, influential, and blessed (in the truest sense of the word). But he took on many foreign wives and became idolatrous.

How could "God's man" fall so far? we ask ourselves. And look at the price the next generation paid.

Perhaps the question we should really be asking ourselves is, *Will my lifestyle set an example that makes it easier for my children to know, trust, and follow the Lord, or will they stumble because of me?*

YOUR LIFE IN ACTION

If someone were to ask your children what your most dominant spiritual trait is, what do you think their answer would be?

> *Let us pursue what makes for peace and for mutual upbuilding.*
> *Do not, for the sake of food, destroy the work of God.*
> *Everything is indeed clean, but it is wrong for anyone to*
> *make another stumble by what he eats (Romans 14:19–20).*

Consider these two verses phrase by phrase, beginning with, "Let us pursue what makes for peace and for mutual upbuilding." These words summarize what Paul had to say about spiritual freedoms and stumbling blocks.

God's message through him was this: Even though you have legitimate freedom to do certain things as a believer, you will sometimes need to set your freedom aside. Why? Because in God's family:

- Pursuing peace is of greater value than promoting personal rights. This comes down to the very essence of what it means to walk in love (v. 15). Our lives are devoted to those things that exalt God and encourage our brothers and sisters in the Lord.

- Mutual upbuilding means putting "we" above "me." We bear the responsibility, and the honor, of being members of God's household. Even if we attempt to act as individuals, others are still affected by what we do. Therefore, we should make our choices based on what will please the Father and strengthen the household.

YOUR LIFE IN ACTION

What are you doing to pursue peace and build up the household of God? On the other hand, what are you doing that hinders these from happening as they should?

> *Let us pursue what makes for peace and for mutual upbuilding.*
> *Do not, for the sake of food, destroy the work of God.*
> *Everything is indeed clean, but it is wrong for anyone to*
> *make another stumble by what he eats (Romans 14:19–20).*

As you consider these two verses phrase by phrase, think now of this: "Do not, for the sake of food, destroy the work of God."

Does it shock you to think that your actions have the potential to *destroy* the work of God? It should, and that's precisely why Paul wrote in such heavy terms—so that you and I would hear the alarm and, if needed, immediately correct our course.

Replace *food* with any of your favorites, and then listen for the alarm once again. Is there any substance, activity, or possession that you insist on having no matter what?

Keep in mind that the argument of "but this is not a sinful thing" has no bearing here. Whereas yesterday we saw that it is sometimes necessary to set aside personal freedoms (of things that are permissible) out of love for the members of God's household, today we see that it may likewise be so for the sake of God's work.

Sometimes certain personal pleasures must take a hiatus (or in some cases, be given up altogether) so that gospel work is unhindered where you are.

YOUR LIFE IN ACTION

Ask God if there are any lifestyle adjustments
He wants you to make for the sake of His work.

> *Let us pursue what makes for peace and for mutual upbuilding.*
> *Do not, for the sake of food, destroy the work of God.*
> *Everything is indeed clean, but it is wrong for anyone to*
> *make another stumble by what he eats (Romans 14:19–20).*

Today consider the last sentence of these verses: "Everything is indeed clean, but it is wrong for anyone to make another stumble by what he eats." (Keep in mind that "everything" refers specifically to food, not to anything and everything we may desire.)

God, writing through Paul, does not mince words. It is *wrong* to intentionally carry on in doing something when we know our activity will be a stumbling block to another's faith.

Out of love for that person and for God, we should willingly restrict ourselves for their sake. To do otherwise—at that time and in that place—is selfish.

Lest you think this is legalistic, remember that such an approach "makes for peace." You are one of the beneficiaries; this peace will prove to be more of a delight than whatever "food" you may have to give up.

YOUR LIFE IN ACTION

Pray today for the lost in your family and community.
Pray that God will open their hearts to believe in Christ.

It is good not to eat meat or drink wine or do anything that causes your brother
to stumble. The faith that you have, keep between yourself and God.
Blessed is the one who has no reason to pass judgment on himself
for what he approves. But whoever has doubts is condemned if he eats,
because the eating is not from faith. For whatever does not
proceed from faith is sin (Romans 14:21–23).

When it comes to identifying sin, certain things should be on everyone's list, but everyone's list will not be the same.

Because God speaks to us through our conscience (of course, this is not the only way that He does), some will feel guilt where others will not. Rather than listen to our own conscience with reluctance, the Bible instructs us to pay attention to what it says.

In *The Hole in Our Holiness*, Kevin DeYoung observes, "The conscience is no substitute for the Bible and must never be in opposition to it. But a good conscience is a gift from God. As we pursue holiness we must always be mindful of God's voice speaking to us through a tender conscience informed by the Word of God."

In reference to Romans 14:23 he adds, "If you don't believe what you are doing is acceptable, then it's not acceptable for you to do it. You must not ignore your conscience."

Conscience-driven beliefs are often referred to as personal convictions. They are to be kept "between yourself and God," and not imposed on others.

YOUR LIFE IN ACTION

What are some of your conscience-driven beliefs?

*Since we are his children, we are his heirs. In fact, together with Christ
we are heirs of God's glory. But if we are to share his glory,
we must also share his suffering (Romans 8:17 NLT).*

You've no doubt heard that as a believer in Christ, you will suffer. This is a statement of realism.

We should also think of suffering in stronger terms—not only *will* we suffer, we *must* suffer. Why?

Today's Bible passage makes it clear that our future glory can in no way be separated from Christ. We will know this glory because we know Him. What is His will become—and in fact is becoming—ours.

The ministry of Paul also made the connection between present suffering and future glory when the Scriptures say he went about "strengthening the souls of the disciples, encouraging them to continue in the faith, and saying that through many tribulations we must enter the kingdom of God" (Acts 14:22).

Christ's sufferings were for our salvation, and they came about because He dwelt in our sin-loving, sin-cursed world. He was not of this world, but He took its iniquity on Himself.

And now, as a believer in Him, you are as out of place as He was. Your suffering is proof that you are made for another time and another place—a glory that will be revealed. *Maranatha!*

YOUR LIFE IN ACTION
Pray for your brothers and sisters who are suffering,
that God will turn their thoughts toward Him and His glory.

*The Spirit helps us in our weakness. For we do not know what to pray for
as we ought, but the Spirit himself intercedes for us with groanings
too deep for words. And he who searches hearts knows what is the mind
of the Spirit, because the Spirit intercedes for the saints according to
the will of God (Romans 8:26–27).*

The promise of John 14:14, "If you ask me anything in my name,
I will do it," is best understood alongside Romans 8:26–27. We
aren't promised to get everything we want; we are promised what we
ask "in [Christ's] name."

There's a significant difference between our telling God what we want
and God directing us to ask Him for what He wants us to want.

Even the strongest of prayer warriors is weak in the sense that he or
she must rely on the Holy Spirit to intercede. This means that the
Holy Spirit transmits our prayers (as it were) from what we ask to
what we should ask; from what we demand to what God wants us to
receive. He scrubs the selfishness, shortsightedness, and foolishness
from our prayers and addresses the Father on our behalf.

Prayer is a sacred interaction with the Godhead—we pray to the Father
in the name of the Son as the Holy Spirit intercedes. What a privilege
is ours to be invited to join in!

YOUR LIFE IN ACTION

Read Romans 8.

We have this treasure in jars of clay,
to show that the surpassing power
belongs to God and not to us (2 Corinthians 4:7).

In moments of honesty, some of us would have to admit that we want to be popular, even famous. We'd like for people to know who we are and to think we are something special.

Setting aside the way these aspirations feed our pride and give rise to an unhealthy—and ungodly—spirit of competition, the real crime herein is attempted robbery.

When we make much of ourselves, we make little of Jesus. The jar tries to seize the glory of the treasure, but the treasure will not allow it: "My glory I will not give to another" (Isaiah 48:11).

Be content with who God has made you and where He has placed you. There is great honor in being His display case.

YOUR LIFE IN ACTION

What are some of the behaviors or attitudes you sometimes adopt that hide rather than display God's glory?

If in Christ we have hope in this life only,
we are of all people most to be pitied (1 Corinthians 15:19).

Christians are faced with a dilemma that reveals itself nearly every day. Though we are citizens of a perfect land, we live—for now—in a degenerate place.

On the outside we see evil being applauded while righteousness is scorned, leaving us weary. On the inside, we long to be what we can't yet achieve, leaving us unfulfilled.

This is as it will continue to be for a time, but thankfully not forever. "For now we see in a mirror dimly . . ." (1 Corinthians 13:12).

To be sure, our union with Christ makes a great amount of difference in how we approach this life, deepening our character and strengthening our integrity.

Even so, our great hope in Him is in future glory. God has not made us better people, He has made us new people . . . and citizens of a new land.

YOUR LIFE IN ACTION
In what ways does the hope of heaven motivate you in this life?

*Let no one deceive himself. If anyone among you thinks that he is wise
in this age, let him become a fool that he may become wise.
For the wisdom of this world is folly with God (1 Corinthians 3:18–19).*

Let's become fools! There's a charge that's sure not to rally many
troops. Yet it's a call we should answer, for the road to wisdom
runs through foolishness.

In Romans 16:19 Paul addressed the same issue from the opposite
end: "I want you to be wise as to what is good and innocent as to what
is evil." Christians are to be wise toward that which is pleasing to God
and "foolish" or innocent in that which is ungodly.

In our pursuit of true wisdom, we must maintain a foolishness—a
personal disregard—for all that is evil.

Even when our drive to fit in pulls us to "be in the know" about the
latest trends, we should rather abandon every effort to be "wise in this
age." Such things have no kingdom value; they only drag us backward
and downward.

YOUR LIFE IN ACTION

Do you ever find yourself acting foolishly for the sake of
fitting in? Ask God to deliver you from this trap and to
help you avoid it in the future.

To have lawsuits at all with one another is already a defeat for you.
Why not rather suffer wrong? Why not rather be defrauded? (1 Corinthians 6:7).

Paul shamed the Corinthian believers because of their public dis-play of retaliation. More than that, he went on to suggest that they should actually overlook some offenses that might bring them into court.

This was not because justice didn't matter, but because gospel-cen-tered living mattered far more. If believers could not settle their differences "within the family," the next step was to . . . let it go.

Our minds have a hard time entertaining this mindset, let alone accepting it. We're saturated with the notion that rights and free-doms outreach nearly every other worldview. And, to our shame, we've brought this thinking into the church.

The gospel is proclaimed in words and is best seen against the back-drop of Christians living Christianly.

On a personal level, that means that sometimes when you are wronged, you need to let it go. There's far more at stake than your rights.

YOUR LIFE IN ACTION

Pray that you and your church would live gospel-centered lives
for the sake of those in your community who need Christ.

We are ambassadors for Christ, God making his appeal through us.
We implore you on behalf of Christ, be reconciled to God. For our sake
he made him to be sin who knew no sin, so that in him
we might become the righteousness of God (2 Corinthians 5:20–21).

Jesus "preached peace to you who were far off and peace to those who were near" (Ephesians 2:17). As His ambassador, Paul preached the same, and you and I should continue in the same way.

Though we may not "preach" in the traditional sense, each and every believer has been given a commission to make the gospel known. This is not a light calling. God Himself is making His appeal to the world through us.

We are carriers of the eternal message of God's love and God's wrath. Nothing matters more. *Nothing.*

Still, knowing we should and doing as we should are separated for many by fear and indifference. For this reason Paul appealed to us to think of Christ—who He was and who He became on our behalf. The sinless one became sin, and not by just a little.

This is all the motivation we need: "Looking to Jesus, the founder and perfecter of our faith, who for the joy that was set before him endured the cross, despising the shame, and is seated at the right hand of the throne of God" (Hebrews 12:2).

YOUR LIFE IN ACTION

Read 2 Corinthians 5.

God, who comforts the downcast, comforted us by the coming of Titus,
and not only by his coming but also by the comfort with which he was comforted
by you, as he told us of your longing, your mourning, your zeal for me,
so that I rejoiced still more (2 Corinthians 7:6–7).

Have you ever been encouraged simply by a visit from a friend? Did you stop to think that God sent them to you?

Paul had been in pretty rough shape before Titus came along. In his own words, Paul had "had no rest . . . afflicted at every turn—fighting without and fear within" (v. 5).

Have you been there? Most of us have. And then God sends along a Titus who, simply by being present, restores our soul, refreshes our thoughts, and resets our motivation.

In this case, the one who came also represented many who could not make the journey. Titus carried messages from other friends of Paul who wanted him to know of their concern and love for him.

But more than that—and this is what you and I need to remember most of all—God Himself sent Titus. He (Titus) was a living reminder to Paul that God was fully aware of the needs of His despairing servant. God always knows.

YOUR LIFE IN ACTION
Do you need to be a Titus for someone today?

> *I bless the LORD who gives me counsel; in the night also*
> *my heart instructs me. I have set the LORD always before me;*
> *because he is at my right hand, I shall not be shaken (Psalm 16:7–8).*

God is everywhere all the time. This truth gives us great comfort at times and conviction at other times, depending on what we're doing, thinking, or saying.

Given the fact of God's omnipresence, is it strange for the Psalmist to write that he had "set the LORD" before him, as if God were movable (and removable)?

Of course we know what David is saying—that he is actively telling his heart and mind what to think. God is near, that is a fact; but it is a fact we need to remind ourselves of often. In this way, our heart "instructs" us of truth that our minds forget.

D. Martyn Lloyd-Jones asked, "Have you realized that most of your unhappiness in life is due to the fact that you are listening to yourself instead of talking to yourself?" He is echoing what the Psalmist wrote—we need to actively engage our minds in telling ourselves the truth.

This is why the intake of God's Word is so vital, and should not end when church is dismissed or when we close our Bibles.

YOUR LIFE IN ACTION

Take 5–10 minutes right now to talk to yourself,
telling yourself truths about God.

The servant said, "Alas, my master! What shall we do?"
He said, "Do not be afraid, for those who are with us are more than
those who are with them." Then Elisha prayed and said, "O LORD,
please open his eyes that he may see" (2 Kings 6:15–17).

Whatever wars against our soul can convince us that it is too much for God to handle. Our feelings of unrest and of being overwhelmed will endure for as long as we forget how great God is.

Temptations, worries, and even the onslaught of all the evil in all the world cannot stand up to God. But how quickly and how often we forget!

We must remind ourselves of God's greatness, and we must remind our brothers and sisters of the same. We should pray like Elisha did for his servant: "Lord, open our eyes that we may see."

Up until that prayer, the servant saw only what his *this-world* eyes could take in. Afterward, God opened his eyes to take in the greater reality. The threat of the advancing army was only a matter of limited (forgetful) perception. God was greater. God is greater.

Someone you know needs this reminder today. Pray for them.

YOUR LIFE IN ACTION

Do you know someone who feels overwhelmed and afraid?
Pray for them, that they will "see" that God is greater.

> *The heart knows its own bitterness,*
> *and no stranger shares its joy (Proverbs 14:10).*

There are emotions too deep to be shared with anyone but God—grief so piercing you cannot express it, or joy so overpowering you cannot let it out.

These occasions remind us of just how personal God is, and how attentive. Even though the days (or weeks, or months) are lonely, they crowd us to God and enlighten us to His nature in ways we aren't able to see on the "normal" days.

Here are a couple of ways to frame our thoughts when we are alone with God:

- We should be on guard against hurt feelings. Our friends cannot fathom what we cannot express. They may pray for us, celebrate with us, or cry for us, but we are "alone with God" in this part of our journey. Let it be so.

- We can be glad that God is both aware and attentive. God goes beyond knowing what our hearts feel; He takes care of us in ways that are ultimately personal. He understands us as no one else can.

YOUR LIFE IN ACTION

Are you in a time of being "alone with God"?
How does your current outlook align with
the two points shared in today's reading?

Above all, keep loving one another earnestly, since love covers a multitude of sins. Show hospitality to one another without grumbling (1 Peter 4:8–9).

Hospitality is an expression of love and, when done without expectation of reciprocity, shows the nature of Christ.

We can show hospitality in myriad ways—inviting guests to share a meal, accepting invitations that are extended to us, engaging in friendly and meaningful conversation, acknowledging special days and events in the lives of others, expressing our appreciation and affirmation, giving a cup of cold water . . .

To show hospitality is to show honor. It is to take on the form of a servant.

It is to say that Jesus loves you . . . through me.

YOUR LIFE IN ACTION

To whom will you show hospitality this week?
How will you show it? (Don't just think about it; do it.)

Encourage one another and build one another up,
just as you are doing (1 Thessalonians 5:11).

Praying alone is good. It needs to be part of your regular spiritual activity.

And you should add to that the practice of praying with others, if you are not doing so already. (If you are married, and your spouse is agreeable, you will find great unity in the habit of praying together daily.)

God has made a great promise to those who pray: "The peace of God, which surpasses all understanding, will guard your hearts and your minds in Christ Jesus" (Philippians 4:7). Imagine living with that kind of peace and security, and being able to share it with others as you agree together in prayer, acknowledging that you want God at the center of all things.

Help to build up the body of Christ by praying for your brothers and sisters, and by praying with them.

YOUR LIFE IN ACTION

Seek out someone to pray with during the next week.

*Therefore a man shall leave his father and mother
and hold fast to his wife, and the two shall become one flesh.
This mystery is profound, and I am saying
that it refers to Christ and the church (Ephesians 5:31–32).*

Do you ever think about God's design for marriage? In the midst of family life, it is easy to think mostly about ourselves and whether we're happy or not. We easily forget that God instituted marriage and has plans that are far beyond our experience.

The Bible is clear: The relationship between husband and wife is to demonstrate the depth of God's love for His people.

Marriage is a high calling, and in many ways, a holy one. That's not meant to be an intimidating statement, but it does bring a fuller perspective.

Marriage is not just about two people getting along, as important as that is. It's about two people interacting in ways that demonstrate the presence of God in the world.

Interestingly, when God's designs for marriage matter most to us, we are happier and more fulfilled. "Delight yourself in the LORD, and he will give you the desires of your heart" (Psalm 37:4).

YOUR LIFE IN ACTION

Pray for the marriages in your family and church
(including yours, if you're married), that each husband and wife
would concern themselves with God's design for marriage.

*Do nothing from selfish ambition or conceit, but in humility
count others more significant than yourselves.
Let each of you look not only to his own interests,
but also to the interests of others (Philippians 2:3–4).*

The longer and deeper a relationship goes, particularly in marriage and family, the more clearly the differences between individuals can be seen. Sooner or later, the inclination toward selfishness is revealed.

While this opens the door to conflict, it also leaves plenty of room for personal growth and for love for one another to deepen. Here are some ways to pray for your closest relationships:

- Thank God for your differences, knowing that through them you can grow in wisdom, understanding, and love. Because you are different, you are given a broader view of the world and greater understanding of how others think and feel.

- Ask God to make you intentional within your friendships. Guard yourself from taking the other person(s) for granted. Show concern and care for the things that matter to them. Bring their burdens to the Father in prayer.

- Admit to God that you tend to be selfish, and ask Him to deliver you from self-centered ways. Ask Him to make you alert to ways you can serve others, perhaps even without being asked.

YOUR LIFE IN ACTION
Think of your closest friends, perhaps your spouse
and other family members, and pray according to
the three thoughts from today's reading.

Let no corrupting talk come out of your mouths,
but only such as is good for building up, as fits the occasion,
that it may give grace to those who hear (Ephesians 4:29).

You're well acquainted with the power of words. Communication—including what you say, how you say it, and even when you say it—is a vital part of life. Whatever power it has to build up love, hope, trust, respect, and admiration, it also has the power to tear down.

People who care about the quality of their communication understand the role it plays in keeping unity and love alive within the body of Christ. They know that words are tools, not weapons.

Learning to communicate well is a lifelong pursuit, but it's well worth the effort. Pray that God would help you break any bad habits of communication and replace them with the goals of understanding, loving, and encouraging others.

Perhaps the best place to start is by determining what the purpose of your communication will be. If you only wish to "speak your mind" or persuade others of your opinion, chances are you will be harsh in tone and closed to what others have to say.

If, however, you choose to communicate in a way that honors God, you will use words that "build up" and "give grace." People will listen to that, and will probably want to hear more.

YOUR LIFE IN ACTION

Do you have someone in your life who communicates in
the spirit of Ephesians 4:29? Thank God for them today,
and tell them how much you appreciate their wisdom.

But I will stay in Ephesus until Pentecost, for a wide door for effective work has opened to me, and there are many adversaries (1 Corinthians 16:8–9).

Paul was in a situation that would have driven many of us away. Let's admit: the "wide open door" and "effective work" portion of what he encountered would have been canceled out by the "many adversaries" part.

The ministry is being well received? Great! I'm in.

The work is going well, and real life change is taking place? Sign me up!

A lot of people are against it? Let me think about it and get back to you.

Here's the difference, the anchor of Paul's commitment: a wide door "has opened."

In other words, Paul recognized that God was the One who had set the work in motion and had deployed him to serve there. How could Paul say no to God's yes, no matter how great the opposition?

YOUR LIFE IN ACTION
Has God opened any doors of ministry to you
that you have refused to enter?

Since we are surrounded by so great a cloud of witnesses, let us also lay aside every weight, and sin which clings so closely, and let us run with endurance the race that is set before us, looking to Jesus, the founder and perfecter of our faith, who for the joy that was set before him endured the cross, despising the shame, and is seated at the right hand of the throne of God (Hebrews 12:1–2).

Let's settle this in our minds: the Christian life is more like a marathon than an evening walk around the neighborhood. We are not on a stroll to see where it takes us, but on a mission that leads to the very presence of God.

From start to finish, everything that happens has spiritual significance. Therefore, we should: (1) run in faith, (2) run with endurance, and (3) run to finish.

Your faith is developed both by looking back and by looking ahead.

You can recall those times when God allowed you to be tested beyond your own capacity, and how He used those times to build your confidence in Him. You can also look ahead and acknowledge that in the things you can perceive—and certainly in those you cannot—God will *have to* be your strength and shield.

And you can look to the great cloud of witnesses—those whom God has raised up as examples for the rest of us. Learn from them. Know that the God who delivered them will also deliver you.

YOUR LIFE IN ACTION

What have you learned about faith in God by looking back at your own history? What have you learned about faith in God by looking into the life of someone in the Bible?

Since we are surrounded by so great a cloud of witnesses, let us also lay aside every weight, and sin which clings so closely, and let us run with endurance the race that is set before us, looking to Jesus, the founder and perfecter of our faith, who for the joy that was set before him endured the cross, despising the shame, and is seated at the right hand of the throne of God (Hebrews 12:1–2).

In the marathon that is your Christian life, you will need endurance. At times you will be called on to face situations or to help others face situations that exceed your limits and theirs.

Here is the Bible's answer for what you should do when this happens:

"Consider him who endured from sinners such hostility against himself, so that you may not grow weary or fainthearted" (Hebrews 12:3).

Great strength can be found in the suffering Savior who died for our sins. He who suffered because of us now suffers with us.

He whose suffering brought the end of sin's control will someday bring the end of sin's existence. He who left His own grave will one day bring every saint out of theirs.

Through Him we live, and in Him we endure.

YOUR LIFE IN ACTION
Read Hebrews 12.

Since we are surrounded by so great a cloud of witnesses, let us also lay aside every weight, and sin which clings so closely, and let us run with endurance the race that is set before us, looking to Jesus, the founder and perfecter of our faith, who for the joy that was set before him endured the cross, despising the shame, and is seated at the right hand of the throne of God (Hebrews 12:1–2).

The Christian life is one of faith, endurance, and completion—all made possible by Christ in us.

Do not rush past this description of our Savior: the "founder and perfecter of our faith."

Jesus pioneered our faith, blazing a trail of unbroken surrender to the Father in whom He wholeheartedly trusted, thereby proving that God alone is all powerful.

Christ also perfected—that is, completed—our faith. There is nothing we must overcome that He has not already defeated, nothing we must acquire that He has not already put on layaway. Our faith flows from His and follows His lead.

Have faith in the Father . . . as Jesus did. This faith will not fail, because God cannot and will not fail. There is an end to setbacks and suffering. Christ has seen to that.

YOUR LIFE IN ACTION

Describe what it means for Christ to be the founder and perfecter of your faith.

Man does not know his time. Like fish that are taken in an evil net,
and like birds that are caught in a snare, so the children of man are snared
at an evil time, when it suddenly falls upon them (Ecclesiastes 9:12).

We are not in control of our lives. This is not an excuse for a care-free existence, but a nod to the realities of earthly life.

No matter how much we plan, prepare, and set up guards against misfortune, there is an unpredictability which we should always factor in. Healthy people get sick, wealthy people go bankrupt, intelligent people make foolish choices.

Do we then give up? Is there no point in living circumspectly? Why not "eat and drink, for tomorrow we die" (1 Corinthians 15:32)?

Throughout his writings in Ecclesiastes, Solomon observed that even wisdom—for which he was famous—is subject to life's uncertainties. This is a fact we should keep in mind as we make plans and set our hopes.

A similar point is made in James 4: "You do not know what tomorrow will bring. What is your life? For you are a mist that appears for a little time and then vanishes. Instead you ought to say, 'If the Lord wills, we will live and do this or that'" (vs. 14–15).

God sees and knows what we cannot. He alone is our certainty, not our hopes, plans, or dreams.

YOUR LIFE IN ACTION

Pray that God will help you hold your plans loosely,
that you will truly trust His will in all things.

*As the Father has loved me, so have I loved you. Abide in my love.
If you keep my commandments, you will abide in my love, just as I have kept
my Father's commandments and abide in his love (John 15:9–10).*

The secret to intimacy with Christ is really no secret at all. It is obedience—not *intended* obedience, but *actual* obedience. Not what you plan to do later, but what you are doing now.

Many times we find ourselves lacking in motivation to obey. We settle instead for a compromised level of doing what we want while banking on God's grace to give us a pass.

If and when we think this way, we are forgetting how rich and full an "abiding" relationship with Christ can be—the kind that only comes about through obedience.

Imagine being so certain and rested in Christ's love for you that it matches what Christ enjoys with the Father: "As the Father has loved me, so have I loved you."

To abide, then, is to obey, and to obey is to abide.

YOUR LIFE IN ACTION

Read John 15.

So now finish doing it as well, so that your readiness in desiring it may be matched by your completing it out of what you have (2 Corinthians 8:11).

Intent is of little value. We should start *and finish* what God puts in our hearts to do.

The Christians in Corinth heard about the needy saints in Jerusalem, and they were so moved that they began taking up a collection. But they had not finished; the money they collected was still in Corinth. What good was it doing there when the need was 800 miles away in Jerusalem? Neither their intentions nor their half-way executed plan helped anyone.

Have you ever been moved to take action? Perhaps you heard of a need and planned to help meet it. Perhaps you became acutely aware of changes you needed to make in your own life and promised God that you would. Perhaps you committed to a friend to help them in some way but never followed through.

Have you taken a Corinthian approach—heard, planned, started, didn't finish?

If you know that your intent is God's will . . . go all the way with it. If you stopped, start again. Make no excuse about it being too late or too little. If God has put it on your heart, obey Him.

YOUR LIFE IN ACTION

Ask God if there is anything He moved you to do that you have not completed. Commit to Him to start again, and see it through to the end.

Hezekiah prayed before the LORD and said: "O LORD, the God of Israel, enthroned above the cherubim, you are the God, you alone, of all the kingdoms of the earth; you have made heaven and earth" (2 Kings 19:15).

We can learn a great deal from the prayers recorded in Scripture. In this case, Hezekiah and the people of Judah were under threat. As a wise leader and God-fearing man, Hezekiah knew that his first and best act of strategy was to pray.

In the way that Hezekiah approached God, in the words that he spoke to God and about God, we see great reverence and absolute trust. Though he spoke to God, it seems that Hezekiah spoke to himself at the same time, recalling to heart and mind that God was great, majestic, and immanent.

By the time he got to the point of request, of verbalizing his cares and burdens to God, Hezekiah had "strengthened himself in the LORD his God" (1 Samuel 30:6).

When teaching His disciples to pray, Jesus said, "Pray then like this: 'Our Father in heaven, hallowed be your name'" (Matthew 6:9). These are not filler words to signify that a prayer has begun, but words that acknowledge there is none greater than the One to whom we pray.

YOUR LIFE IN ACTION

Look up other prayers in the Bible,
and see what they teach about the nature of God.

*Jesus said, "Father, forgive them,
for they know not what they do" (Luke 23:34).*

Being Christlike sounds like something we want . . . until it costs us. Even the slightest irritations, let alone large offenses, can switch our reactions from graceful to vengeful within a moment.

While our human nature is warring against the Spirit within us, we should remind ourselves that Christlikeness demands patience, forgiveness, and showing grace to the undeserving (as if we could make such a judgment).

Showing grace is an honor, especially when it's being given in the form of forgiveness. Those who give grace cannot help but remember the great price Christ gave for their redemption, and those who receive grace encounter Christ in action.

When you are wronged, "consider him who endured from sinners such hostility against himself, so that you may not grow weary or fainthearted" (Hebrews 12:3). And remember that He prayed "Father, forgive them" *from* the cross.

He forgave long before His suffering was complete. Can you do that? Yes. Will you?

YOUR LIFE IN ACTION
Are you holding on to any offenses?
Will you ask God for the strength and love to forgive?

When he saw the crowds, he had compassion for them,
because they were harassed and helpless,
like sheep without a shepherd (Matthew 9:36).

Even in crowds, some are lonely, and all are needy. Jesus knew this, and He approached them with compassion.

He knew that the heart of every man and woman was sinking beneath regrets, fears, longings, and temptation. They were tormented from the inside and the outside.

While these heart conditions might elicit our sympathy, the way they present themselves usually does not. People whose hearts are harassed often come across as angry, bitter, manipulative, and obnoxious. Many are troublemakers; some are criminals.

We like to celebrate the occasional story of redemption when one such person believes in Christ, but we'd rather someone else did the dirty work of loving them when they're still in the mess.

Christ was drawn to the helpless. And we should be as well. We once were as they are.

YOUR LIFE IN ACTION

Begin praying courageously about how God might want you to minister to the marginalized of our society.

Do not be anxious about anything, but in everything
by prayer and supplication with thanksgiving
let your requests be made known to God (Philippians 4:6).

Why is it so important that when we bring requests before God in prayer, we do so with thanksgiving? Surely there are many reasons we should—here are three:

- Because God listens to our prayer. Never lose the wonder of this simple truth: God hears us when we pray. Prayer is not an empty ritual; it brings us into dialogue with the Almighty.

- Because He is able to provide what we ask. God alone can give us all things. No one is richer, stronger, or more generous.

- Because of what we've received from Him in the past. If anything, our history with God assures us of what He can do based on what He has done.

When you pray, remember to give thanks.

YOUR LIFE IN ACTION

Think of other reasons for giving thanks to God when you pray.

Thus shall you say to my servant David, "Thus says the LORD of hosts, I took you from the pasture, from following the sheep, to be prince over my people Israel, and I have been with you wherever you have gone and have cut off all your enemies from before you" (1 Chronicles 17:7–8).

David was not a self-made man. None of us are, and the more we remind ourselves of this, the greater our success will be. God will see to it.

Jesus said a similar thing: "You did not choose me, but I chose you and appointed you that you should go and bear fruit and that your fruit should abide, so that whatever you ask the Father in my name, he may give it to you" (John 15:16).

While it is true that we responded in faith, we must remember that it was God who initiated the call and who gave us the faith to believe. This was not our doing.

Your life has a divine purpose, a high call. God began a work in you that includes both your salvation and your service. Be faithful to the One who chose you.

YOUR LIFE IN ACTION

Reflect on the ways God has worked in and through your life.
Thank Him for choosing you, and humbly submit to His plans for you.

From the day we heard, we have not ceased to pray for you, asking that you may be filled with the knowledge of his will in all spiritual wisdom and understanding, so as to walk in a manner worthy of the Lord, fully pleasing to him, bearing fruit in every good work and increasing in the knowledge of God (Colossians 1:9–10).

Praying the words of Scripture is one of the best ways to pray for your brothers and sisters in the Lord. Today's passage offers some clear guidance:

- Pray that they will be filled with the knowledge of God's will. This will keep their thoughts on God as they seek to know His will, and it will give them confidence in Him when they are discouraged or tempted.

- Pray that they will have spiritual wisdom and understanding. Again, this is a prayer that your brothers and sisters will keep seeking God wholeheartedly so they will be able to discern the best ways to accomplish God's will. It is a prayer that they will not be deceived into using worldly (unspiritual) wisdom and try to do God's work in ungodly ways.

Paul prayed this on behalf of those who were already active in doing God's work and pursuing His will (see verses 4–5). We often focus our prayers on those who are backslidden, which is right and good to do. But we must not neglect to pray for those who are walking with God and bearing fruit.

YOUR LIFE IN ACTION

Think of three to five people you know who are walking with God, and pray these things for them today.

From the day we heard, we have not ceased to pray for you, asking that you may be filled with the knowledge of his will in all spiritual wisdom and understanding, so as to walk in a manner worthy of the Lord, fully pleasing to him, bearing fruit in every good work and increasing in the knowledge of God (Colossians 1:9–10).

Continue to pray today for your brothers and sisters in the Lord who are actively seeking and serving Him. Use the words of Scripture to guide your prayer:

- Pray that they will walk in a manner worthy of the Lord. It is easy for humans to think of ourselves more highly than we ought, and to limit our obedience to only those things that make us look good and bring affirmation. Pray that God will keep us all mindful of the fact that we are here to represent Christ, not ourselves.

- Pray that they will bear fruit in every good work. John 15:8 reads, "By this my Father is glorified, that you bear much fruit and so prove to be my disciples." We should pray that our work results in nothing short of people coming to know the Lord and growing in Him.

Your brothers and sisters need your prayers, and you need theirs. Be faithful to God and to each other.

YOUR LIFE IN ACTION

Find one or two people to share the four prayer points from Colossians 1 (in yesterday's and today's readings) and pray together for each other.

*May you be strengthened with all power, according to his glorious might,
for all endurance and patience with joy (Colossians 1:11).*

The principle of cause and effect is often at play in our spiritual formation. The thing we need (the effect) comes about through the God-directed collaboration of circumstances, events, and people (the cause). Sometimes the effect is not clear to us; we don't understand what God is doing or why He is doing it.

In Colossians 1:11, God's man, the apostle Paul, prayed for God's people. Paul knew they were in need of endurance and patience, so he prayed they would be strengthened with God's power.

He recognized the spiritual significance to what others might have passed off as random circumstances. What some might have brushed off as the "stuff that happens" in life, Paul saw as God's activity. He knew God was building endurance, patience, and even joy into the believers' lives, and he participated in that work through prayer.

God is not random; He is purposeful, intent on completing the work He began in each one of His children. Let us then accept His divine cause-and-effect, even when we can't see the whole picture. Let's also pray for each other, that His work will be complete and that our joy will be full.

YOUR LIFE IN ACTION
Read Colossians 1.

---

*Saul died for his breach of faith. He broke faith with the L*ORD
*in that he did not keep the command of the L*ORD,
and also consulted a medium, seeking guidance (1 Chronicles 10:13).

All must die, but not shamefully. Sadly, Saul's was a disgraceful death.

On one level, his death occurred by the thrust of a sword. On a level of deeper reality, his death occurred because of his breach of faith.

Saul's demise did not begin on the day of his death. Little by little he had walked away from the Lord, making hasty decisions and then haughty ones. He shifted from awe-filled wonder that God would choose him, to believing that he actually deserved to occupy the throne.

The breach of faith began as a crack, but it grew wider with each act of self-importance.

We can learn a lot from the way Saul lived. And the way he died.

YOUR LIFE IN ACTION
Pray that God will make you sensitive to
any ways you might be straying from Him.

Put off your old self, which belongs to your former manner of life and is corrupt through deceitful desires, and . . . be renewed in the spirit of your minds, and . . . put on the new self, created after the likeness of God in true righteousness and holiness (Ephesians 4:22–24).

The transformation Christ brings about in our lives is amazing. Think about what you were before you knew Him—it was worse than you knew—and the way He has changed you since.

Transformed is the right word for it. You aren't a better version of the old you; you are a new you, "created after the likeness of God in true righteousness and holiness."

Times of discouragement sometimes come into the lives of Christians, and we may even occasionally drift toward spiritual indifference. Yet even in our listlessness, we can be certain that God has not ceased *His* work within us.

Give thanks today that God will not abandon you for even a moment.

˙YOUR LIFE IN ACTION

Meditate on the words of Psalm 68:19, and pray them back to God:
Blessed be the Lord, who daily bears us up; God is our salvation. Selah

*Put off your old self, which belongs to your former manner of life
and is corrupt through deceitful desires, and . . . be renewed in the spirit
of your minds, and . . . put on the new self, created after the likeness of
God in true righteousness and holiness (Ephesians 4:22–24).*

While we rest in the completed work of Christ that has brought about our salvation, and His sanctifying work that never ceases even when we falter. We must also report for duty.

Our relationship with Christ is not passive. We have work to do.

"We are his workmanship," Ephesians 2:10 tells us, "created in Christ Jesus for good works." If we are not doing the works of God, we are not being true to our new nature. Furthermore, we are missing out on the soul strengthening that comes through spiritual works.

It is not that God started something in us that we must complete, but that God initiated something in us that we are privileged to join Him in continuing.

Do not dread the journey of spiritual growth that lies ahead, though there will surely be difficult days. Rather, look to the One who began it, and who promises never to leave. Abide in Him.

YOUR LIFE IN ACTION
Read Ephesians 4:17–32.

> *Let no corrupting talk come out of your mouths,*
> *but only such as is good for building up, as fits the occasion,*
> *that it may give grace to those who hear (Ephesians 4:29).*

How differently would yesterday's conversations, texts, and emails have gone had you observed the boundaries of Ephesians 4:29? In other words . . .

- Did you speak in corrupting ways? Were people left with evil, unwholesome, angry, or vengeful thoughts because of things you said? Did your communication pull them away from pursuing godliness?

- Did your words build up the hearers? Did you leave them encouraged, uplifted, hopeful?

- Did you speak in a timely way? Were you aware of what needed to be said and what should be left unsaid?

- Did your words deliver grace? Did you leave your listeners with thoughts of God's goodness?

Once spoken, words cannot be recalled. They find their target and do their worst, or their best. Take care of your hearers by showing caution with your words.

YOUR LIFE IN ACTION
Encourage someone today by speaking words of grace to them.

In [Christ] the whole fullness of deity dwells bodily, and you have been filled in him, who is the head of all rule and authority (Colossians 2:9–10).

Do not be deceived into thinking that you must add to the work of Christ, or that you *can* add to it. Christ is complete; He is perfect, and He brings "fullness" to everything He does.

In obeying Him you are not adding; you are achieving. You are advancing into territory He has already won.

Kevin DeYoung wrote, "Once you understand the doctrine of union with Christ, you see that God doesn't ask us to attain to what we're not. He only calls us to accomplish what already is. The pursuit of holiness is . . . the fight to live out the life that has already been made alive in Christ" (from *The Hole in Our Holiness*).

Growing in Christ is both the birthright and the destiny of every believer.

Second Peter 1:3 assures us that Christ's "divine power has granted to us all things that pertain to life and godliness." This means that Jesus provides what He demands, and that while our obedience is *for* Him, it is only possible *through* Him.

YOUR LIFE IN ACTION

In what ways have you experienced God's power to accomplish His will?

If then you have been raised with Christ, seek the things that are above, where Christ is, seated at the right hand of God. Set your minds on things that are above, not on things that are on earth (Colossians 3:1–2).

Those who think low thoughts lead lowly lives. Because values and emotions are linked—"Where your treasure is, there your heart will be also" (Matthew 6:21)—we emphasize in our affections and actions what our thoughts have led us to love.

Even those who believe in Christ can often fall into a pattern of thinking and doing that pushes the temporal over the eternal, the earthly above the heavenly—thoughts below rather than thoughts above.

May God deliver us from such. May we embrace the habit of seeking and setting our minds "on things above" so that we will know and do the will of God and experience the joy of the Lord.

Unless we take on the responsibility to adjust our way of thinking, our thoughts will fall short of our identity, and our lives will be barren. We will be like withering branches, attached to a flourishing vine but rejecting the life it freely gives.

YOUR LIFE IN ACTION

What are you doing to set your mind on things that are above?

No longer do I call you servants, for the servant does not know
what his master is doing; but I have called you friends, for all that I have heard
from my Father I have made known to you (John 15:15).

Jesus Christ is our friend. Amazing, is it not, that we who were once His enemies have been brought into such closeness?

We killed Him. He loves us.

The great indication of this friendship is that He has brought us "into the loop." Jesus tells His disciples what the Father has told Him.

Of course, this does not mean that we know every jot and tittle about our individual futures—what joys and sorrows are in our path. But God has brought us in on His eternal plan and purpose. Why? Because He's chosen us to play a role.

The best of friends share not only a mutual trust but also a mutual ambition. They want the same things and will work together to accomplish them. Do that . . . with Jesus.

YOUR LIFE IN ACTION

Describe some of the differences between
being Christ's servant and being His friend.

You did not choose me, but I chose you and appointed you that you should go and bear fruit and that your fruit should abide, so that whatever you ask the Father in my name, he may give it to you (John 15:16).

Jesus sought you, found you, and made you His. Think on these things. Now you are His friend (see verse 15), and He has given you purpose for life.

Some people struggle with feelings of futility, thinking they are of no value to anyone or for anything. But a true believer has no grounds for such feelings. He or she has been *chosen* and *appointed*.

These are contiguous acts that make up our calling (1 Corinthians 1:9), setting us on a path of sanctification by God and service to Him. There is no expiration date on our calling; it will not end, it will only be made complete.

You are in the family business, as it were. No matter your vocation or location, you are a disciple maker. That is your calling; it is why you were chosen and appointed. Be doing this, and Christ will evict any feelings of futility that may have bothered you in the past.

YOUR LIFE IN ACTION
Read Romans 8:31–39.

When words are many,
transgression is not lacking (Proverbs 10:19).

What do quiet people know that others seem not to know? Perhaps they have nothing to prove. They are not driven to be accepted, so they don't throw out words and opinions in hopes of gaining the approval of others.

Perhaps they do not want to call attention to themselves. They don't need to steer conversations back in their direction, because they are not searching for affirmation. (This is not the same as being "reserved." Quiet, contented people are not necessarily slow to share their emotions or to open their heart. They will do these things readily if it will help.)

Perhaps they are enjoying an intimate, inner conversation with God and do not want to interrupt it unless and until He prompts them to speak.

Perhaps they understand that "when words are many, transgression is not lacking" (Proverbs 10:19). That being the case, one can be talked into—or talk themselves into—discontentment and foolishness. Many words are the breeding ground of sin.

YOUR LIFE IN ACTION

Strive to limit your words today to
only those that are necessary, helpful, and loving.

A NEW WAY OF SEEING OTHERS

From now on, therefore, we regard no one according to the flesh.
Even though we once regarded Christ according to the flesh,
we regard him thus no longer (2 Corinthians 5:16).

Some people will annoy you, even within the family of God. Sometimes this happens because the two of you have fallen out—have moved from disagreement to dislike.

Of course, you know what you should do about that, but what if there has been no such rift? What if your differences are just because you are . . . different?

Here's some help: Don't see that person as someone you may or may not like, someone you could "take or leave." Instead, see them as someone God fully loves.

As you contemplate the fact that God loves them so much, be very grateful that His love extends to a person who needs His love so much. If His love did not run that far, it wouldn't have reached you either.

The mutual receiving of God's love is more than just a factor in our Christian friendships—it is the foundation for them.

YOUR LIFE IN ACTION

Give thanks today for the height, depth,
and breadth of God's love for the whole world.

Besides that, they learn to be idlers, going about from house to house,
and not only idlers, but also gossips and busybodies,
saying what they should not (1 Timothy 5:13).

Idle people are often in motion. Their minds are filled with thoughts, their mouths speak many words, and their bodies move from place to place without resting. They are busy people—busy doing nothing.

Idle thoughts are wandering thoughts. They lead a person to be self-centered, nursing wounds and reliving hurts over and over. Idle thinkers hold their opinions as superior to anyone else's. They are proud and overly sensitive.

Idle deeds are actions without purpose. Our social media-driven culture is taking this to a sickening level. A person can spend hours "communicating" their gripes, dislikes, and every sort of grievance imaginable. But to what end? Who is helped? What is solved?

Idle words have no grace attached to them. They do not exalt God or help the hearer in any way.

We've been blessed with time, opportunity, and yes, even technology. Why be idle? Why serve ourselves? Why stay busy doing nothing when there is so much good that needs to be done (and said)?

YOUR LIFE IN ACTION

Describe the difference between resting—which is a good
and necessary thing—and being idle.

Each person is tempted when he is lured and enticed by his own desire.
Then desire when it has conceived gives birth to sin,
and sin when it is fully grown brings forth death (James 1:14–15).

When you want something so badly that you can hardly think of anything else—when you're rearranging your life to be able to pursue it—stop and ask: *Am I wanting this because God has put the desire for it in my heart?*

What will change if I get it? What will change if I don't get it? Am I willing to sin in order to have it?

Am I violating my faith or my conscience by seeking it?

C. S. Lewis wrote, "A thing may be morally neutral and yet the desire for that thing may be dangerous."

Desire is a power that can cause us to do unholy things, even if what we want isn't unholy in and of itself. This is why, when we are sensing a strong pull of desire, we should increase our praying and open our heart to some wise and godly influencers.

Desire is not a road that should be walked alone. Let God and the godly in on your "wants," and be open to their guidance

YOUR LIFE IN ACTION

Who are the godly influencers in your life that will
challenge you and help you make wise decisions?

A man of God came to him and said, "O king, do not let the army of Israel go with you, for the LORD is not with Israel, with all these Ephraimites. But go, act, be strong for the battle. Why should you suppose that God will cast you down before the enemy? For God has power to help or to cast down" (2 Chronicles 25:7–8).

Under threat by the Edomite army, Amaziah, king of Judah, was about to make a foolish decision. He planned to hire mercenary soldiers from Israel to fight alongside his own troops.

God sent a prophet, whose name we never learn, to urge Amaziah to cancel this unholy alliance, because:

- The plan was made in fear rather than faith.

- The plan would open the door to an ungodly influence.

Both errors in judgment show that Amaziah had forgotten that "God has the power to help or to cast down." In his panic he pushed God to the side and rationalized a scheme that might (nothing definite about it) bring some relief. He was willing to risk long-term spiritual decline for a quick victory on the battlefield.

Thankfully, he listened to God's warning and turned back. May we ever remember the encounter of Amaziah and the nameless prophet.

YOUR LIFE IN ACTION

Describe some of the ways we may make unholy alliances
in our lives today—things we do for relief or happiness
that do not center on God.

We ought always to give thanks to God for you, brothers, as is right, because your faith is growing abundantly, and the love of every one of you for one another is increasing. Therefore we ourselves boast about you in the churches of God for your steadfastness and faith in all your persecutions and in the afflictions that you are enduring (2 Thessalonians 1:3–4).

Spiritual growth is sometimes difficult to measure. While this isn't something we should try to quantify (there's no formula to ensure its advancement and therefore no metric to calculate its progress), there are discernible ways to know we are growing stronger in Christ. There will be evidence.

While telling the believers in Thessalonica that he prayed for them, and sometimes even boasted about them, Paul pointed to three clear indications that displayed forward spiritual momentum:

- Their faith continued to grow. Because our faith is not in ourselves but in God, a believer's experiences make him more and more aware of how desperate he would be without God.

- Their love for one another was increasing. Paul had been concerned about this at one time (1 Thessalonians 3:12), but not any longer. Genuine love reveals authentic faith.

- They were steadfast in the midst of affliction. Rather than raging at God for the hardship He allows, believers seek Him all the more during such times, knowing that only He can give the grace of endurance.

YOUR LIFE IN ACTION

Prayerfully consider your own life in light of these three evidences of spiritual growth.

*To this end we always pray for you, that our God may make you
worthy of his calling and may fulfill every resolve for good
and every work of faith by his power, so that the name of our Lord Jesus
may be glorified in you, and you in him, according to the grace of our God
and the Lord Jesus Christ (2 Thessalonians 1:11–12).*

Paul prayed for his disciples. He carried them in his heart even when he was separated from them. This shows how much he cared for them—people were not projects—and how greatly he relied on prayer as a means of discipleship.

What did he pray for his disciples, and what can we learn from how he prayed?

- Pray that your disciples—those you directly influence in their spiritual growth—will be made worthy of their calling. This means they will live up to the salvation Christ gave them. It does not mean they have to earn or preserve it, but that they will strive to live according to all its joy and purpose.

- Pray that your disciples will undertake and fulfill everything God puts in their hearts to do. In doing so they live with greater purpose than any they could discover on their own.

If your disciples do these things, the name of the Lord Jesus Christ will be glorified in them, and they will find great fulfillment in His glory.

YOUR LIFE IN ACTION

Think of those for whom you have any degree of spiritual responsibility,
and pray these two things for each one specifically
and for yourself today.

Do not regard him as an enemy,
but warn him as a brother (2 Thessalonians 3:15).

Being on the right side of a disagreement does not give us the privilege of snobbery. Quite the opposite, we are to be more loving than ever. Love demands a severe compassion.

In the circumstances Paul addressed here, some people rejected his teaching and were leading lives of intentional disobedience. Paul instructed the others to withhold social interaction from these rebels, hoping the isolation would shame them into a change of heart.

Even so, he urged those "on the right side" to treat to them as brothers, not enemies—not to bully them, but to warn them; not to fight *against* them, but to fight *for* them.

Our modern culture is opening many doors to conflict and increasing divisiveness among true believers. These are days that call us up to godly behavior and the need for biblical responses. Severe compassion may be required.

Let's be sure to do it right, treating real brothers and sisters not as enemies to reject but as family to restore.

YOUR LIFE IN ACTION

How are you responding to those in the church (seemingly true believers) who are leading lives of intentional disobedience? Does your response align with Scripture?

---

*The Lord will rescue me from every evil deed and bring me safely
into his heavenly kingdom. To him be the glory
forever and ever. Amen (2 Timothy 4:18).*

Will life ever get better? Definitely. Soon? Maybe not. (Perhaps
you hoped for a brighter response, but a true answer is better
than false hope.)

Paul was a realist. Shipwrecks, snake bites, slander, and other suffering
will bring a person to that.

He knew better than to expect an easy life, especially when so much of
what he taught was an affront to what people wanted to hear. Yet he
also knew that God would one day rescue him to eternal safety.

On a scale of 1–10, let's say that Paul's sufferings registered an 8.
Because Christ's were a 10, and because of his sure and certain hope
of heaven, Paul only thought of his hardships as "light momentary
affliction" (2 Corinthians 4:17).

He would have rebuffed labeling them as an 8, because his perspective
was fed not by circumstances of yesterday or dreams of a better tomorrow, but of eternity in the undisturbed presence of God—a future that
is ours as well. Perhaps we should think more like Paul.

YOUR LIFE IN ACTION
Read 2 Corinthians 4:7–5:10.

He was thirty-two years old when he began to reign, and he reigned eight years in Jerusalem. And he departed with no one's regret. They buried him in the city of David, but not in the tombs of the kings (2 Chronicles 21:20).

He [Jehoram] departed with no one's regret." The New Living Translation words it, "No one was sorry when he died."

The Scripture is not being lighthearted here, just stating a fact—a direct and sad fact. Life got better for his survivors after Jehoram died.

Imagine living in such a way that no one mourns your death! To be sure, dying well is not a contest where the one whose death registers highest on the sadness scale wins. But Jehoram's epitaph should sober us into contemplating how we're living and what our lingering influence will be.

Today accounts for one more stone you lay on the wall that will become your legacy. What form is that wall taking?

Is it a monument to selfishness, anger, complaining, discontentment—all things that deny the life-changing gospel you profess?

Or is your legacy shaping into a monument of God's goodness displayed daily through your love, peace, joy, and gratitude?

YOUR LIFE IN ACTION

Thinking of how you've been living, what do you think others would say about your legacy?

> *The Spirit of God clothed Zechariah the son of Jehoiada the priest,*
> *and he stood above the people, and said to them,*
> *"Thus says God, 'Why do you break the commandments of the LORD,*
> *so that you cannot prosper? Because you have forsaken the LORD,*
> *he has forsaken you'" (2 Chronicles 24:20).*

God's desire is to support His children, to bless them. This is His default position. Therefore, when we find ourselves being opposed by God, it is not because He is being unreasonable or manipulative.

There is no bait and switch going on. Obedience brings blessing, while disobedience brings about the forfeiting of His pleasure (though never His acceptance).

What's at issue here is not our getting what we want from God, as if we could hold Him hostage to our demands. *(I did ____, so You owe me!)* No, the issue is that we have believed many lies about God, one of the biggest being that He eagerly waits for us to cross over into disobedience so He can punish us, because that's what makes Him happy.

The truth: God wants to bless you, though He defines what that means, not you. He wants your soul to prosper. He wants you to have His joy inside you (John 15:11). So . . . obey Him.

YOUR LIFE IN ACTION

What Scripture passages can you think of that speak of the joy of the Lord? Write out a few of these today, and perhaps memorize them.

> *These all died in faith, not having received the things promised,*
> *but having seen them and greeted them from afar, and having acknowledged*
> *that they were strangers and exiles on the earth (Hebrews 11:13).*

How much do you trust God—*really* trust Him? This is an important question because trust is a true indication of love.

Put your love for God in the context of waiting . . . something we humans rarely do well.

What if God were to promise you something—not a trinket or a slight life improvement, but something so grand that it would literally change your life? Imagine wanting this promise fulfilled so badly that your longing became an ache, and you adjusted your whole life around it coming true.

The days of waiting turned into years, yet because God was the One who promised, you were certain He would come through. Even on your dying day, though you had not received the fulfillment of His promise, you still trusted Him, still loved Him.

Do you trust God that much?

There is much we can enjoy and experience about God today, but the greatest of Him we can only greet from afar . . . for now.

YOUR LIFE IN ACTION

Read Hebrews 11.

Do not withhold good from those to whom it is due,
when it is in your power to do it (Proverbs 3:27).

Sometimes our reluctance to help may be traceable to our lack of love for the person or people in need, but sometimes it's because we don't think our help will make enough difference to truly matter. On this point, pastor and author Andy Stanley offers some good advice: "Do for one what you wish you could do for everyone."

The title of an old hymn, "Little Is Much When God Is In It," unmasks the mindset of our occasional reluctance. When we think God is limited to only what He can accomplish through our efforts and resources, it's not a lack of love we're showing, but a deficiency of faith.

Can God not still feed a crowd with five loaves and two small fish? Yes. God can indeed multiply whatever you bring—perhaps by using your example to draw others to join or even moving you to give more than you had originally planned.

However God chooses to extend your giving beyond your own reach, yours is to give what you have, however much or little, and leave the results to Him.

YOUR LIFE IN ACTION

Is God prompting you to give or help in some way that seems
beyond your ability? Ask Him what He would have you do.

When he was strong, he grew proud,
to his destruction (2 Chronicles 26:16).

Had you met Uzziah a few years earlier, you would have been impressed. He was intelligent, creative, influential, and highly respected. He was a good leader. Under him the kingdom had prospered.

Sadly, when Uzziah's life is analyzed by historians and commentators, it is often divided into two parts: (1) faithfulness and blessing, and (2) sin and punishment.

Uzziah fell from God's favor. His was a slow decline, brought on by pride as he allowed his dependence on God to be eclipsed by a belief that he was a self-made man. And self-made men, he reasoned, could do whatever they wanted.

May Uzziah's decline and fall be a warning to us all: Pride is dangerous. It is a slow-moving debilitation that can turn servant-leaders into megalomaniacs.

Pride is not an issue to ignore or attempt to excuse away. If you see it in yourself, even a little, be aggressive in repenting of it.

YOUR LIFE IN ACTION

What are some of the results of unchecked pride
that you have observed?

All Scripture is breathed out by God and profitable for teaching,
for reproof, for correction, and for training in righteousness,
that the man of God may be complete,
equipped for every good work (2 Timothy 3:16–17).

George Müller, known to be mighty in prayer and faith, once observed, "The vigor of our spiritual life will be in exact proportion to the place held by the Bible in our life and thoughts." There's a reason disciple makers emphasize Bible reading, memorization, study, and meditation.

It is a terrible mistake to think we can treat God's Word with indifference and still know Him well. Intimacy with God requires a faithful intake of Scripture.

This goes beyond the reading of printed words on a page or screen. It is a readiness of heart and mind to be taught, reproved, corrected, trained, and equipped in matters of God's will and ways.

As long as the habit of Bible reading and meditation is optional, you choose to increase your vulnerability to Satan's maneuvers. He takes note and will therefore take advantage.

On the other hand, you could be growing stronger and wiser each day. It's your choice.

YOUR LIFE IN ACTION

Look up the meaning of these words from 2 Timothy 3:16—
teaching, reproof, correction, training—to see the importance of
each way the Word of God affects you.

Keep your life free from love of money, and be content with what you have, for he has said, "I will never leave you nor forsake you" (Hebrews 13:5).

Here are two grand ideals that are seldom connected to each other as they should be:

- Keep yourself free from the love of money.
- God will never forsake you.

What does one have to do with the other? Perhaps the logical connection is obvious—a person who is secure in God's loving presence does not look for security or happiness in "things."

Knowing that God is here, and always will be, *should* bring about a holy contentment. Yet the connection of these two ideals is lost when we choose to live on a lower level than we should.

C. S. Lewis described this disconnect in *The Weight of Glory*: "We are half-hearted creatures, fooling about with drink and sex and ambition when infinite joy is offered us, like an ignorant child who wants to go on making mud pies in a slum because he cannot imagine what is meant by the offer of a holiday at the sea. We are far too easily pleased."

Let's admit that we sometimes try to appease our spiritual desires with activities that are not good for our souls. We promise ourselves to make more room for God later, but now is not convenient. May God deliver us from such foolish thinking and low living!

YOUR LIFE IN ACTION

Ask God to search your heart and show you any areas where you are trying to satisfy your spiritual appetites in ways that do not please Him.

Whoever covers an offense seeks love,
but he who repeats a matter separates close friends (Proverbs 17:9).

Replace the word *covers* with the word *overwhelms* (that is how the same word is translated in other verses) and read the passage above again. This raises the question, "How can we overwhelm an offense?"

Picture a fire flashing up in a pot on a stove. One of the quickest ways to extinguish the fire is to smother it by putting a lid over the pot. Deprived of oxygen, the fire dies.

In this illustration, the fire is the offense and the lid is our silence—our choice to keep the offense from spreading. Repeating something to others, who were not involved in the first place, only keeps the offense alive and even spreads its destruction. Love would never drive us to do such a thing.

You can't always control what you hear or see, but you do have a choice regarding stemming the tide of the damage. You can spread the fire, or you can smother it. Love, in this case, rightly chooses to smother.

YOUR LIFE IN ACTION
What are some of the dangers of gossip and slander?

Take care, brothers, lest there be in any of you an evil, unbelieving heart, leading you to fall away from the living God. But exhort one another every day, as long as it is called "today," that none of you may be hardened by the deceitfulness of sin (Hebrews 3:12–13).

Are you your brother's keeper? In many ways, yes. While we are "individually" members of the body of Christ, we are members "one of another" (Romans 12:5). We are joined; therefore, what I do or do not do (of the will of God) affects you.

Pastor and author Brian Hedges made this observation regarding a sizable portion of the New Testament: "Sometimes we forget that most of Paul's letters were written to churches. When he exhorts us to kill our sins and grow in grace, he speaks in a corporate context. We pursue holiness *together*."

The point is, as believers we are better together. We learn from each other's example, encourage each other when necessary, and refresh each other when weary. Our burdens are shared, and our joys are multiplied.

Some want to pull away from the body of Christ and worship God on their own. This is a mistake that brings leanness to the soul.

Through our interactions and relationships, we learn to forgive, show patience, serve, and share. We experience the joy of meeting the needs of others and the grace of having our needs met as well.

YOUR LIFE IN ACTION

Think of ways you have benefited through being joined with other members of the body of Christ. Is there someone you can thank today for how God has used them in your life?

Hezekiah did not make return according to the benefit done to him,
for his heart was proud. Therefore wrath came upon him
and Judah and Jerusalem (2 Chronicles 32:25).

A change for the better in circumstances does not necessarily indicate a change of heart. Sometimes proud hearts are not moved by God's goodness right away. Hezekiah is proof of that.

Even though God had miraculously helped him and promised to extend his life (he had been near death), Hezekiah remained a self-centered man. But God brought him low once more; and this time his people suffered with him—because of him—and Hezekiah eventually repented.

We can see two remarkable dynamics here, and both are as formidable as ever: (1) The human heart has a surprising capacity for arrogance, even to the point of resisting God's grace, and (2) God is relentless in pursuing repentance from His children. This is a mercy that cannot be matched, for "the LORD **will** fulfill his purpose for [us]" (Psalm 138:8).

Hezekiah's obstinacy seems foolish to us, yet our reaction to God's conviction is often the same. We want to hold to our way just a little longer. We must know, then, that God will not allow this to go on and on; He will bring us low.

YOUR LIFE IN ACTION

Do you find yourself resisting God today,
intending to obey at a later time? If so, why?

> *Whoever knows the right thing to do and fails to do it,*
> *for him it is sin (James 4:17).*

The book of James, short as it may be, is brimming with practical teachings of Christian obedience and behavior. One reading of its five chapters provides the believer with rich instructions for living in a way that exalts God and blesses others. It is, in many ways, a primer for discipleship.

So much is taught in this book that James concluded one section with a "you are without excuse" warning to his readers. He told them (us) that there could be no basis for appeal in which a Christian could say, "I didn't know I was supposed to live like that." No, they had been instructed through his letter (as have we) and were accountable to its teaching (as are we).

The point James makes in this warning is worth giving our attention today: Sins of omission—failing to do what we know is right—are as critical as sins of commission in which we flagrantly disobey. Ours is not a life of "don'ts" but of "do's" as well.

YOUR LIFE IN ACTION

Read the book of James.

*If these qualities are yours and are increasing, they keep you from being
ineffective or unfruitful in the knowledge of our Lord Jesus Christ.
For whoever lacks these qualities is so nearsighted that he is blind,
having forgotten that he was cleansed from his former sins (2 Peter 1:8–9).*

God provides everything we need to live godly lives (2 Peter 1:3). The fulfillment of this promise begins with the faith He gives us to believe in Him in the first place.

The life we lead as a result of salvation continues on in faith as we abide in (draw our life from) Christ, who is the true and life-giving vine (John 15). Yet we are called to participate in this faith through obedience and action.

Indeed, the absence of our participation calls our faith into question. We are active agents in our own spiritual growth, partaking of the divine nature that is ours in Christ.

Peter specifies seven attributes that should be present and growing in every believer: virtue, knowledge, self-control, steadfastness, godliness, brotherly affection, and love. When these are true of us, and are on the increase, we will be more and more spiritually effective and enjoy a deepening intimacy with Christ.

YOUR LIFE IN ACTION

Define each of the seven attributes: virtue, knowledge, self-control, steadfastness, godliness, brotherly affection, and love.

If these qualities are yours and are increasing, they keep you from being
ineffective or unfruitful in the knowledge of our Lord Jesus Christ.
For whoever lacks these qualities is so nearsighted that he is blind,
having forgotten that he was cleansed from his former sins (2 Peter 1:8–9).

God provides everything we need to live godly lives (2 Peter 1:3). The faith He initiated, which enabled us to believe in Him, has given us access to His divine nature.

As we grow in our spiritual lives, by partaking of that nature, seven attributes become more and more a part of who we are and how we live: virtue, knowledge, self-control, steadfastness, godliness, brotherly affection, and love. These seven attributes bring about two grand transformations in us—we increase in our spiritual effectiveness, and we enjoy a deepening intimacy with Christ.

On the other hand, when these attributes are not present and growing, the believer is nearsighted and blind. This means he is living as one who does not even know Jesus, and he stumbles when he should be able to walk confidently.

He is also forgetful of the most glorious mercy he will ever know—forgiven and reborn. He carries a phantom guilt.

Oh, the sadness of knowing Christ and living as if we do not!

YOUR LIFE IN ACTION

Which of the descriptions best fits you—increasing in spiritual
effectiveness and enjoying a deepening intimacy with Christ,
or spiritually nearsighted and forgetful of God's mercy?

We are slaves. Yet our God has not forsaken us in our slavery,
but has extended to us his steadfast love before the kings of Persia,
to grant us some reviving to set up the house of our God, to repair its ruins,
and to give us protection in Judea and Jerusalem (Ezra 9:9).

In our quest for revival, let us be certain of a few things. For one, let us be sure to seek the Lord Himself, the Reviver.

To want only the "times of refreshing" and not the One who refreshes (Acts 3:20) is to accept an invitation to a lavish celebration and then snub the host. This would be a foolish reversion to the arrogance that had delayed revival all along. Could we be so shortsighted in faith?

Let us also be certain that God revives His people for kingdom-expanding purposes. Because Ezra and his countrymen knew "some reviving," worship of the one true God was restored, and His exalted glory brought peace and security to the nation.

It is understandable that God's people now feel oppressed by the state of things in our culture. But perhaps God is preparing the way for "some reviving" again—where His light will be seen all the brighter against the backdrop of this present darkness.

YOUR LIFE IN ACTION

Pray today for the Christians in your country to be revived—
to turn wholeheartedly to the Lord in repentance and faith.

> *The fear of man lays a snare,*
> *but whoever trusts in the LORD is safe (Proverbs 29:25).*

This principle plays out clearly in 1 Samuel 13. Samuel had told Saul to wait for him in Gilgal for seven days, at which time he would offer sacrifices to God and advise Saul what he was to do next.

When Samuel was delayed in coming and some of the people grew restless, Saul responded in foolish haste. He did what he was not allowed to do (because he was not a priest) and offered the sacrifices himself.

Author John Piper summarizes Saul's actions and motives, revealing the snare he stepped into: "Why did Saul obey the people instead of God? Because he feared the displeasure of the people more than the displeasure of God."

Interesting that this proverb contrasts fearing man with trusting God, for it is often our impatience with God—believing He either won't come through at all or won't come through soon enough—that leads us to give in to the pressure of others and "just do something."

The *something* we choose to do in those instances becomes a snare, prolonging our stay in a place from which God was soon to deliver us. Trust frees; impatience ensnares.

YOUR LIFE IN ACTION

Recall a time when you gave in to the fear of man and
made your situation even more difficult.
Now, recall a time when you chose to wait on God and trust in Him.

*At that time the Jews who lived near them came from all directions
and said to us ten times, "You must return to us." So in the lowest parts of
the space behind the wall, in open places, I stationed the people by their clans,
with their swords, their spears, and their bows (Nehemiah 4:12–13).*

Nehemiah and the people were doing God's work—they were rebuilding the wall around the city of Jerusalem.

As is often the case, this activity stirred up the enemies of God, and they threatened harm and even death to any servant of the Lord. Day after day the threats came, and some of the people grew worried enough that they urged their brothers to stop working.

Nehemiah was a wise and God-fearing leader. He knew where his workers were vulnerable—some of the most fearful lived closest to the enemy and could therefore hear the threats with high and frequent volume. He also knew there were gaps in the wall that would be easy targets for the enemy to breach if they chose to attack.

Nehemiah took action, urging the people to remain in the city so they could be farther from the threats and nearer their families and countrymen. He filled the gaps—the "open places"—with armed workers and called the people to remember their God and their families, and to concentrate on finishing the job.

YOUR LIFE IN ACTION

Do you know where you are vulnerable to the enemy,
where he may draw your focus away from God and righteousness?
What actions are you taking to close the gaps in your life?

*Whoever meddles in a quarrel not his own
is like one who takes a passing dog by the ears (Proverbs 26:17).*

Grabbing a stray dog's ears is ill-advised behavior. It is generally not going to end well for the grabber . . . which makes this a fitting metaphor for the foolishness of joining an argument you are not part of.

In our day of advancing technology, we have hundreds of opportunities to grab stray dogs' ears by way of social media. We should therefore use even more caution when choosing to comment or to remain silent.

Proverbs 10:19 is a good verse to keep in mind when in a face-to-face conversation or a digital one: "When words are many, transgression is not lacking, but whoever restrains his lips [stops typing] is prudent."

YOUR LIFE IN ACTION

Look up other Bible verses that have to do with
controlling our tongue.

The LORD is my chosen portion and my cup; you hold my lot.
The lines have fallen for me in pleasant places;
indeed, I have a beautiful inheritance (Psalm 16:5–6).

There is great delight found in anticipating eternity, and renewed contentment for what will be between now and then. George Müller put it like this: "Self-denial is not so much an impoverishment as a postponement: we sacrifice a present good for a future, greater good."

We live in an on-demand world where any sort of happiness we want is expected immediately and without interruption. We want what we want, and we want it now. But the Christian life differs from this worldview in two key ways:

- We know that true joy is not found in getting everything we want, but in receiving what God gives. There is no guilt, no impatience, no lust, and no corruption with God's gifts.

- We are certain that our hunger for unending joy is legitimate and that it will be met, although not in this life. We are citizens of another place . . . for another time. Eternity is our greater reality.

Today's joys and sorrows find their order in the context of eternity. We endure sorrow with hope, knowing it will come to an end; we embrace joy with anticipation, knowing it is a foretaste of what will forever be our lot.

YOUR LIFE IN ACTION

Can you think of any songs of praise or hymns that speak
of heaven and eternity? Look up the words to a few of these today,
and sing them in worship to God.

*When [God] summoned a famine on the land and broke all
supply of bread, he had sent a man ahead of them, Joseph,
who was sold as a slave (Psalm 105:16–17).*

God is always doing more than we can see at the moment, which brings context to our pain. This does not mean that God is a cosmic manipulator, knocking our lives against others in uncaring ways. It means He is building His kingdom, and you are playing a part that is beyond the hardships of today.

God may give you a glimpse of what your role is, and He may not. Sometimes the lessons to be learned, the changes to be made, and the blessings to be received are not fully known until the next generation, or even the next.

Joseph is a good example. He suffered many setbacks, insults, false accusations, and broken hopes. Brothers and friends turned against him. The favored son became an inmate. Yet all this was part of God's plan; Joseph was the man God had sent ahead.

We may hope for God to explain Himself, to tell us why we are in a storm; God is not put off by our asking. But we must understand that sometimes our suffering indicates we have been sent ahead. It may not be to save a starving nation, as in the case of Joseph, but it may be to turn the tide of your family from spiritual darkness to light, or to display the grace of God within your circle of friends and neighbors, or to set about a chain of events that will bring the gospel to a people group you don't even know.

YOUR LIFE IN ACTION

What people can you think of that God sent ahead
to accomplish His purposes?

They forgot God, their Savior, who had done great things in Egypt,
wondrous works in the land of Ham,
and awesome deeds by the Red Sea (Psalm 106:21–22).

Do you remember what your life was like before Christ? Without recalling specific acts of sin, it is encouraging to remember the hopelessness of your life before Christ, and even better to think about the people, events, and circumstances He used to draw you to Himself. In other words, remember the great things God did to bring you out of your "Egypt."

In many biblical accounts, the spiritual decline of people can be traced back to their forgetting the works of God. As a countermeasure, throughout both the Old Testament and the New, God's people are encouraged to remember.

They also were not to keep these memories to themselves, but to tell them to one another. In this way, their own faith was bolstered, others were encouraged, and God was publicly exalted.

Remembering the works of God in your life and in the lives of friends and family can set your heart on a path of thanksgiving, praise, and faith. Be intentional about such remembering. Talk to yourself and to others about the goodness of God and how He brought you out of Egypt.

YOUR LIFE IN ACTION

Look for an opportunity today to tell a friend about
a way God has worked in your life.

Blessed be the God and Father of our Lord Jesus Christ, the Father of mercies and God of all comfort, who comforts us in all our affliction, so that we may be able to comfort those who are in any affliction, with the comfort with which we ourselves are comforted by God (2 Corinthians 1:3–4).

All who live will suffer. All who live in Christ Jesus will be comforted by God. All who have been comforted by God should become comforters to others.

We know we are to be stewards of our money, time, and talent in order to serve and support the kingdom work of God. We see ourselves as a manager of these things rather than the owner, knowing that all we possess, we have been given (1 Corinthians 4:7). Therefore, we are ready to pass some or all of it on to others as God directs.

And so it is with comfort. We should not keep it to ourselves.

Do you remember the comfort of God that made you able to endure your dark days? Don't keep that comfort to yourself.

Someday—perhaps today—there will be a person in your sphere of influence whose sense of hopelessness is as deep as yours once was. God wants you to carry His comfort to them.

YOUR LIFE IN ACTION

Reflect on the times and ways God has comforted you.
Thank Him, and then also pray for those you know who are
presently in a time of suffering.

Wisdom is justified by all her children (Luke 7:35).

Are you a child of God, an offspring of the gospel? Does your life validate your profession of faith?

It is your very life as a follower of Christ that gives evidence of His saving grace. This does not come about by your "trying to be a better witness," as if you were changing your appearance with a new hairstyle and wardrobe. Rather, this validation comes about as your inner growth in Christ becomes outwardly apparent.

Paul put it this way when writing to the Christians in Corinth: "You yourselves are our letter of recommendation, written on our hearts, to be known and read by all. And you show that you are a letter from Christ delivered by us, written not with ink but with the Spirit of the living God, not on tablets of stone but on tablets of human hearts" (2 Corinthians 3:2–3). He recognized that the authenticity of their faith would be obvious through the way they conducted themselves in all areas of life.

This did not mean for them—nor does it for you—that they should be silent witnesses who never put the gospel into words. It meant for them—as it does for you—that their life would represent not their own claims, but the very claims of Christ.

YOUR LIFE IN ACTION

How was your belief in the gospel influenced by the lives of Christians you knew?

Humble yourselves, therefore, under the mighty hand of God
so that at the proper time he may exalt you,
casting all your anxieties on him,
because he cares for you (1 Peter 5:6–7).

Offloading our anxieties onto God is sometimes an act of desperation, and it is always an act of humility. When the pain of a certain trial begins to dominate our thoughts, we have little strength to do anything but worry. And with whatever energy we may muster, in a state of anxiety, we will likely do or say something that makes matters worse.

Our troubles should drive us first to call on God. In so doing we are humbling ourselves and acknowledging our need for God's care. This is the only reliable exit strategy from our worries. So if humility takes the pressure off, pride puts (or keeps) the pressure on.

The way of the proud man (or woman) grows increasingly difficult throughout his life. All of us encounter anxiety-producing situations, some more threatening than others.

Those who humble themselves in the face of these challenges by turning them over to God will endure and grow stronger. But those who try to handle these matters on their own become weak, harsh, and miserable. Pride exacts a higher price than humility ever will.

YOUR LIFE IN ACTION

If you are facing a challenging circumstance in your life
right now, have you yet cast your anxieties about this situation on God?
If not, will you take this step of humility today?

"Why are you sleeping? Rise and pray that you may not enter into temptation" (Luke 22:46).

The enemy is emboldened by our procrastination in prayer, and he will use it to his advantage. The longer we delay praying against temptation, the more likely we are to give in to it.

Of course we should pray when we find ourselves facing temptation. It is appropriate to call out to God in the heat of battle.

But how much better off we would be if we prayed in advance, even to the point of praying to be spared temptation entirely. This kind of praying raises our awareness of sin's approach, equipping us to recognize sin that can otherwise camouflage itself as harmless and even appealing.

It is not wrong to reactively pray. Sin is ever present in our world, and we have a cunning enemy who relentlessly pursues our downfall. But if our praying is always and only reactive in nature, we will lose more battles with temptation than we win.

However, proactive, watchful praying positions us to overcome sin by outmaneuvering the enemy. For this reason, Jesus called on His disciples to "rise and pray."

YOUR LIFE IN ACTION

Knowing the ways in which you are weak and likely to be tempted, pray that God will protect you from falling today.

He said to them, "Pay attention to what you hear:
with the measure you use, it will be measured to you,
and still more will be added to you.
For to the one who has, more will be given, and from the one who has not,
even what he has will be taken away" (Mark 4:24–25).

Having direct access to Jesus didn't guarantee that the disciples would always understand His teaching. On more than one occasion, we find them asking Jesus clarifying questions after the crowds had departed. Even when Jesus taught using parables, the disciples didn't necessarily get the point.

In at least one instance, described in Mark 4, Jesus used their confusion to reveal an underlying issue: Their obedience was lagging behind their knowledge. In other words, obeying the truth they knew would increase their capacity to understand more truth, while not acting on the truth they knew would prove a hindrance.

Disobedience—whether in the form of defiance (acting in opposition to God's will) or indifference (taking no action on God's will)—stunted the disciples' spiritual growth. Is it also stunting yours?

Many times we want to *know* more than we are willing to *do*. Our motive for acquiring biblical knowledge is often for the purpose of making an impression rather than making disciples. We want the reputation of being spiritually mature without doing the real work of our mission, "Go therefore and make disciples of all nations" (Matthew 28:19).

YOUR LIFE IN ACTION

Is your obedience in sync with your biblical knowledge,
or does it lag behind? What do you understand of the truths
in Scripture that you have not yet acted on?

Behold, is not their prosperity in their hand?
The counsel of the wicked is far from me (Job 21:16).

Here is a paraphrase of what Job said, and it's a good indication that he was going to be okay, despite his suffering: *The godless think their prosperity is a result of their own doing, but I reject such foolish thinking. It is worse than foolish, it is wicked.*

Why is it a good thing that Job would think this way? In the thick of suffering, Job might have been expected to give in to bitterness, thereby blaming God for his misery.

Furthermore, he might have reasoned that he himself had been the actual source of the good he had known in the past, and that God had only lately entered the picture to "bring him down a notch." But Job could not and would not think that way.

A man or woman who acknowledges God in seasons of prosperity as well as in hardship knows that He does not change—that He never lays aside His mercy for the godly. He does not grow weak, indifferent, or vindictive.

The righteous trust God regardless of the weather, the bank account, or the doctor's diagnosis. They believe God is near, and always the same.

YOUR LIFE IN ACTION
Think of some of the ways God has displayed His mercy to you.
Thank Him!

Be subject for the Lord's sake to every human institution, whether it be to the emperor as supreme, or to governors as sent by him to punish those who do evil and to praise those who do good. For this is the will of God, that by doing good you should put to silence the ignorance of foolish people. Live as people who are free, not using your freedom as a cover-up for evil, but living as servants of God (1 Peter 2:13–16).

Paul said that everything he did, he did for the sake of the gospel (1 Corinthians 9:23). This is a necessary frame of reference for believers to have when it comes to the matter of submitting to civil authorities.

As laws are written or changed to affirm godlessness, opening the way for the rejection—and perhaps the persecution—of a biblical worldview, Christians must align themselves all the more with right thinking in this area.

Does the Bible address civil *dis*obedience? Of course. There are recorded instances where it was necessary for God-fearing people to reject evil laws that would have forced them to do evil things (Daniel comes to mind).

But before wrestling with particular laws, we should consider the general standard of our conduct in Christ toward human authorities. Our obedience is a witness that lends a credible voice to the gospel.

Evil laws aside, Christians should be the best of law-abiding citizens. And not just to avoid fines and jail time, but to "do good" for the sake of the gospel.

YOUR LIFE IN ACTION

Pray for the human authorities in your life today.

> *Be angry, and do not sin; ponder in your own hearts on your beds,*
> *and be silent (Psalm 4:4).*

Do you know what to do with your anger? Anger is a reality and it should not be ignored.

- Pray that God will prevent you from releasing your anger in a sinful way.

- Keep silent until you know what more you are to do about the situation, if anything.

- Ponder the cause of your anger. Do not shut down your thinking, as some would suggest; rather, think it through prayerfully, until you have clear and peaceful direction from God.

- Do not discuss the matter with others; ponder it alone before God ("on your beds"). Have many private conversations with God before ever uttering a word to anyone else. This will lead you to a good solution while keeping the anger contained.

YOUR LIFE IN ACTION

Are there any situations in your life that you need to take through these four steps? Do so prayerfully.

Shout for joy in the LORD, O you righteous!
Praise befits the upright (Psalm 33:1).

In Colossians 3:2 we're told to "set [our] minds on things that are above." This means we are to direct our thoughts, to tell our minds what to concentrate on.

One of the best ways we can do this is through the beauty of worship—singing in particular.

We often offer praise in response to God's activity in our lives, or because of some blessing He has bestowed on us; and so we should.

But we need to be proactive in our worship, too. We need to take our thoughts to God, to sing of and proclaim His glorious deeds.

Don't just praise when you feel right; praise *until* you feel right, and then praise some more. Praise befits you.

YOUR LIFE IN ACTION

Do you have some favorite hymns or worship songs?
Sing some of them today to God alone.

Many are the afflictions of the righteous,
but the LORD delivers him out of them all (Psalm 34:19).

God never gets weary. Unfortunately, it seems that our enemy doesn't get weary either.

The devil does not curtail his activity after we have believed in Christ; he merely changes tactics. Since he can no longer prevent our faith from leading us to salvation, he concentrates on making us doubt God's daily goodness.

Have you ever said to yourself, *I hate to bother God with this*, or wondered if God would be "happy" to hear from you if you prayed about one more personal struggle you were having? These thoughts expose the devil's work; he is happy to see you falter in your trust, because he knows that once a small doubt has been let in, bigger ones can follow.

Think on today's verse throughout today: "**Many** are the afflictions of the righteous, but the LORD delivers him out of them **all**." God stands with us against each and every affliction.

YOUR LIFE IN ACTION
Read Psalm 34.

*Teach me your way, O LORD, and lead me on a level path
because of my enemies (Psalm 27:11).*

Many have rightly observed that Christian discipleship cannot be found in observing a prescribed regimen of do-these-and-don't-do-those. Truly, the life we lead in Christ could never be reduced to checklists and inventories.

The Bible often uses a "path" to describe our ongoing spiritual formation. This word picture illustrates the progress we make in knowing God and enjoying Him more fully as we walk with Him day by day.

This is the way of a relationship. God Himself, through His Word and by His Holy Spirit, is our instructor and companion. He does not drop us off at the trailhead, give us our instructions, and then arrange to meet up with us again at journey's end. He walks with us, every step.

Today will be filled with opportunities to experience God's presence and to learn from Him as He leads you on the path. Remind yourself throughout the day that God is at your side.

YOUR LIFE IN ACTION

In what other ways does a path represent
the nature of your relationship with God?

God is our refuge and strength,
a very present help in trouble (Psalm 46:1).

By its nature a refuge must be stronger than the storm from which it protects us. A refuge has a known history of saving lives, of restoring peace, and of never failing.

Our God is such a refuge. He is . . .

- a strong tower (Proverbs 18:10)

- a mighty rock (Psalm 62:7)

- a shield, stronghold, and savior (2 Samuel 22:3)

- our light and salvation (Psalm 27:1)

- an everlasting rock (Isaiah 26:4)

God is your refuge, so give fear no place. When it comes—and it will—reject it as a ploy from the enemy designed to undermine your faith.

God has not changed. He has not grown weary. Though the form of your trials may change—one time it may be a heartbreak, another time an illness—God does not. He is able, always able, to deliver your soul from the snare of fear and worry. He is stronger than every storm.

YOUR LIFE IN ACTION
Look up and read the words of the hymn
"A Mighty Fortress Is Our God."

This is my commandment, that you love one another as I have loved you. Greater love has no one than this, that someone lay down his life for his friends (John 15:12–13).

The love of Christ cannot be overlooked. His sacrificial death on the cross—"No one takes it from me, but I lay it down of my own accord" (John 10.18)—makes it clear for all to see. All who *will*, that is,

And lest we ever come to believe that even in the smallest way we deserved His love, we should likewise "remember that [we] were at that time separated from Christ, alienated from the commonwealth of Israel and strangers to the covenants of promise, having no hope and without God in the world" (Ephesians 2:12).

Sacrifice, even when not made in the name of Christ, is a reminder of Him—which makes it all the more remarkable when it *is* done in the name of Christ. For this reason alone, Christ's call to love one another should always be heard within earshot of Calvary.

He is our example and our divine enabler; we can love because of Him. Even when that love demands our sacrifice.

YOUR LIFE IN ACTION

Are you needing to love a difficult person? Look to Calvary.
Meditate today on the love of Jesus seen in His
dying on the cross for you.

*If then you have been raised with Christ, seek the things that are above,
where Christ is, seated at the right hand of God. . . .
When Christ who is your life appears, then you also will appear
with him in glory (Colossians 3:1, 4).*

Believers in Jesus Christ are future-dwellers with present obligations. It is because of what *will be* true of us that we *can do* what is required of us.

In his book *Licensed to Kill*, author Brian Hedges observes, "The certainties of our past justification and our future glorification empower us for present sanctification." This is why Paul instructed the Colossians how to live and grow in the present (referring to their sanctification) after first reassuring them of what their eternal condition would be (referring to their glorification).

Before they could put to death the sin that entangled them (Colossians 3:5–11) or put on godly behaviors and attitudes (vv. 12–17), they needed to comprehend the truth of one day appearing with Christ in glory (v. 4).

No amount of self-urging can motivate loving obedience to God, but a look to our sure and certain future can. Do those things God has placed before you to do, but with an eternal perspective.

YOUR LIFE IN ACTION

What do you think it means to
"seek the things that are above"?

> *I acknowledged my sin to you, and I did not cover my iniquity;*
> *I said, "I will confess my transgressions to the LORD,"*
> *and you forgave the iniquity of my sin (Psalm 32:5).*

Ignoring guilt is neither healthy ("my bones wasted away") nor helpful ("my strength was dried up," Psalm 32:3–4). David learned these things the hard way, by trying to evade his guilt, yet all the while becoming a weaker man in every way. But he could not outrun God.

Sometimes we try to escape guilt when what we really need to do is spend some time listening to it—that is, listening to what the Holy Spirit is saying to us through it.

Yes, we're all too aware of Satan's use of (false) guilt, where he tries to ensnare us in either the shame of that which we've been forgiven or in trumped-up accusations. But if he cannot pin us down with false guilt, Satan will switch tactics by urging us to evade real guilt.

Sometimes we feel guilty because we *are* guilty. It is best then to stop and seek God's answer to guilt's cause. His purposes are to restore us, and guilt is the divine alarm that signals this work.

Embrace the work of God, not by evading guilt but by examining, with the Holy Spirit, its legitimacy and doing as God says.

YOUR LIFE IN ACTION

Read Psalm 32.

*For you, O Lord, are good and forgiving, abounding in steadfast love
to all who call upon you. Give ear, O Lord, to my prayer;
listen to my plea for grace. In the day of my trouble I call upon you,
for you answer me (Psalm 86:5–7).*

There are prayers we voice right away. Our distress drives us because our need is either urgent or immediate, or both. We need God's help and we need it now. Quite often this urgency is brought on by the pain and panic of unexpected trouble. Aren't you glad God hears urgent prayers?

Realizing the attentiveness of God in every moment of our lives ("In the day of my trouble . . . you answer me"), does it not seem foolish then to postpone His grace, to put His help on hold? But this is the very thing we do when we stubbornly refuse to confess sin.

Is God any less attentive to prayers of confession than He is to pleas for help? Are not deliverance and restoration His response to both kinds of prayer?

When we live with guilt for a long time, we make room for it through excuses, such as, *That was so long ago, why bother with it now?* But there is no statute of limitations on guilt . . . or on God's forgiveness.

Refusing to confess sin, and deal with it biblically with God and any who may have suffered because of it, is postponing grace. Why would anyone do that?

YOUR LIFE IN ACTION

Read Psalm 86.

*Against you, you only, have I sinned and done what is evil
in your sight, so that you may be justified in your words
and blameless in your judgment (Psalm 51:4).*

Confessing our sin amounts to more than words; it is an awakening that should bring us low. Even the popular description of confession, "agreeing with God about the nature of our sin," doesn't really get to the heart of the matter—especially if *agreeing* means merely *assenting*.

It is possible to admit sin without ever confessing it. But that approach will bring about neither repentance nor restoration.

Confession brings us to a place of sadness, of shame, of grieving the fact that we betrayed the lover of our soul. David's confession is an example.

Had his sin affected others? Absolutely. Yet he came to recognize that it was "against you, you only," referring to God. How could he say such a thing? Furthermore, what should we take away from this text to make part of our outlook on our own sin?

Sin is an offense to God (part of which may be the suffering it inflicts on others whom He loves); it put Jesus on the cross. Until we come to terms with the evilness of sin, and the price Christ paid to rescue us from it, we will continue to settle for confession lite—a little regret, a feeble promise to do better or try harder.

YOUR LIFE IN ACTION

Read Psalm 51. How did David's outlook on his sin differ
from how you tend to view your own sin?

They spoke against God, saying, "Can God spread a table in the wilderness? He struck the rock so that water gushed out and streams overflowed. Can he also give bread or provide meat for his people?" (Psalm 78:19–20).

How big is God? How strong is He? What can He do? Is there anything He can't do?

In theory, we'd probably answer these questions, and others like them, with enthusiastic words of praise and admiration. We'd gladly boast in God's unmatched magnificence.

But our faith, as lived out through our day-by-day reality, may communicate something quite different. Like the Israelites in the wilderness, who seemed to think that God was capable of only those things they had personally witnessed, we might present a weaker God—one who can only repeat His past works, as wonderful as they were, but unable to do anything more or "new."

How foolish to think that He who gave them water from a rock could not also feed them solid food. Yet they were no less believing than we . . . *God has redeemed some wicked people, but can He reach my prodigal child? God has restored broken marriages, but surely mine is too far gone.*

Reject these thoughts. Is anything too difficult for God (Jeremiah 32:27)?

YOUR LIFE IN ACTION

Read 1 Corinthians 2:9, and look up other verses that are similar to it.

Reproaches have broken my heart, so that I am in despair.
I looked for pity, but there was none,
and for comforters, but I found none (Psalm 69:20).

Have you heard the story of the starfish? A man walked along the beach at low tide. Seeing what seemed like hundreds of stranded starfish, he wondered if there was anything he could do to help.

Realizing there were too many to help, he walked on. Soon he came upon a child who was picking up starfish one by one and throwing them back into the ocean.

"What are you doing?" the man asked. "You can't save them all. What does it matter?"

Reaching down, picking up another starfish and hurling it into the water, the child replied, "It mattered to that one."

Sometimes we do nothing, because we think we can't do enough. But there are people around us who are clinging to the hope that just one person will listen to their plea and offer help.

They are looking for a comforter, just one. It could be you.

YOUR LIFE IN ACTION
Ask God if there is one person you can help today.

Because your steadfast love is better than life,
my lips will praise you (Psalm 63:3).

We discover the most profound truths when we are at our lowest. Stripped of everything but the basics, we find that even life has a better rival (not *bitter*, but *better*).

God's steadfast love is more precious, more essential than air, water, and sunlight.

The capstone of this truth is this: "The steadfast love of the LORD never ceases" (Lamentations 3:22). God's love is unending.

Furthermore, His love is irrevocable: "For I am sure that neither death nor life, nor angels nor rulers, nor things present nor things to come, nor powers, nor height nor depth, nor anything else in all creation, will be able to separate us from the love of God in Christ Jesus our Lord" (Romans 8:38–39).

God holds us by His love; He will never let go. This is better than life.

YOUR LIFE IN ACTION
Think through some of the ways God has demonstrated
His love to you. Thank Him for each one.

In him the whole fullness of deity dwells bodily, and you have been filled in him,
who is the head of all rule and authority (Colossians 2:9–10).

What a wonder is Jesus Christ! Let us not drift off into a ditch by becoming enamored with what He does or what He gives. Let us rather fix our thoughts on who He is. Let our minds be "stayed" on Him.

Jesus is God; all the fullness of deity indwells Him. He was in the beginning with God, and He was and is God (John 1:1).

He is the One who awakens our faith to believe in Him, and He perfects that faith into eternal salvation (Hebrews 12:2). Jesus alone is able to give us the "right" to become children of God (John 1:12). All this, and so much more, Jesus does because He is Lord, Savior, Redeemer, the Lamb that was slain, the Head of the Body, the Alpha and Omega . . .

We could spend a lifetime trying to understand and explain all that Christ is, and while we would never reach the height, depth, or breadth of Him, it would not be time wasted. Let everything and everyone else fall in line behind Him in your love and affections. Be glad in Him.

YOUR LIFE IN ACTION

What other biblical names or descriptions of Christ can you think of?
Write each one down, and describe what it means.

*Teach us to number our days
that we may get a heart of wisdom (Psalm 90:12).*

The wise observe two basic conventions. First, they keep an eternal perspective in life.

When we understand that, as Leonard Ravenhill described, "This life is merely a dressing room for eternity," we are better equipped to make purposeful choices and set meaningful priorities. We are also less likely to become entangled in pettiness and discontentment.

The second convention of the wise is that they number their days. This means they live with an awareness of the brevity of life.

They are therefore motivated to make the best use of time, to treat their days and moments with gratitude and intentionality. They are also pressed in their spirits to make the proclamation and demonstration of the gospel their highest concern, because everyone else's life is brief as well.

Are you living wisely?

YOUR LIFE IN ACTION

List some of the ways your life would be different if
you were to live in accordance to the conventions of the wise
as described in today's reading.

You are a chosen race, a royal priesthood, a holy nation,
a people for his own possession, that you may proclaim the excellencies of him
who called you out of darkness into his marvelous light (1 Peter 2:9).

A great deal of emphasis is being given to personal identity and how an individual fits into the human population on a meta-scale and in his or her community on a micro-scale. We want to know who we are, where we belong, and why we're here.

For the believer, 1 Peter 2:9 provides a grand answer:

- chosen race—God sought you, pursued you, chose you

- royal priesthood—no matter your occupation (employment), you have a singular vocation (to serve God)

- holy nation—you are a citizen of heaven living in a time and place that is passing

- a people of God's possession—you are secure with Christ in God

These four descriptors are the core of your identity. Walk worthy.

YOUR LIFE IN ACTION

Pray through today's four descriptors of your true identity.
Thank God for making each one true, and ask Him for the courage
and faith to walk in a manner worthy of who He has made you.

*We all stumble in many ways. And if anyone does not stumble in what he says,
he is a perfect man, able also to bridle his whole body (James 3:2).*

We all sin, no surprise there. James employs an interesting word picture to describe the form our sin sometimes takes: we *stumble*.

This tells us that sin is not always premeditated. No one, other than perhaps stunt men or con men, intentionally stumbles.

James, by the Holy Spirit, also does us the good service of pointing out the likeliest way we will stumble: in our words. The fact that we are capable of stumbling at all means we are fundamentally flawed— which is clear evidence of our sin nature.

In Christ we have been delivered from sin's domain; nevertheless, we still battle against the dogged determination of sin to hold us back from fully enjoying this new position in Christ.

When it comes to sinning and stumbling with our words, we must be especially vigilant. For if we win this battle, other victories will come easier.

YOUR LIFE IN ACTION

In what ways are you prone to stumble with your words
(e.g. through lying, exaggerating, gossiping, etc.)?
Ask God to help you overcome these sinful habits.

> *Behold, I am with you always,*
> *to the end of the age (Matthew 28:20).*

The greatest assignment comes with the highest promise: Christ is with you, never to depart. So sure is this promise that it is part of the very divine nature of Christ and even one of His names ("they shall call his name Immanuel," Matthew 1:23).

No ministry, no sacrifice, no kingdom-building undertaking should be approached apart from the assurance that Christ is with us.

If we cannot boldly ask for or be certain of His presence, we cannot depend on His blessing or rest in His approval. We will more likely be "on our own" because we'll be "doing our own thing." This is individualism, not ministry.

When it comes to disciple making, we can be sure that Christ is with us. We can with confidence urge others to know Him and walk with Him.

We will not be hamstrung by self-interests or distracted by worries of whether we are liked. When we're engaged in disciple making, we can be confident of Christ's presence, His pleasure, and His enabling power.

YOUR LIFE IN ACTION

In what ways are you working to make disciples? If you are not, what adjustments do you need to make in order to bring your life into alignment with the Great Commission?

> *He turns rivers into a desert,*
> *springs of water into thirsty ground,*
> *a fruitful land into a salty waste,*
> *because of the evil of its inhabitants (Psalm 107:33–34).*

Revival is "extraordinary" in the sense of how much is accomplished in a short period of time. Jonathan Edwards, describing what we now call the First Great Awakening, wrote, "God in so remarkable a manner took the work into his own hands, and did as much in a day or two that, under normal circumstances took the entire Christian community, using every means at their disposal . . . more than a year to accomplish."

So in its pace, revival is indeed extraordinary; yet what it accomplishes is a matter of returning the church to what should be its "normal" condition. Just as stream beds are meant to hold life-giving water, so the church is to be a place of refreshing and vibrancy. As the ground is meant to be fertile, so Christians are meant to be spiritually reproductive.

Our shameful state comes about by our willingness to settle for dry stream beds and deserts where rivers should run and vegetation should flourish. Sadly, we among the family of God have grown accustomed to our unrevived condition. We have settled for less water, less life, less God.

YOUR LIFE IN ACTION

Read Psalm 107, and pray for revival in your church and family.

His glory is great through your salvation;
splendor and majesty you bestow on him.
For you make him most blessed forever;
you make him glad with the joy of your presence (Psalm 21:5–6).

The glory of God is our good. Every blessing we enjoy, every victory we celebrate, and every gift we receive is from Him and for Him. ("Every good gift and every perfect gift is from above, coming down from the Father of lights with whom there is no variation or shadow due to change," James 1:17).

Notice that every "you" and "your" in this psalm refers to God, while every "he" and "his" refers to David. As king, David knew a higher level of success and celebration than most (and also a great deal of suffering and setback). One of the things that kept him on track spiritually was his faithful recognition that God was the source of his every blessing.

There are no self-made men or women in God's household. We are each the recipient of God's moment-by-moment grace, provision, and enabling. When we forget this one central truth, we open ourselves to the hollowness of pride.

YOUR LIFE IN ACTION

Read Psalm 21. In prayer, thank God for the truth of James 1:17.

Who can discern his errors? Declare me innocent from hidden faults.
Keep back your servant also from presumptuous sins;
let them not have dominion over me!
Then I shall be blameless,
and innocent of great transgression (Psalm 19:12–13).

There is more sin in us than we know. This was the disheartening news of the law (think Old Testament)—that we cannot compensate for our evil, even through our very best efforts.

But God's mercy covers all of our sin, including that which we can see and that which we cannot. This is the great news of the gospel. Even though the full extent of our sinfulness is not known to us, we are blameless before God in Christ.

Hallelujah!

When we do become aware of our sin, we most certainly should confess it to God. However, knowing that in our human condition we are unable to see all of the evil that is within our own hearts, we rejoice all the more that God has seen our sinfulness and removes its every stain.

YOUR LIFE IN ACTION

Spend some time today rejoicing in the full work of salvation in Christ. Is there a worship song or hymn you might sing to God today in worship?

He sent redemption to his people; he has commanded his covenant forever.
Holy and awesome is his name! (Psalm 111:9).

Our salvation is whole, our ransom fully paid, our debt permanently canceled, because God was the One who completed the transaction. He didn't have to mortgage heaven or put a lien on our goodness. He paid it all because only He *could* pay it all.

Once it was paid, God made a covenant with those He ransomed. This is not a contract whereby He requires any amount of repayment or any form of recompense. It is a covenant that He initiated—the superior with the inferior, the King with the pauper—that by His own stipulation cannot be repealed.

It is an eternal covenant that guarantees life, joy, and unbroken love in His presence. It is a promise of imputed righteousness.

We must remember that we were guilty and condemned, but now we are pardoned and free. May we give our lives to praising our Deliverer, praying for those still imprisoned, and urging them to believe in the one and only hope of salvation.

YOUR LIFE IN ACTION
Pray for your family and friends who have not yet
believed in Jesus Christ.

O LORD, who shall sojourn in your tent?
Who shall dwell on your holy hill? (Psalm 15:1).

Why is the act of worship so important in the life of a believer? Does it really affect our devotion to God or make a difference in the way we live?

In this psalm, using words like *sojourn* and *dwell*, the writer describes what it means to be a welcomed guest of God. This foreshadows our future and eternal living arrangement, our heavenly home, by pondering the lives of those who seek to earnestly worship God now.

Worship gives us the opportunity to express our amazement of God and proclaim His greatness. It is also transformative. It helps us grow in godliness. Consider just a few of the ways this is so, as described in Psalm 15. Worship . . .

- increases our integrity—"walks blamelessly and does what is right"
- raises our sensitivity to falsehood—"speaks truth in his heart"
- pulls us away from worldliness—"a vile person is despised . . . honors those who fear the LORD"
- makes us trustworthy—"swears to his own hurt and does not change"
- gives us a love for justice—"does not take a bribe"

One of the most needed activities in our lives is to worship God. Do it privately, and join others in doing it publicly.

YOUR LIFE IN ACTION

Are you meeting regularly with the family of God to worship
and seek Him? Make sure this is part of your life.
Do not neglect private worship, either.

Continue steadfastly in prayer, being watchful in it with thanksgiving.
At the same time, pray also for us, that God may open to us a door for the word,
to declare the mystery of Christ, on account of which I am in prison—
that I may make it clear, which is how I ought to speak (Colossians 4:2–4).

We have been invited, even commanded, to pray for the matters that concern us directly. In lifting these issues to God, we are acknowledging our dependence on Him and hopefully surrendering our will to His.

Yet our prayers need to reach even further, to other places where the gospel is being proclaimed. We need to pray for the proclaimers and for the hearers. It is our duty and our joy to participate in the work of God in places we will never visit.

You need to hear what God is doing throughout the world; if you're not hearing these stories, seek them out. Modern technology has brought a steady stream of reports from mission agencies, churches, and other organizations God is using to make disciples throughout the world. Pay attention to what God is doing, and pray that His kingdom will grow wherever the seed of His Word is planted.

As you pray for the global witness of the church, listen carefully for news of what God is doing. Your joy will increase, and your faith will enlarge.

YOUR LIFE IN ACTION

Spend time seeking out stories of the gospel at work in your community and other places in the world. Take extra time to thank God for those He is delivering from the domain of darkness.

*We regard no one according to the flesh. Even though we once
regarded Christ according to the flesh, we regard him thus no longer.
Therefore, if anyone is in Christ, he is a new creation. The old has passed away;
behold, the new has come (2 Corinthians 5:16–17).*

Christ brings about many "never again" changes in us. These deep transformations are especially clear in our interpersonal relationships. Good ones are made better, and bad ones can be restored.

Before being in Christ, we could really only relate to others on a superficial level. Even what we might have considered good friendships had a limit to them. We had only our best love, compassion, understanding, or patience to offer.

But that all changed through Christ, because we were made new. Every relationship now has eternal significance and spiritual meaning. Our "regard" has shifted from the limits of our humanity to the unbounded nature of Christ's sacrificial love. Therefore, we . . .

- cannot give up praying for the salvation of those who may be lost

- will never lose the hope or pursuit of reconciliation where a relationship is broken

- set aside any desire for revenge

- rejoice wherever and upon whomever we see God's mercy come

YOUR LIFE IN ACTION

Four items are listed today that characterize
the possible state of various relationships in your life.
What actions do you need to take in any one of these?

Rejoice in hope, be patient in tribulation,
be constant in prayer (Romans 12:12).

Look always forward with the anticipation of eternal rest and glory in the presence of God. This is not naive optimism, for it is coupled to the reality of tribulation and the call to constant prayer. These three—rejoicing in hope, being patient in tribulation, and being constant in prayer—are not easy to do, and we need the reminder today.

Rejoice in hope. This means more than rejoicing that you *have* hope; it is recognizing the condition that will be true in the future no matter how strongly the circumstances of today argue against it. Sick today? You will be perfectly and eternally whole someday. Burdened today? You will be emptied of sorrow and filled with joy someday. Weary or wrestling with sin? Someday you'll live where there will never be the slightest hint of evil.

Be patient in tribulation. Rejoicing in hope will put tribulation in its proper perspective: temporary and fading. No matter how challenging or even agonizing the tribulation of a believer may be, it will ultimately give way to God's glorious restoration brought about through Christ.

Be constant in prayer. How foolish we are to spend a day or an hour without praying to our Father who is in heaven! When we fail in this, we forget that He has all things under control.

YOUR LIFE IN ACTION

Which of these three do you need most today?
Commit this short verse to memory.

*Not that I am speaking of being in need, for I have learned
in whatever situation I am to be content (Philippians 4:11).*

Our human nature drives us to seek comfort, sometimes to the
point of risking friendships and reputation. We need to learn
that contentment is far better.

Paul's words in Philippians 4:11 reveal three truths about contentment:

Contentment must be learned. It is not in our human nature to be
settled and joyful when there are still things we want that we don't
have; but when our hearts are turned to God, the switchover to contentment begins. We learn to want what He wants and to accept what
He gives.

**Contentment recognizes circumstances but does not depend on
them.** Content people have good days and bad ones. Some content
people are wealthy, and some are poor. Paul slept in palaces and
dungeons, and ate the food of kings and criminals. Contentment
took him to places of ministry opportunity that comfort would
never have gone.

Contentment makes one generous. Paul wanted the readers of his
letter to understand that he was not playing on their sympathies or
trying to manipulate them. He was verbalizing a truth that had so
liberated his life, he hoped they would learn it too.

YOUR LIFE IN ACTION

How has God used your various life circumstances, whether wealth,
need, health, sickness, etc., to give you opportunities for sharing
and demonstrating your faith in Christ?

Jesus, perceiving in himself that power had gone out from him, immediately
turned about in the crowd and said, "Who touched my garments?" . . .
But the woman, knowing what had happened to her, came in fear and trembling
and fell down before him and told him the whole truth. And he said to her,
"Daughter, your faith has made you well; go in peace, and be healed
of your disease" (Mark 5:30, 33–34).

All that mattered to this woman was getting to Jesus. After years of suffering, trying this cure and that, she was desperate. So broken was this dear lady, she was down to her last hope. Suffering had brought her to simple faith in Christ alone. She believed He was the only one who could help her.

God had arranged matters so that Jesus was in her vicinity that very day (divine appointments often look like coincidences), so she put all her energy into getting to Him. Something (Someone) told her that if she could just touch Jesus' garment, she would be healed.

This story should not be taken as a universal promise of healing. Doubtless there were other sick people in the crowd that day who went away just as ill as when they arrived. The point is this: Regardless of the nature or cause of your suffering, know that there is One who cares about you supremely.

In your desperation, move toward your Savior, not away from Him. Draw near. Seek, as it were, to touch His garment. The hardships we encounter shape us more than most other circumstances, because desperation will activate either our fear or our faith.

YOUR LIFE IN ACTION

Are you in a season of hardship and suffering right now?
Are you moving toward Jesus?

We have not made use of this right, but we endure anything rather than put an obstacle in the way of the gospel of Christ (1 Corinthians 9:12).

How much does the gospel mean to you? Imagine loving the gospel so much that you would endure anything to see it spread, bringing the message of eternal life to family members, friends, neighbors, strangers, and even enemies.

Again, how much does the gospel mean to you? To Paul and others like him, the gospel meant everything. He was willing to set aside every desire and right he had if these proved in any way to be an obstacle to others hearing the good news about Jesus Christ.

To a world (and sadly, often to the body of Christ) that elevates the selfish demands of the individual above the call to righteousness, this sounds strange. And it should, for we are "indeed sojourners and exiles" here (1 Peter 2:11). Our outlook should be firmly set on the advance of the gospel; and that means we will sometimes, perhaps often, need to relinquish our grip on what we want, if getting it would mean the spread of the gospel would be hindered.

Our pursuit of all earthly things, even those that are not sinful, and sometimes even those we rightly deserve, should be seriously and prayerfully thought of alongside the role God has for us in the advance of the gospel to the world. Would such prayerful consideration lead us to set any of these aside?

YOUR LIFE IN ACTION

Ask God: Is there anything I am pursuing that, if I get it,
might be an obstacle to others hearing and believing
the message of the gospel?

I will praise you with an upright heart,
when I learn your righteous rules (Psalm 119:7).

An unmistakable correlation exists between our obedience to God and our capacity for thankfulness. In fact, our obedience is an expression of gratitude—a classic case of actions speaking louder than words.

We know that thankfulness is a core characteristic of believers. Sadly, we sometimes try to replace the heart of gratitude with mere words of appreciation.

This is not to say the words are meaningless, but they are really only currency, whereas a truly thankful heart is the gold standard. Our heart assigns value to our words, never vice versa.

Even more telling than our words, however, is our behavior—displayed through both actions and attitudes. Behavior is the grand revealer of the heart.

Obedience compels us to be thankful, and thankfulness compels us to obey. The growth of one brings vibrancy to the other.

YOUR LIFE IN ACTION

Today, concentrate on obeying God in the things you know
He wants you to do. Let these acts of obedience be
your expressions of true thankfulness.

Let the insolent be put to shame, because they have wronged me with falsehood;
as for me, I will meditate on your precepts (Psalm 119:78).

Are you familiar with the phrase "driven to distraction"? It could be used to describe a condition that many believers suffer from at various times along the way.

One day we are living with purpose and intention, and the next we are unmotivated and uncertain. What should we do when we are spiritually adrift?

For the writer of this psalm, the answer was clear: do the will of God that you *know* is the will of God ("meanwhile I will concentrate on your commandments" NLT), and don't allow any bit of uncertainty to stop your overall progress.

Even in a whirlwind of circumstances he could neither understand nor control, the psalmist knew enough of God's will to keep himself joyfully occupied. Most likely you do too.

YOUR LIFE IN ACTION

As specifically as you can, list five things you *know* are
God's will for you to do today.

> *Greatly have they afflicted me from my youth,*
> *yet they have not prevailed against me (Psalm 129:2).*

You may sometimes be down, but you'll never be out. Why, because you are strong? No, because you are in Christ.

It would be wise to keep this truth close at hand: "In the world you will have tribulation. But take heart; I have overcome the world" (John 16:33). Persecution and other hardship will not let us go until we leave this world. As long as we align our lives with Christ, some people will oppose and even hate us.

Our best response to this hostility will come by knowing that we are not the real target—Christ is. He told us so long ago, "If the world hates you, know that it has hated me before it hated you. . . . Because you are not of the world, but I chose you out of the world, therefore the world hates you. . . . All these things they will do to you on account of my name" (John 15:18–21).

Those who mistreat, slander, and abuse the gospel and its followers need our prayers, not our vengeance.

YOUR LIFE IN ACTION

What anti-Christian activity are you seeing or hearing about
in our culture? Pray for those who are being deceived by it,
and for those who are behind it.

*I bow down toward your holy temple and give thanks to your name
for your steadfast love and your faithfulness,
for you have exalted above all things
your name and your word (Psalm 138:2).*

The Word of God is backed by the honor of His name. Its every warning carries His signature, its every promise comes with His personal guarantee. He has spoken its truth and endorsed its teaching.

Therefore, we must never take God's Word as a mere helpful text for enduring life's challenges, for He has exalted His Word as He has exalted His name. His Word represents Him, and as such is a principal way through which we know Him.

The Word of God is holy. We often hear the Word of God described as being "personal," and it is—not because it is *to* us but because it is *from* Him. We are not its theme—God is.

To be a student of God's Word is to be a seeker of God Himself. Approach His Word with the reverential anticipation of coming to understand more about Him, and you will come away with unshakable peace and confidence. Anchor your thoughts in God's Word, and you will establish yourself in the security of His unending presence.

YOUR LIFE IN ACTION

What other Scripture passages can you think of that speak
about the power and holiness of God's Word?

> *Search me, O God, and know my heart!*
> *Try me and know my thoughts!*
> *And see if there be any grievous way in me,*
> *and lead me in the way everlasting! (Psalm 139:23–24).*

This psalm opens with the recognition that God has searched and known the heart of the writer, and closes with a prayer that He will continue to do the same. Why this desire, this longing to be known by God, and then to have Him reveal what He finds?

When it gets quiet enough to listen, the Christian soul wants nothing more than it wants intimacy with God; and by its very nature, intimacy requires honesty. There can be nothing hidden, nothing off limits from being known.

And then, once known, it is revealed so that the behavior, or attitude, or fear, or loss, or whatever it may be can be properly dealt with. Is it a sin to be repented of, a longing to be pursued, a relationship to be mended . . . ?

God searches that He might reveal; He reveals that He may put right that which is broken, unwholesome, or incomplete. Be sure of this, and make this psalm your prayer.

YOUR LIFE IN ACTION

Are you allowing God to search and know you? If you are, how has this level of intimacy deepened your love for and trust in God?

OUR BENEVOLENT FATHER

---

*The LORD upholds all who are falling
and raises up all who are bowed down (Psalm 145:14).*

The Lord is good. He is kind and benevolent. He treats His children with great care and affection. He is attentive to their needs and quick to show them mercy.

It is through His benevolent nature that we experience the height, depth, and breadth of God's love. He does for us what we cannot do for ourselves. He literally helps the helpless, for such we all were before Christ.

Following Christ's ascension, the body of Christ became the feet that go and the hands that serve; we are the visible demonstration of God to the world. He is benevolent through us.

Our acts of mercy—giving "to the least of these," serving the needy and distraught, showing kindness to the hostile, or being patiently persistent with the self-destructing—foreshadow the gospel. We give what we have received.

YOUR LIFE IN ACTION

In what ways can you exercise benevolence in your community,
praying that it will open hearts to the gospel?

> *If you were of the world, the world would love you as its own;*
> *but because you are not of the world, but I chose you out of the world,*
> *therefore the world hates you (John 15:19).*

Hatred is an ugly and unsettling thing. No one wants to be truly hated, yet hatred exists. In fact, it seems to be on the upswing in our world. People are filled with rage and triggered for outburst.

It is not a new phenomenon for Christians to be hated for the mere fact that they are Christians. They love the One the world hates most of all.

So, how do we handle being hated for our association with Christ? By first of all recognizing that the target of this hatred is Christ in us.

This reality should awaken mercy in us rather than revenge—a longing that those enslaved to hatred will themselves be delivered from the domain of darkness and transferred to the kingdom of Jesus Christ (Colossians 1:13).

Speaking of which, another means of enduring hatred is to remember that we have been chosen out of the world. Were it not for Christ, we would be among the haters.

YOUR LIFE IN ACTION

Pray for those who oppose you for your faith in Christ;
for haters of Christ worldwide; and for your brothers and sisters
whose lives are in danger because of this hatred.

*"The simple are killed by their turning away,
and the complacency of fools destroys them;
but whoever listens to me will dwell secure
and will be at ease, without dread of disaster"* (Proverbs 1:32–33).

Indifference can be deadly. Surely this is true in terms of rejecting the gospel, yet we must also wonder what damage we do to our own and others' souls through complacent living.

Has God warned you of the presence of sin in your life? Have you explained away your disobedience as only delay (*I'll deal with it later*)?

Has the Holy Spirit urged you to give assistance or encouragement? Have you stiff-armed His prompting because what He asks is inconvenient? Are you putting off obedience in any way for any reason?

Dietrich Bonhoeffer observed, "Silence in the face of evil is itself evil: God will not hold us guiltless. Not to speak is to speak. Not to act is to act."

Our indifference may not be deadly in the literal sense, as in the case of Bonhoeffer standing up to Hitler's evil forces; but if we try to side-step God's will in lesser things, how likely is it that we will be faithful if and when lives are on the line? Let's be honest enough to admit that souls are on the line every day, and not a solitary believer can be indifferent to that.

YOUR LIFE IN ACTION

Ask God to reveal any indifference in your life, and commit to taking whatever action He may lead you to take.

*So you will walk in the way of the good
and keep to the paths of the righteous (Proverbs 2:20).*

There is nothing but good in seeking wisdom, which in biblical terms means seeking Jesus Christ, who is wisdom personified. The second chapter of Proverbs describes both the honor and the value of wholeheartedly pursuing wisdom.

One of the benefits is the great companionship you find among those who are on the same path—the fellowship of the wisdom seekers. They are from every ethnicity, income level, and background. That which binds them is Christ alone; in light of Him, any differences fade away.

They are mutually strengthened as they hear and observe the work of God in one another's lives. Each living testimony expands their understanding of how God works, increases each one's faith regarding their own circumstances, and enriches their thanksgiving and joy in God.

You don't walk this way alone, so do not isolate yourself from the fellowship you need. It is a gift from God.

YOUR LIFE IN ACTION

Are you living in true heart connection with other saints?
If not, ask God to bring you into fellowship with others who are
serious about knowing and serving God.

If you are wise, you are wise for yourself;
if you scoff, you alone will bear it (Proverbs 9:12).

In our humanity we are prone to finger-pointing. We claim that our failures and shortcomings are mostly the fault of someone else.

Blame is our factory setting. Even if we eventually accept personal responsibility, we've probably had a long hard fight with our emotions to get there.

The wise person takes responsibility. He "owns" his infirmity—and propensity to sin—with graceful humility.

This is a strange concept to the worldly and foolish, who see any such admission as weakness. But it is quite the opposite; those who blame push away wisdom and continue on in self-delusion. Their pride weakens them.

On the other hand, the wise are made stronger and more secure through their humble and honest self-perception. They know how dependent they are on God and are quick to admit it. And at the very least, their wisdom is rewarded with more wisdom.

YOUR LIFE IN ACTION
Read Proverbs 8.

> *When words are many, transgression is not lacking,*
> *but whoever restrains his lips is prudent (Proverbs 10:19).*

Some Scripture doesn't require much commentary. The words are clear and the message straightforward—and in this case more than a little convicting.

The more we talk, the greater the likelihood we will say something regrettable, even sinful. This doesn't mean that words are in themselves evil, though a few certainly are, but that speaking them (or writing them, or texting them) requires a great deal of wisdom, thoughtfulness, and restraint.

Proverbs aren't commands per se, but observations about life to guide those who want to be wise. It comes as no surprise, then, that biblical proverbs point to words as the dominant tipping point between wisdom and folly.

Therefore, if we want to live wisely—and godly—we should concentrate on our speech. We should measure our words, always remembering that careless speech edges us toward the sin zone.

YOUR LIFE IN ACTION

Be alert to what you say and how much you talk today.
What did you learn today that will help you
measure your words tomorrow?

HONESTLY?

*The righteousness of the blameless keeps his way straight,
but the wicked falls by his own wickedness (Proverbs 11:5).*

Many people like to think of themselves as being "an honest person," and will boldly profess to being so. The problem is that this profession is generally made at a time when their credibility is in doubt. Their walk brings their talk into question.

The truth of the matter is that honesty is much more than an event-based behavior, wherein we might tell outright lies in one circumstance, hide a few facts in another, and tell the whole truth in yet another.

Honesty is not situational; it is a lifestyle of blamelessness (some Bible versions interchange the words *blameless* and *honest*). An honest person is one whose conscience is clear of any and all duplicity; and this covers more territory than just lie- or truth-telling.

On one level, Christ has made us blameless, and our sins can no longer condemn us. But until we reach our glorified state, we will contend with sin.

We strive to live out now, albeit imperfectly, what we one day will actually be. For this reason every believer should work to be "an honest person" (a blameless person) who lives obediently toward God and is quick to seek forgiveness from Him and others when necessary.

YOUR LIFE IN ACTION

In your own words describe what it means to live a blameless life.

> *Righteousness exalts a nation,*
> *but sin is a reproach to any people (Proverbs 14:34).*

We may want many things for our nation—we want it to be debt-free, prosperous, strong, secure, peaceful, unified . . . And if we're honest, we probably want these things for what they could mean to us personally and to our family.

Here's a question that every believer should ponder: If the standing of our nation is ultimately a matter of righteousness, as today's passage indicates, are you a contributor to or a detractor from our nation's strength?

To be sure, only those who know God can be righteous, so our nation's best hope is not in the branches of government but in the branches that abide in the "true vine" (John 15:1, 5).

Proverbs 14:34 is a call to holiness and therefore a compelling vision for revival.

"We" inside the church, not "they" on the outside, are the hope of the nation. As citizens of the eternal kingdom, let us be light to this and every kingdom that is fading away.

YOUR LIFE IN ACTION

Pray today for your church and the church throughout our nation.
Pray that believers will live righteously and with
an urgency for spiritual awakening.

The LORD has made everything for its purpose,
even the wicked for the day of trouble (Proverbs 16:4).

Faith and understanding are not contradictory, but there is often tension between the two. When God's ways or purposes are not clear to us, we strive to understand, while at the same time positioning our hearts to accept what we cannot know.

This is why we so often get to the point of clinging to the goodness of God in the darkness. We lean on the fact that "my thoughts are not your thoughts, neither are your ways my ways, declares the LORD. For as the heavens are higher than the earth, so are my ways higher than your ways and my thoughts than your thoughts" (Isaiah 55:8–9). Where our understanding falls short, faith takes the lead.

"The LORD has made everything for its purpose" should be viewed as a fact, not a promise. We won't always comprehend His purposes, or in some cases even agree with them.

We can always know—and therefore rest in the fact—that God is in control. His purposes are good and will be accomplished. It is our privilege to participate in them, even when (perhaps especially when) they are beyond our understanding.

YOUR LIFE IN ACTION

Give thanks today that God includes you in the
working out of His purposes.

*The heart of the wise makes his speech judicious
and adds persuasiveness to his lips (Proverbs 16:23).*

Wise people say wise things because they think wise thoughts. Their minds are disciplined; that is, they are under control—not just under their own control, but under the Savior's control.

Therefore wise people are on alert to keep their minds from wandering. They do this by *setting* their minds (Colossians 3:2) and *taking* "every thought captive to obey Christ" (2 Corinthians 10:5).

Where have your thoughts been today? Did they get there by free-ranging, or did you take them there? More importantly, did the Savior take them there?

Our words carry great influence; we can transmit either high or low ideas, words of life or words of death. And because our words are transmitted from our thoughts, our words will move the hearer in the same direction our thoughts have directed us.

YOUR LIFE IN ACTION

Think back over your conversations of the past twenty-four hours.
In what ways have your words influenced others?

Fine speech is not becoming to a fool;
still less is false speech to a prince (Proverbs 17:7).

Sometimes our words are weaponized. Having been both the sender and the receiver of hurtful speech, we are acquainted with the damage it can bring.

Gossip, slander, degrading comments, false accusations, and rumor mongering are but a few of the missiles we fire at people who are not our enemies.

Lying is perhaps the most destructive way in which we can launch our words. Once spoken, we have no control over the range of our words or their effect.

Even if we apologize and seek forgiveness, there is often irreparable damage to those we have disappointed, misled, or involved in our deception. Beyond that is the cloud we've cast over our own integrity.

As believers in truth, we ought to be truth-tellers.

YOUR LIFE IN ACTION

Purpose to be truthful in all things, big and small.
How does a basic commitment to always telling the truth
help you grow in godliness?

From the fruit of a man's mouth his stomach is satisfied;
he is satisfied by the yield of his lips.
Death and life are in the power of the tongue,
and those who love it will eat its fruits (Proverbs 18:20–21).

Have you ever walked away from a conversation and thought, *I wish I would have said* _____, or, *I wish I hadn't said* _____?

Wise people—godly people—try to be selective with their words. They want their words to be life-giving. They have not only the motive to express themselves properly, but also the desire to help the hearer and to exalt God.

Our words have consequences, sometimes lingering ones. What we say, or fail to say, often hangs in the hearer's memory and heart. Our communication has given them a dose of life or an inkling of death. We've moved them forward in their pursuit of God, or we've perhaps caused them to stumble over doubt and discouragement.

We will be more careful with our words when our focus is first on exalting God, second on loving the listener, and a distant third on saying what's on our mind.

YOUR LIFE IN ACTION

Whose words have recently encouraged you and helped you
progress in your spiritual life? Reach out to that person
and thank them.

A man's steps are from the LORD;
how then can man understand his way? (Proverbs 20:24).

The fact that God is always in control—if we believe it so fully that we live accordingly—is a tremendous help in applying the means of grace in our every situation.

Because we know that we are never alone, and that God is at the helm of the universe (and beyond), we can live with a holy and settled confidence. God enables us to:

- rest in His irrevocable salvation
- rejoice in Him equally in seasons of happiness and in days of difficulty
- respond to loneliness as a call to draw nearer to Him
- return good for evil
- love and pray for our enemies
- remember His past goodness in the face of present need

There are two things we need to tell ourselves every day: (1) God is great, and (2) God is good. So long as He does not change, we are safe.

YOUR LIFE IN ACTION
Read Romans 8:31–39.

> *A man without self-control is like a city*
> *broken into and left without walls (Proverbs 25:28).*

An undisciplined person is an endangered person, and his greatest threats come from within. Having given in time and again to lust, anger, or any other self-indulgence, he is bombarded by nearly relentless temptation. His foolishness has made him weak.

The image of a city that has been "broken into and left without walls" is of a place that will be pillaged repeatedly. It represents the man who has given himself over to low living and no longer gives even a show of resistance. He lives with chronic infirmity, leanness of soul.

There is good news, however. Christ is a rebuilder of walls.

Many defeats do not mean that victory is impossible. But that man must choose to surrender now to a different victor—one who will be his Savior.

We were all without walls at one time, and still would be were it not for Christ. Let us remember what He has done in us, and remain surrendered to Him.

YOUR LIFE IN ACTION

In what areas of your life do you need God to help you become more disciplined? How can you surrender to Him in these areas?

As in water face reflects face,
so the heart of man reflects the man (Proverbs 27:19).

Your heart is an open book to God (Proverbs 21:2) and perhaps to others. Is this good news to you or bad? Would you rather hide "the real you" or be known?

When it comes to being known by God, you really have no choice. And because His intentions for His children are always good, you can be assured that God's intimate knowledge of your heart is a good thing. You should welcome it.

Being fully known and still lavishly loved is a constant reminder that your salvation was all one-sided. There was no earning on your part, only receiving.

Being known by God also frees you from pretending for others to be someone you are not. You can live and therefore love them from a place of liberty, no longer bound up by trying to make the right impression in hopes of their acceptance.

God's acceptance has made you real, true, and right. This posture of soul then enables you to speak to others with gladness about the Savior who can set them free as well.

YOUR LIFE IN ACTION

What does it mean to you that God knows everything about you?

> *Whoever rebukes a man will afterward find more favor*
> *than he who flatters with his tongue (Proverbs 28:23).*

When rebuke is needed but we choose to flatter instead, we miss out on an opportunity to help someone grow in godliness. We choose to take the easy road rather than the best road. For the price of our own insecurity (*"They may not like me if I say _____"*), we let a friend continue down a path of sin, failure, or (in worst cases) destruction without a word of warning.

To be sure, we should never be so quick to rebuke that we overlook our own motives. We must be prayerful and thoughtful.

However, when rebuke is needed, let us not hold back in fear. This means, as today's verse indicates, that we must keep the long view in mind.

What matters most is not how the one rebuked responds initially, but whether he returns to a trajectory toward godliness. We really do have this kind of responsibility for one another in the body of Christ.

So do not be hasty in rebuke, but do not neglect it either. Do not flatter, but speak the truth in love.

YOUR LIFE IN ACTION

Have you ever been rebuked in a way that helped restore you?
What have the results of that rebuke been?

---

*Let us come into his presence with thanksgiving;
let us make a joyful noise to him with songs of praise! (Psalm 95:2).*

This is a season of thanksgiving in the United States. Thanksgiving Day is a day theoretically set aside to acknowledging the goodness and provision of God to our nation.

And while it is true that God is revered less and less in our culture, as members of His household let us never neglect—on this day or any other—the beauty of counting our blessings and thanking God for each one.

Here are five simple prompts to help you. Thank God for:

- Faith—for awakening your heart to believe in Jesus Christ for salvation

- Family—both immediate and extended

- Friends—the people with whom you share life and influence

- Provision—food, clothing, shelter, and so much more

- Mission—a purpose for living that is eternal

YOUR LIFE IN ACTION

Pray through each of these five categories, and thank
God for what He has done for you and given you in each one.
Be as specific as possible.

> *Bless the Lord, O my soul,*
> *and forget not all his benefits (Psalm 103:2).*

Remembering is the beginning point of thanksgiving. Those who most remember what God has done are faithful to give thanks, thereby keeping their faith in Him vibrant.

On the other hand, those who are ungrateful and take God's goodness for granted are generally weak in faith and long in doubt.

Pastor and author Crawford Loritts wrote, "Finding it hard to be grateful? There is a relationship between memory and gratitude. Think about where you came from."

As a personal expression of thanksgiving during this special season, think of the many ways God has spiritually developed and formed you.

Beginning with salvation, think of the occasions, people, and circumstances He has used to move you forward in your journey of Christianity. Thank Him for each one.

YOUR LIFE IN ACTION

Today, let your memory of God's work in you
move you to give thanks.

*Thus says the One who is high and lifted up, who inhabits eternity,
whose name is Holy: "I dwell in the high and holy place, and also with him
who is of a contrite and lowly spirit, to revive the spirit of the lowly,
and to revive the heart of the contrite" (Isaiah 57:15).*

When God disciplines us, He generally does so by bringing one of the following into our lives:

- a difficult person
- a traumatic event
- a heightened sense of conviction over personal sin

Do you have any irritating people in your life? Are you willing to accept the possibility that God placed them there for your good, perhaps to teach you to be longsuffering and forgiving?

Have you suffered any trauma to your soul? Can you allow room for God to use that deep hurt to soften your heart and increase your endurance and compassion?

Are you aware of particular sins in your life that are causing shame to you and pain to loved ones? God may be preparing you for greater fruitfulness by first putting you into an attention-getting season of endurance.

Whatever the trouble might be in your life, there is generally more at stake than just that issue. Does God want you to make every legitimate effort to love that difficult person? Yes. Does God want you to heal from trauma? Yes. Does God want you free from sin's power? Yes. And through it all God wants to produce in you a humble, contrite spirit.

YOUR LIFE IN ACTION

Take stock of the people and circumstances troubling you
right now. Ask God to open your heart to the ways He wants to work
in your life, through these, to make you more like Jesus.

> *"And though a tenth remain in it, it will be burned again,*
> *like a terebinth or an oak, whose stump remains when it is felled."*
> *The holy seed is its stump (Isaiah 6:13).*

The faithful ones—the remnant—are evidence that Christ is still advancing His kingdom. Though history records several instances when Christianity seemed to be in decline, it has never reported its demise.

Nor will it. Christ and His church are very much alive; throughout the world people are being born again every day.

"The holy seed is its stump." Though God had disciplined His people, and many of them literally died, He did not destroy them. Those He left on earth were more sure than ever that their purpose was to live for His glory and not their own. The remnant was vibrant—not just breathing, but multiplying.

Our presence on earth today as believers is no less a call to kingdom living than was the preservation of God's faithful ones in the Old Testament. We too are here for Him and not for ourselves. We are representatives of His eternal kingdom.

YOUR LIFE IN ACTION

How are you serving the kingdom?

> *You did not look to him who did it,*
> *or see him who planned it long ago (Isaiah 22:11).*

The people of God are prone to commit two follies when they encounter hardship and testing.

- We don't consider the possibility that God is disciplining us, even though the Bible makes it clear that He sometimes does this very thing. Hebrews 12:7 says, "It is for discipline that you have to endure." This means that our difficulties sometimes come directly from the hand of God for the best of reasons: to draw us back into an obedient and loving closeness to Him.

- We don't ask for God's help. As foolish as it sounds, we may find ourselves hours, days, or even longer into an overwhelming situation, only to realize that we have not called on God to intervene. We've limited our perspective to only what we see, feel, and think, and are therefore extending our stay and increasing our stress.

What a shame and folly it would be to endure your present hardships without seeking the Lord in the midst of them. Who knows what God has in mind?

YOUR LIFE IN ACTION

What are some of the ways God has shaped your life through hardship and testing?

> *Not that I am speaking of being in need,*
> *for I have learned in whatever situation I am*
> *to be content (Philippians 4:11).*

Contentment is learned. After wrestling through days of abundance, or need, or both, we come out knowing that God is faithful to His promises. Yet we may still choose to waste days wanting things we do not need, distracted from seeing just how good God is to us.

Lust and covetousness make our journey more difficult than it needs to be. By looking at what others have, and wanting it for ourselves, we are entangling our souls in a weave of comparison that leads to discontentment.

If we were to look up from the here and now and realize that we can trust our heavenly Provider to know what we need—and to be sure that we get it when we need it—we could free our hearts to enjoy Him again. This would also move our thoughts forward into the reality of His eternal presence, which we will one day know forever and ever.

Discontentment in a believer's life comes not so much from not having things we want as it does from not believing that the One who has promised to care for us really does. Discontentment signals a move away from God; therefore the remedy cannot be found at the outlet mall. Instead, let our discontentment drive us back to our faithful, life-giving, promise-keeping God.

YOUR LIFE IN ACTION

Have you been living a distracted life due to discontentment?
Read Ephesians 2 to be reminded of what God has done for you.

> *Whether you eat or drink, or whatever you do,*
> *do all to the glory of God (1 Corinthians 10:31).*

Think of the glory of God as the sum total of all His attributes on display. Imagine seeing God's love, mercy, justice, grace, sovereignty, eternality (to name just a few) all working together at the same time.

It would be overwhelming, which explains why Moses, Abraham, Isaiah, and others were actually in fear of seeing God. Their humanity could not receive it; neither can ours.

Scripture lays out two primary means by which God displays His glory: through the heavens and earth He created (Psalm 19; 104), and by making mankind to bear His image (Genesis 1:26–28). These showcase His brilliance, beauty, and love, yet they only give a glimpse of all that God is.

Again, we cannot take in His glory. When we reach the end of our comprehension, the outskirts of His glory are not yet in view.

These thoughts actually lead us to ask: How do we glorify God? The answer in part is: We bring Him glory by doing the most common things for the greatest of purposes. All of our activities—even those as basic as eating and drinking—should be done with His glory in mind.

YOUR LIFE IN ACTION

Think about some of the common things you do each day
(things like eating, resting, talking, working).
How can you do these things to the glory of God?

I therefore, a prisoner for the Lord, urge you to walk in a manner worthy of the calling to which you have been called (Ephesians 4:1).

In every twist and turn of his life, Paul saw each event against the backdrop of his relationship with Jesus Christ. If he sorrowed, he sorrowed in Christ. If he rejoiced, he rejoiced in Christ. Suffering, successful, loved, or abandoned, he was who he was and did what he did for the cause of Christ and the gospel. Even as a prisoner.

Paul personified the strength of keeping a godly perspective in all circumstances. Through his example, we learn that trying to figure out the scope, meaning, and purpose of our circumstances, especially the difficult ones, is generally futile.

On the other hand, pursuing Christ within all circumstances builds our faith. Though we may at first wonder why a certain trial has come, we can and should move as quickly as possible to the more productive question, *What now?* This gets us to the place of determining how we can best "walk worthy" in the context of our present realities.

Paul's role as prisoner did not silence or intimidate him. He continued to write, teach, and make disciples from prison. His message only grew in intensity. It was not that he was a "prisoner" that mattered most to him, but that he was a "prisoner for the Lord."

YOUR LIFE IN ACTION

In what various circumstances has God used you to further His kingdom?

Little children, keep yourselves from idols (1 John 5:21).

You probably don't have a graven image in your house. But you might have idols.

The people to whom John wrote lived in an idol-saturated culture. Nearly any desire they had could be expressed by showing allegiance to one god or another.

Idol worship was pervasive, and John knew that a profession of faith in Christ would not ensure that the bonds were broken; some would give up on the invisible God to return to something they could see and feel. Others would grow jealous of their idolatrous neighbors and rejoin them in immediate carnal pleasure, thereby forsaking the promise of fullness of joy that would come at a later time.

Idols are as appealing now as they were then, regardless of what form they may take. Our society is not known for its graven images, but it is as populated with God-replacements as any civilization in history.

For this reason we must be vigilant to keep ourselves from idols—that is, from giving to anything or anyone that which belongs to God Himself, the greatest of our love, loyalty, and worship.

YOUR LIFE IN ACTION

Can you think of any possession, activity, person, or desire in your life that competes with your true heart devotion to God? What changes do you need to make to keep yourself from idols?

> *Give thanks to the LORD, for he is good,*
> *for his steadfast love endures forever (Psalm 136:1).*

Does your life have a reprise? In musical or lyrical terms, a reprise is a repetition—a phrase that is repeated in order to point to its significance. A reprise is a memorable way to capture truth in words.

Psalm 136 employs the reprise "his steadfast love endures forever" twenty-six times. The theme of the psalm is God's supremacy over all—a supremacy that can never be detached from His enduring love.

God's rule over us is never tyrannical but always paternal; He is an ever-present and connected Father. Because this truth dominated the psalmist's thinking, and because he wanted others to understand its significance, he worded his reprise accordingly: *[God's] steadfast love endures forever.*

What is your reprise? What truth about God do you want to dominate your thoughts?

YOUR LIFE IN ACTION

Using ten words or fewer, write your reprise about God.

When the Helper comes, whom I will send to you from the Father,
the Spirit of truth, who proceeds from the Father, he will bear witness about me.
And you also will bear witness, because you have been with me
from the beginning (John 15:26–27).

What do you and the Holy Spirit have in common? As seen in today's Scripture, you share a divine purpose: to "bear witness" about Jesus Christ.

As a believer, you are indwelt by the Holy Spirit. He is ever present and always pressing you to do the Father's will.

This explains why you have feelings of futility or of being unfulfilled when you neglect your personal spiritual development and service. You are, in those days, failing to live out your purpose.

No matter how busy you may keep yourself, or even how successful you may become at other things, if you are giving no part of your life (and it should be the best part) to bearing witness about Christ, you are adrift.

Have you set aside your true and highest purpose? It is time to reengage.

YOUR LIFE IN ACTION

What does it mean for you personally to
"bear witness" about Christ?

The earth will be filled with the knowledge of the glory of the LORD as the waters cover the sea (Habakkuk 2:14).

What a majestic scene this Scripture puts before us! As far as the eye can see, there is only God's glory. No blemish, no interruption.

Can you imagine such an exhibition? Wouldn't it be . . . heavenly?

It would be, and it will be, for it is reality. *The earth [shall we say, "The new earth"] will be filled with the knowledge of the glory of the LORD.*

Everywhere we look and in any direction we may go, we will be in the midst of God's glory. It will be.

To know that it will be so makes us long for it, sometimes even to the point of impatience.

But may we also be compelled to pray for our neighbors and for the nations, that many more will come into the kingdom of God through Christ before it is too late. Let us remember that this time of waiting is God's mercy on them.

YOUR LIFE IN ACTION

Pray with urgency for those in your community who are not believers in Jesus. Choose a nation that needs to hear the gospel, and pray for the people to receive it and believe it.

Wait for the LORD; be strong, and let your heart take courage;
wait for the LORD! (Psalm 27:14).

What does it mean to wait for the Lord? When we think of waiting, two images typically come to mind: (1) being suspended in time until a particular need is met, certain news is delivered, or our name is called, or (2) serving the needs of another. A job applicant illustrates the first form of waiting, and a restaurant server illustrates the second. And both illustrate what it means to wait on the Lord.

If we are waiting on the Lord, we are in a faith-filled environment. But be warned—and surely you already know this—that this faith will be tested. We are waiting rather than moving out on our own because we acknowledge that God knows best. He sees what we cannot, and He can move obstacles that our best efforts could never budge. We need God to act.

Yet we also know that much like the wait staff at a restaurant, waiting is not passive. In fact it can be some of our most active days. Waiting is a call to fervent prayer and to warring against our own impatience.

And interestingly, while we wait on God, He often deploys us to wait on (serve) others. It's as if He has awakened in us a sensitivity that has been long dormant, and we are compelled to be part of meeting the needs we suddenly see. Waiting, you see, changes us.

YOUR LIFE IN ACTION

In what ways has God changed your life
during a season of waiting?

Say to them, "Thus says the Lord God: 'Any one of the house of Israel who takes his idols into his heart and sets the stumbling block of his iniquity before his face, and yet comes to the prophet, I the Lord will answer him as he comes with the multitude of his idols, that I may lay hold of the hearts of the house of Israel, who are all estranged from me through their idols'" (Ezekiel 14:4–5).

God's holy purpose is to make Himself known—to sooner or later convince every doubter and denier that He alone is Lord.

When the rebellious leaders of Israel approached Ezekiel to give them a prophetic utterance (Why? They certainly had no intention of obeying it . . .), it was God they provoked more than Ezekiel.

To the prophet it was just a waste of time and words; to God it was rebellion. Even so, God spoke through His prophet, and the message would serve His purpose even though the hearers did not receive it.

Why would God not rather meet their demands with silence (or a lightning bolt)? Because there was still hope for some. A few hearts and minds in the crowd of eavesdroppers could still be captured and restored to the Lord.

Rejecting the idolatrous rebels would prove Him Lord, as would restoring the repenters. This has not changed; may God's men and women therefore continue to speak of Him.

YOUR LIFE IN ACTION

What Scriptures and truths about God have made
the greatest impression on you about His divine nature?

I lift up my eyes to the hills.
From where does my help come?
My help comes from the LORD,
who made heaven and earth.
He will not let your foot be moved;
he who keeps you will not slumber.
Behold, he who keeps Israel
will neither slumber nor sleep (Psalm 121:1–4).

God is awake, aware, alert, and attentive . . . always. God is never distracted; He never looks away. There are no gaps in His watchfulness, no lapses in His love.

Do you not marvel that this is so—that God is constantly watching over you? This is not because you (we) are so interesting. It's not because we've earned His attention.

This is the extension of His abundant mercy. He never abandons those He has set His love on.

What joy there is, what freedom and security in being watched over by God in this way!

YOUR LIFE IN ACTION
Write out a prayer of thanks today for God's watch care over you.

My soul continually remembers [my affliction and my wanderings]
and is bowed down within me. But this I call to mind, and therefore I have hope:
The steadfast love of the LORD never ceases; his mercies never come to an end;
they are new every morning; great is your faithfulness.
"The LORD is my portion," says my soul,
"therefore I will hope in him" (Lamentation 3:20–24).

Grief provokes memories, some of remorse and regret and others of "the good old days" when life was so much better. Lamentations, as the name implies, is a book of grieving—grieving with a purpose, that is. These verses make up its most recognized passage.

Remembering is a bridge that transitions us from remorse and sadness toward hope and new beginnings. Recalling God's goodness is restorative, breaking through the gloom and offering forgotten perspective. We dare not forget what God has done and who He is.

How do we protect our hearts from forgetting God's love, mercy, and faithfulness—the attributes that lifted the lamenter's spirit? By choosing to remember, by calling God's love to mind, by letting each new day awaken in us the memories of His fellowship. Therefore, we will have hope.

YOUR LIFE IN ACTION

Reflect on your past twenty-four hours.
Think of the ways God has demonstrated His love,
mercy, and faithfulness to you.

O Lord, by these things men live, and in all these is the life of my spirit.
Oh restore me to health and make me live! Behold, it was for my welfare that
I had great bitterness; but in love you have delivered my life from the pit
of destruction, for you have cast all my sins behind your back (Isaiah 38:16–17).

There is both good and bad in the way Hezekiah lived out his last years, and there are lessons for us in both. First, the good.

Hezekiah faced death realistically and honorably, though not perfectly. He didn't want to die (not yet anyway), and he pled with God to spare his life.

God then added fifteen years to his life. These verses record some of Hezekiah's response to the illness that nearly killed him and the lessons he learned on (what he thought was) his deathbed.

Hezekiah's sick days were not wasted; He sought the Lord—possibly more intensely than ever. In his suffering Hezekiah saw God's hand of discipline at work and recognized that the pain was for his good.

For Hezekiah, as for all, it was not how he responded to adversity that mattered, but how he responded to God in the adversity. Suffering days are days to turn *to* God, not away from Him.

YOUR LIFE IN ACTION

Describe a lesson you have learned in adversity
that you might not have learned otherwise.

> *Then Hezekiah said to Isaiah, "The word of the Lord*
> *that you have spoken is good."*
> *For he thought, "There will be peace and security*
> *in my days" (Isaiah 39:8).*

In contrast to his response to suffering, and the good way in which Hezekiah responded to God, here we see a different response of self-centeredness. Sadly, this a smudge on Hezekiah's record.

Having faced death, and being given a fifteen-year reprieve, Hezekiah lived a grateful life. He had received his adversity as discipline (Hebrews 12: 7–11) and yielded himself more fully to God.

But in time he seems to have softened and to have begun taking God's goodness for granted. His humility was overshadowed by presumption, leading him to make some serious blunders in leadership. This time, when God pronounced punishment, Hezekiah received the news with shallow self-centeredness, happy that he himself would not suffer the consequences and unconcerned that his sons would.

It is spiritually myopic to fail to consider the effect our choices will have on our descendants. Yes, we are each accountable for our own sins, but that doesn't mean others are spared the consequences.

In his self-centeredness, Hezekiah's failed to prepare the next generation for what was to come. Are you repeating Hezekiah's error, or are you establishing a legacy of godliness?

YOUR LIFE IN ACTION
Read Isaiah 38–39.

> *[Jesus] holds his priesthood permanently, because he continues forever.*
> *Consequently, he is able to save to the uttermost those who*
> *draw near to God through him, since he always lives*
> *to make intercession for them (Hebrews 7:24–25).*

Because Jesus is a permanent priest (think of Old Testament priests), He is always doing priestly things. This means that He is always interceding for His children. He is our representative, our advocate. And He prays for us.

Think of it. Jesus Christ prays for you!

Robert Murray M'Cheyne, Scottish minister in the nineteenth century, wrote, "If I could hear Christ praying for me in the next room, I would not fear a million enemies. Yet distance makes no difference. He is praying for me." This is an outlook every child of God needs, not just when he is praying, but also when he is in need of prayer.

There is fear in feeling alone and outnumbered, and certainly even the "strongest" of saints feel this way at times. But it is never our reality. Our permanent Priest is always praying.

YOUR LIFE IN ACTION

In addition to praying for you, what does it mean that
Jesus Christ is making intercession for you?

*In all their affliction he was afflicted, and the angel of his presence
saved them; in his love and in his pity he redeemed them;
he lifted them up and carried them all the days of old (Isaiah 63:9).*

Just as God endured the pain of Israel's afflictions under the old covenant, so Jesus endured—and endures—ours in the new.

Jesus is our suffering Savior. "He was pierced for our transgressions; he was crushed for our iniquities; upon him was the chastisement that brought us peace, and with his wounds we are healed" (Isaiah 53:5).

Jesus is our understanding intercessor who "sympathizes with our weaknesses" (Hebrews 4:15).

The so-called gods of all other religions are set above and beyond their followers. They inflict suffering, but they do not endure it, and certainly not on behalf of those who worship them.

But in Christ, God "takes away the sin of the world" (John 1:29) by bearing every bit of it Himself. There is no God like Him!

YOUR LIFE IN ACTION

Sing one of your favorite hymns or
songs of praise that exalts Christ.

Your iniquities have turned these away,
and your sins have kept good from you (Jeremiah 5:25).

Why do we sin? When you think about it, sin isn't very logical; it robs us of blessings and happiness.

We sin because we want to feel good—or feel better—whether that means escaping from pain, avoiding a challenge, or simply feeding our cravings. Sin, therefore, is often a matter of our insisting on something sooner than God wants us to have it, or demanding it in a different form than He wants us to enjoy it.

And certainly sin is sometimes a heartbreak wrapped in enticement from which God wants to spare us altogether.

Whatever form your sin may take, you can be sure that it will not deliver greater happiness than what God wants to give you through obedience and trust.

YOUR LIFE IN ACTION

In what ways has sin "kept good from you"?

> *We are ambassadors for Christ, God making his appeal through us.*
> *We implore you on behalf of Christ, be reconciled to God (2 Corinthians 5:20).*

Are you distracted from your mission? As a believer, you have a singular mission: to show and tell friends, neighbors, relatives, and strangers how to be reconciled to God through Christ.

In all that you do—*all* that you do—this mission is your highest purpose in life. Yet it is so easy to get distracted and disinterested. The noise of our culture and the demands of daily life easily pull us off course.

Perhaps one of the greatest distractions comes as a result of our cultural angst and "wishing" conditions were better so life would be calmer. Sometimes this angst turns into an anti-culture stance, isolating ourselves from the needs and the needy of our society.

As a follower of Jesus, you are here on assignment. Rather than wasting your emotions and energies on anger and angst, invest them in the mission God has given you and in the culture where He has placed you.

Do not withdraw. Do not surrender. Do not quit.

YOUR LIFE IN ACTION

Pray for our nation and your community. Ask God to keep Christians, including yourself, focused on the mission of the gospel.

We are ambassadors for Christ, God making his appeal through us.
We implore you on behalf of Christ, be reconciled to God (2 Corinthians 5:20).

It has never been easy to be an ambassador for Christ, and it was never meant to be. The church needs to realize this once again and rise to its heavenly obligations.

In fact, the darkening of our cultural conditions could prove to be the very wake-up call that is needed in the body of Christ. We are on God's mission in enemy territory.

Does this mean that people who disagree with us politically, morally, and/or ethically are our enemies? No, not at all. They, and the ones they influence, are our mission objective. We are sent to them as ambassadors of the only One who can set them free from the darkness.

In his book *Onward*, Russell Moore observes, "To rail against the culture is to say to God that we are entitled to a better mission field than the one he has given us."

Rather than railing against the culture, let us love each and every soul within that culture. May we, like Jesus, see the multitudes and be moved with compassion.

YOUR LIFE IN ACTION
Pray for the believers in your community to be
gospel-centered in all they do.

*The darkness is not dark to you; the night is bright as the day,
for darkness is as light with you (Psalm 139:12).*

There is no escaping God's presence; let us rejoice in this truth. May it comfort us when we are sad, enlighten us when we are confused, turn us when we are rebellious, and embolden us when we are afraid.

God's presence is constant. He is not limited to daylight hours or restricted by earthly boundaries.

He does not drop in for brief visits. He came to abide.

God is here—now and always. Rejoice in His presence. Rest in it.

Rest in Him. You are never alone.

YOUR LIFE IN ACTION
Read Psalm 139.

Thus says the LORD: *"The people who survived the sword found
grace in the wilderness; when Israel sought for rest,
the* LORD *appeared to him from far away" (Jeremiah 31:2–3).*

In the wake of our brokenness, God makes a way of beauty.
Sometimes we bear the scars of our resistance, and God transforms
them into marks of restoration. They tell the story of our rebellion
and God's restorative grace.

Every believer has—or will have—restoration marks on their soul.
These are meant to enamor us with God's mercy, not cause us to wallow in the guilt of sin that has long been forgiven. Memories of our
waywardness should end in celebration of God's loving intervention.

The devil will try to re-enter our scars into evidence, attempting to
prove us guilty once again. But he will be overruled every time.

The scars show what was, who we were before Christ. They do not
prove guilt; they document grace.

YOUR LIFE IN ACTION
Thank God today for specific ways and times
He has forgiven and restored you.

When they saw the boldness of Peter and John, and perceived that
they were uneducated, common men, they were astonished.
And they recognized that they had been with Jesus (Acts 4:13).

Prayer can transform us. Time spent in the presence of our Savior renews us and makes us men and women who are mighty in Spirit.

C. S. Lewis admitted what all who are given to prayer also know: "I pray because I can't help myself. I pray because I'm helpless. I pray because the need flows out of me all the time—waking and sleeping. It does not change God, it changes me."

How often we wrestle and become discouraged over things about ourselves that we so desperately want to change, yet we neglect the one spiritual discipline that would make the greatest difference—prayer. This is our way to *be with Jesus*.

YOUR LIFE IN ACTION

Bring your list of worries and the things about yourself that
you know are not as they should be, and truly pray about them today.

"The LORD is right," Jerusalem says, "for I rebelled against him. Listen, people everywhere; look upon my anguish and despair, for my sons and daughters have been taken captive to distant lands." . . . I say to myself, "The LORD is my inheritance; therefore, I will hope in him!" (Lamentations 1:18; 3:24).

Lamentations is an intriguing book. In it we read of disturbing sin, great sadness, God's discipline, personal repentance, and corporate restoration. It portrays the major themes of how God and His children interact.

The ESV Study Bible says that Lamentations shows a "movement from horrible loss and personal shame, to restored hope and prayer for renewal"—which explains the dichotomy (rather than discrepancy) of today's two verses. Together, they tell us something of God's response to our sin and our response to His mercy.

One by one, as God's people repent and return to Him, they begin to pray that He will restore their brothers and sisters, and God's people as a whole. Revival in our own lives should always drive us to pray for others to encounter God. In fact, our own revival experience raises the intensity of our praying. Faith (knowing God can) connects to hope (believing God will).

Are you praying for your brothers and sisters in the Lord, for your church, and for other churches in your community to be revived? Are you praying with both faith and hope because of what God has done in your life?

We often hear the phrase "and let it begin with me" associated with the plea for revival. Let's add to that: "but let it not end with me."

YOUR LIFE IN ACTION
Pray for revival in your church
and other churches in your community.

> *The LORD is merciful and gracious,*
> *slow to anger and abounding in steadfast love (Psalm 103:8).*

In one short verse we are introduced to four of God's attributes—four things that are true about Him and that stand between His holiness and our humanity. God is:

Merciful – He is aware when we are distressed, and He is able to deliver, comfort, and restore us.

Gracious – He extends favor to those who deserve punishment, and never on the basis of merit or our promise to do better and try harder.

Patient – He restricts His anger and gives us one opportunity after another to repent.

Abounding in steadfast love – His is not an on-again, off-again kind of love. It is lasting—that is, *ever*lasting.

There is no one like our God.

YOUR LIFE IN ACTION

Think of ways you have encountered each of these four attributes, and worship God accordingly. Give Him thanks and praise.

The Lord will not cast off forever, but, though he cause grief,
he will have compassion according to the abundance of his steadfast love;
for he does not afflict from his heart
or grieve the children of men (Lamentations 3:31–33).

We tell ourselves many falsehoods about God. Consequently, we sometimes try to keep away from Him when we should be drawing near.

When His children sin, God's intent is to restore them, not reject them. Having given the precious life of His only begotten Son for our salvation, God delights in keeping near to those He has redeemed.

He may sometimes cause us to experience the grief of sin, not to suspend us in sorrow but to sever our ties with iniquity. It is this godly sorrow that produces repentance (2 Corinthians 7:10), and this repentance that leads to restoration.

If you are experiencing the grief of sin (some call it guilt), do not run from God; run *to* Him. He is gracious and ready to restore.

YOUR LIFE IN ACTION

In your own words, describe the meaning and purpose
of grieving over our sin.

*By your great wisdom in your trade you have increased your wealth,
and your heart has become proud in your wealth (Ezekiel 28:5).*

Success can be good, but it brings certain risks to our spiritual vitality. Lest you think this is an overstatement, think of all the individuals, cities, nations, and civilizations whose downfall the Bible records.

There are so many who owed their success to God's favor but eventually came to believe that they had done it all on their own. They saw themselves as a cut above the rest and deserving of a higher station.

Oh, how near pride is to the successful, how dangerously close! This risk is not limited to the executive or the aristocrat; it can overtake anyone whose talent or skill has given them a "platform" of any size. Where there is the possibility of getting affirmation, there is the risk of expecting it more and more. And this expectation indicates that pride is creeping in.

If you have been given a talent with which to serve God, and that service puts you in front of others, be humbly thankful. Consider it an honor to serve.

Count your blessings, yes, but never take credit for them.

YOUR LIFE IN ACTION

Pray for those you know (and yourself, if applicable)
whose ministry often puts them in front of other people.
Pray that God will protect them from pride.

*When you pray, go into your room and shut the door and
pray to your Father who is in secret.
And your Father who sees in secret will reward you (Matthew 6:6).*

Prayer is a high and holy calling that is best done without an audience. It is never meant for show.

When we pray, one of the first things we should do is *shut the door*. We should seek solitude.

Many people look on prayer as a means of showcasing their spirituality—a way to impress others by turning a (spiritual) phrase that is sure to get God's attention.

In this way, prayer becomes a performance rather than an intimate connection between a child and his heavenly Father. It is speaking to hear oneself and hoping that those who are listening will think well of us. In other words, it is hypocrisy.

Even when we pray in public, our thoughts need to be focused on the Father. The door should always be shut to every desire that competes with seeking Him.

YOUR LIFE IN ACTION

Read Matthew 6.

Suddenly there was with the angel a multitude of the heavenly host praising God and saying, "Glory to God in the highest, and on earth peace among those with whom he is pleased!" (Luke 2:13–14).

The one thing we must not do, particularly at this time of year, is allow sentimentality to replace spirituality. We must be on guard against letting holiday celebrations push aside holy worship.

Christmas is an annual reminder of what (Who) matters most every day of every year. Jesus!

The angels sang, the shepherds hurried, the wise men set out, Mary pondered . . . all because of Jesus Christ. His coming was life changing, not just a notable event.

And as it was for them, so it is for you.

There is much to enjoy in our holiday traditions, but be sure to "make much of Jesus" in these days. Celebrate Him, and His coming to redeem the lost.

YOUR LIFE IN ACTION

What new tradition could you add to your Christmas celebration that would be all about Jesus?

---

*I have fought the good fight, I have finished the race, I have kept the faith.
Henceforth there is laid up for me the crown of righteousness, which the Lord,
the righteous judge, will award to me on that Day, and not only to me
but also to all who have loved his appearing (2 Timothy 4:7–8).*

What do you most look forward to? Is there anything that daily captures your attention, your longings? What are you passionate about?

To "love his appearing" means to wait expectantly for the return of Christ. It means to build one's life on the hope, the certainty, of that coming day. It is a matter of eternal perspective, where one views all of life through the lens of being fully united with Christ in His presence.

Two outliers in the biblical narrative surrounding Christmas personify this: Anna and Simeon. Their stories are recorded in Luke 2:22–38.

While they waited for Christ to come to earth the first time, to be incarnated in human form, we wait for Him to return and take us with Him. They looked forward in anticipation, faith, and hope. To them, all of life hung on this coming day.

May we also live with such expectancy. May we be fixated on our coming Savior!

YOUR LIFE IN ACTION
Read Luke 2.

Since then we have a great high priest who has passed through the heavens,
Jesus, the Son of God, let us hold fast our confession. For we do not have
a high priest who is unable to sympathize with our weaknesses,
but one who in every respect has been tempted as we are, yet without sin.
Let us then with confidence draw near to the throne of grace,
that we may receive mercy and find
grace to help in time of need (Hebrews 4:14–16).

To be our Redeemer, Jesus had to leave heaven and come to earth. He had to take on the form of human flesh to suffer and die; yet He also had to retain His divine nature in order to be the perfect, sinless sacrifice. Only Christ could save us, because only He was God and man. He alone met the requirements.

In one sense, could our salvation not have been accomplished in days rather than years? Could Christ have come one day, been killed the next, resurrected three days later, and then received back into heaven?

But that was not God's way. God provided a Savior whose sufferings culminated at the cross but did not begin there. He gave us a sympathizing Savior who encountered the pains and drains of years of humanity and who intercedes as One who—much more than observed—experienced the weakness that is our life on earth.

Christ lingered here. So, every time we sin, struggle, and grow weary, and then call out to Him for help, let us remember that He is "able to sympathize."

YOUR LIFE IN ACTION

Read the lyrics to some of your favorite Christmas hymns that celebrate Jesus and our redemption through Him.

> *As you sent me into the world,*
> *so I have sent them into the world (John 17:18).*

With the meaning and message of Christmas still fresh on our hearts, it is important to remember this: As the Father sent Jesus, so Jesus is sending us.

It is easy to raise objections to this calling and make excuses for our spiritual stagnation—Christ was sinless, we are not; Christ was perfect, we are not; Christ was God, we are not . . .

But let's call these what they really are—either excuses for outright refusal of God's assignment, or unbelief in His power to equip us for the mission.

We must come back to this one clear biblical statement: "As you [the Father] sent me [Jesus] into the world, so I [Jesus] have sent them [that includes you and me] into the world." We must grasp the reality that this is our purpose. *We have been sent.*

We are the carriers of the gospel, the ones sent to continue the proclamation of God's good news. This is our time for holy action.

YOUR LIFE IN ACTION

Pray that God would overcome any fear or apathy
you may have toward His purpose for you.

> *Cast your burden on the LORD,*
> *and he will sustain you (Psalm 55:22).*

We are never really hopeless, yet the feeling that we are is real at times. People disappoint us, expectations go unfulfilled, longings give way to heartbreaks. Our reality comes up short of our dreams.

In those times when our feelings pull us down, we must turn to God. In fact, our disappointments do us a great service when we are forced to "cast" our burdens on the Lord.

In these broken seasons we rediscover that God is "near to the brokenhearted" (Psalm 34:18). God Himself is the answer to our disappointments—heaven's response to earth's troubles.

When you are hurt or disappointed, it is natural to go on the hunt for someone to blame or punish, or to "give yourself a break" through indulgence.

As believers, let us first be driven to seek God when our heart hurts. He will calm us, heal us, and protect us from turning our let-downs into rampages of anger or disillusionment.

YOUR LIFE IN ACTION

Is your first reaction to disappointment to draw near to God?
Have you even prayed about that which hurts you?

> *. . . that I may know him and the power of his resurrection,*
> *and may share his sufferings, becoming like him in his death (Philippians 3:10).*

What has changed in your life since you believed in Jesus Christ? In what ways are you being made new?

Once Paul came to faith in Christ, his passions and activities were drastically changed. He was no longer a religious zealot trying to earn his way to heaven, but an energetic believer who lived by faith and humble obedience.

He gave up on intimidation (and even persecution) as a means of persuasion and instead became a man of great compassion and service. He learned to see that his sufferings were not setbacks, but means of identifying with Christ.

To live according to the gospel, as Paul did, means appropriating the power of Christ to our struggles with sin and to our mission. Christ's work in us is not yet complete.

By the grace of God we are changed and still changing, being transformed form glory to glory. Praise Him that He never withdraws from us.

YOUR LIFE IN ACTION
What has changed in your life since you believed in Christ?
In what ways are you still being made new?

Jesus, knowing their thoughts, said, "Why do you think evil in your hearts? For which is easier, to say, 'Your sins are forgiven,' or to say, 'Rise and walk'? But that you may know that the Son of Man has authority on earth to forgive sins"—he then said to the paralytic—"Rise, pick up your bed and go home." And he rose and went home (Matthew 9:4–7).

Three truths about sin: We all sin. Sin brings consequences. Christ alone can forgive sin.

It is easy to gloss over the first truth without giving it much thought; yet our salvation springs out of this terrible reality: We are (were) among the guilty.

This then leads to the next and even more sobering truth—that sin has severe and eternal consequences. So severe that, in the words of Ephesians 2:1, we were dead.

The curse of the first two truths is canceled by the third: Christ alone can forgive sin. In this is all our eternal hope.

Like the paralytic man Jesus healed, and those who witnessed this miracle, we have seen and heard the forgiving work of Christ. May each demonstration of His mercy embolden us to pray all the more for those who do not yet know Him. May we also be passionate proclaimers that Christ alone can forgive sin.

YOUR LIFE IN ACTION

Be on the lookout today for demonstrations of the power of God. Each time you see it, take a moment to acknowledge, and thank Him, that He alone has the power to forgive sin.

> *"Let your heart therefore be wholly true to the LORD our God,*
> *walking in his statutes and keeping his commandments,*
> *as at this day"* (1 Kings 8:61).

Sin often begins with our failure to keep commitments or hold to biblical convictions. When we are distracted from pursuing God, and when we neglect basic spiritual disciplines, our resistance to sin is weakened.

Consider the basic commitment of having a daily time alone with God. Such a discipline, when faithfully observed over a period of time, can strengthen your spirit in several ways, including:

- guiding your thoughts to where they need to be

- developing your sense of discernment

- making you mindful of God's constant presence

- giving you greater clarity and confidence in making decisions

These are but a few of the ways our spirits can be strengthened through just one area of discipline, and these are all in addition to the reward of building our resistance to sin.

So, when we find ourselves in a weakening spiritual state, we would be wise to ask, "What commitments have I set aside that I need to pick up again?"

YOUR LIFE IN ACTION

What commitments have you held on to, related to your spiritual development, that have served you well over the years? Which ones have you abandoned that you need to recover?

> *Return to me, and I will return to you,*
> *says the LORD of hosts (Malachi 3:7).*

Let us begin where we started, on January 1. Evan Roberts was grieving over the spiritual indifference of the church in his day. He began preaching a gospel-centered sermon that called for these four responses:

1. Confess all known sin, receiving forgiveness through Jesus Christ.

2. Remove anything in your life that you are in doubt or feel unsure about.

3. Be ready to obey the Holy Spirit instantly.

4. Publicly confess the Lord Jesus Christ.

Many responded to this message, resulting in over 150,000 conversions and innumerable lives transformed during what we now know as the Welsh Revival of 1904–05.

The people of Wales learned to respond to God immediately, without delay. Their prior indifference had only added to their misery.

Is God saying the same thing to His church today? Is He saying it to you?

YOUR LIFE IN ACTION

Pray through the four responses in Evan Roberts' sermon.
What actions do you need to take?

ADDITIONAL RESOURCES

We recommend the following to continue in your pursuit of God, personal revival, and a strong daily walk:

Life Action Events

Life Action offers various in-church conferences designed to communicate the call to personal revival for the entire family: "creating contexts where people can seek and obey God." Our revivalists, musicians, children's and youth ministers, and family instructors can walk your congregation through the principles that lead to revival.
www.LifeAction.org

Revive Our Hearts

The women's ministry of Life Action, led by Nancy DeMoss Wolgemuth, casts a vision for biblical womanhood across the world through daily radio broadcasts, multi-lingual publications and web resources, and women's conferences.
www.ReviveOurHearts.com

OneCry Church Experience

This small group guide and church kit help engage whole congregations in a vision for revival that goes beyond individual change. OneCry offers perspective on what community and

national revival look like, and how God's people can be part of a larger movement of repentance, prayer, and biblical unity. **www.OneCry.com**

Seeking Him

This group-friendly devotional guide has been used by thousands of churches, small groups, and classes across the world. It walks readers through twelve thoroughly biblical and powerfully convicting truths regarding personal revival. **www.SeekingHim.com**